"To my knowledge Vladimír Dzuro's book is the first to explain the complexities, the frustrations, and finally the satisfaction of conducting investigations into the serious crimes that were committed during the conflict in the former Yugoslavia. It is above all the story of the people who suffered from those crimes and the investigators and lawyers who worked tirelessly to try and ensure that the alleged perpetrators faced trial for their part in those crimes."—**Judge Joanna Korner**, former prosecution senior trial attorney, International Criminal Tribunal for the former Yugoslavia

"*The Investigator* is rife with demons. Vladimír Dzuro details his life as an international criminal investigator, and like many of his colleagues at the Yugoslav and Rwanda Tribunals, he witnessed the unfathomable daily. Skills, teamwork, wit, and luck (bad and good) allowed him to squeeze justice out of profound depravity. Dzuro's book chronicles the real slog of international investigators and prosecutors. Hollywood fiction would shrink from his searing view of war crimes from under the wet tarpaulin of a mass grave. Notwithstanding, Dzuro ponders his experience by observing that 'humanity owes it to the scarred and broken people who open up their hearts to you.' It is also true that the best international investigators, like Dzuro, open up their hearts, in turn."
—**Patricia Viseur Sellers**, special advisor for gender to the prosecutor of the International Criminal Court

"For the war to really end, when the military conflict was over, the citizens of the former Yugoslavia needed closure that could only be provided by impartial justice. Our friend Vladimír Dzuro and his colleagues from the International Criminal Tribunal for the former Yugoslavia provided the only option. They put their own lives at risk so that others could have justice, and this book eloquently tells their story."—**Ralph R. Johnson**, U.S. ambassador to Sarajevo (1999–2001); and Lt. Col. Jacqueline M. Johnson, U.S. Army (Ret.), executive officer in the Office of the High Representative, Sarajevo (2000–2001)

"*The Investigator* reminds us that the United Nations is a body that can, at will, search out and hold accountable those individuals who orches-

trate and enforce extreme violence on noncombatants. . . . Vladimír Dzuro's years of work with the International Criminal Tribunal for the former Yugoslavia are a testament to the tenacity of persons dedicated to the investigations of war crimes. He and his colleagues deserve not only our admiration but most certainly our attention, as atrocities and genocide permeate the beginnings of the twenty-first century. Dzuro's narrative is fascinatingly clear and engaging; it also serves as a warning."
—**Ralph J. Hartley**, adjunct professor of anthropology, University of Nebraska–Lincoln

"The International Criminal Tribunal for the former Yugoslavia was an institution that should have never been needed in the twentieth century, but the internal conflict that erupted in the former Yugoslavia in the 1990s precipitated large-scale war crimes committed by both civilian and military factions of the former Yugoslavian republics. The tribunal successfully identified and prosecuted war criminals from different sides of the conflict, which in turn brought at least some closure to those innocent victims who had suffered the most."—**Kevin Curtis**, chief of investigations, UNICEF, and former investigator and team leader at the Office of the Prosecutor, International Criminal Tribunal for the former Yugoslavia

"This is a detective story with a difference. The shallow graves that Vladimír Dzuro examines contain scores, even hundreds, of victims. He investigates the worst war crimes Europe has seen since the Second World War. Dzuro takes us inside the investigation of atrocities committed as Yugoslavia collapsed. He explains what it feels like and smells like when you stand in a mass grave as it is being exhumed. He tracks down suspects and witnesses, flies across the world to authenticate evidence, and finally faces the war criminals at a war crimes tribunal in The Hague. *The Investigator* is a raw and unique firsthand account of an extraordinary pursuit of justice in the face of absolute horror."—**Julian Borger**, Pulitzer Prize–winning journalist and world affairs editor for the *Guardian*

THE INVESTIGATOR

THE INVESTIGATOR

Demons of the Balkan War

VLADIMÍR DZURO

Foreword by Carla Del Ponte,
chief prosecutor, International Criminal
Tribunal for the former Yugoslavia

Potomac Books
An imprint of the University of Nebraska Press

Library of Congress Cataloging-in-Publication Data
Names: Dzuro, Vladimír, 1961– author.
Title: The investigator: demons of the Balkan war /
Vladimír Dzuro; foreword by Carla Del Ponte.
Other titles: Vyšetřovatel. English
Description: Lincoln: Potomac Books, an imprint of
the University of Nebraska Press, [2019] | Includes
bibliographical references and index.
Identifiers: LCCN 2018057899
ISBN 9781640121959 (cloth: alk. paper)
ISBN 9781640122277 (epub)
ISBN 9781640122284 (mobi)
ISBN 9781640122291 (pdf)
Subjects: LCSH: Yugoslav War, 1991–1995—Atrocities. |
War crime trials—Netherlands—Hague. | Trials (Crimes
against humanity)—Netherlands—Hague. | War
criminals—Trials, litigation, etc. | War crimes investigation.
| Detectives—Czech Republic.
Classification: LCC DR1313.7.A85 D9813 2019 |
DDC 341.6/90268—dc23
LC record available at https://lccn.loc.gov/2018057899

Set in Lyon Text by E. Cuddy.

The views expressed in this book are solely the author's
and do not reflect the official policy or position of the
United Nations or the International Criminal Tribunal for
the former Yugoslavia.

This book is dedicated to the innocent
victims of the wars in the former Yugoslavia,
regardless of their nationality or ethnicity.

Setting up the ICTY was truly one of the most important cases I ever took to the Security Council. Despite the fact that people doubted it would work, it has been remarkable. The war was a tragedy and those involved needed to be punished. To this day, I say that the ICTY was essential—by assigning individual guilt we could expunge collective guilt.

MADELEINE ALBRIGHT, former U.S. secretary of state, former permanent representative of the United States to the United Nations

The UN was not created to take mankind to heaven but to save humanity from hell.

DAG HAMMARSKJOLD, second secretary-general of the United Nations

CONTENTS

ILLUSTRATIONS

FOREWORD

After serving for five years as Switzerland's attorney general, in 1999 I was appointed by the United Nations Security Council as chief prosecutor for both international tribunals (ICTY and ICTR) to conduct investigations and prosecutions of war crimes and crimes against humanity in the former Yugoslavia and Rwanda.

When I took up my responsibilities, I was determined that the main objective, justice for the victims of the horrendous crimes committed, required a ruthless and comprehensive effort at both the international and the national level. However, as with my predecessors, Justices Richard Goldstone and Louise Arbour, I also faced huge challenges, the most critical of which was the lack of cooperation by of some of the states developing governments that appeared during the disintegration of the Socialistic Federative Republic of Yugoslavia in 1991.

I had teams of prosecutors, lawyers, and investigators that worked under my supervision who had to deal with not only practical but also political difficulties on a daily basis. Initially there was no access or on occasions only limited access to documents and material witnesses. These obstacles often delayed the progress of the investigations, and the reluctance of governments to apprehend indicted war criminals created problems that could easily have crippled the work of the tribunals and may even have portrayed the international community as inept at dealing with such barbaric acts.

Notwithstanding these difficulties, we managed to investigate, indict, apprehend, and bring to justice 161 individuals accused of war crimes in the former Yugoslavia. This would not have happened without the dedicated work of my staff, one of whom was a Czech investigator, Vladimír Dzuro.

I knew that even before my arrival, Vladimír was instrumental in the first arrest of an indicted war criminal, Slavko Dokmanović. The arrest of Dokmanović demonstrated not only to the leadership of NATO but also to other military contingents deployed in the region that it was possible to bring indicted war criminals to The Hague to stand trial. The success of this arrest operation also sent a very strong message to the people of the former Yugoslavia that nobody with blood on his hands could hide any longer.

During my time as chief prosecutor, Vladimír worked as a leader of a team of dedicated professionals that operated in Serbia, Croatia, Bosnia, and Kosovo on the development of critical witnesses, whom we called "insiders," who were crucial to obtaining hard-to-access information. The lack of cooperation from local governments required the clandestine penetration of systems, specifically police, military, and intelligence agencies, so that documentary evidence could be secured and witnesses from within the ranks could give testimony. These operations were particularly important during the trial of Slobodan Milošević and his conspirators. The "insider project" resulted in numerous successful prosecutions.

At some stage I decided that I should demonstrate to the international community that the Serbian authorities were secretly sabotaging the work of the tribunal. For this I used Goran Hadžić, an indicted war criminal who we knew was hiding in Serbia. I had Hadžić indicted under seal, I placed surveillance around his house, and then I delivered the indictment with international arrest warrants to the Serbian authorities. In less than an hour Hadžić was tipped off and disappeared. Since we did not have jurisdiction to arrest Hadžić in Serbia, Vladimír and his team documented the escape, which allowed me to publicly challenge the national authorities.

I also fondly recall my official trip to Eastern Slavonia in Croatia, during which Vladimír worked as my guide. We traveled to a number of places where atrocities had been committed, including Ovčara, Lovas, Dalj, Erdut, and Vukovar.

During this trip I devoted my time to talking to families of victims and also some of the survivors of atrocities. There I again realized how important it was to the healing process to meet not only with the politicians but also with ordinary people affected by the conflict and to carefully listen to their life stories.

Vladimír spent almost ten years with the ICTY investigating war crimes in the former Yugoslavia. His knowledge of and direct experience with critical events and key people during that time have prepared him well to tell the often horrific, sometimes bizarre, but always interesting stories about the work of the International Criminal Tribunal for the former Yugoslavia.

Carla Del Ponte

PREFACE

In 1918 two of the new countries that arose out of the ruins of World War I were Czechoslovakia and Yugoslavia. Each was dominated by ethnic Slavic peoples who spoke mutually intelligible languages and shared many cultural characteristics. These new countries were nevertheless built on centuries-old wounds that reignited when Germany invaded them at the outset of World War II. Both countries managed to survive the upheaval and reprisals following the war. During the 1990s they began to split apart as political transformation set in.

The dissolution of Czechoslovakia was a peaceful affair. Each side—the Czechs and the Slovaks—felt they could do better without the other. This was not the case in Yugoslavia. When it began to fall apart, the outcome was bloodshed and tragedy not seen in Europe for half a century.

This book is not an analysis of the causes of the war that subsequently raged there, the fifth and last one to consume the Balkans in the twentieth century. Rather it is the story of a Czech investigator who left his job as a homicide detective in Prague to help in the hunt for the criminals of that war. He joined a team of international investigators, lawyers, and prosecutors intent on bringing to justice those responsible for the heinous acts committed in the former Yugoslavia.

This story bears witness to the torture and killing of defenseless civilians, to finding and exhuming their mass graves, to investigating and arresting the perpetrators, and finally to bringing them to trial before the International Tribunal in The Hague.

THE INVESTIGATOR

1

From Interpol to The Hague

I'm Off to War

I'm lying on an iron-frame bunk with an IV tube stuck in my arm. Around me is a makeshift tarpaulin wall, and medical staff are speaking in some strange language. I feel terrible, and everything hurts. My head is buzzing like a beehive, and I have no clue what's going on or why the hell I'm even here.

I look around and slowly realize that I'm probably in a field hospital and the staff are speaking English. I call out to a nurse, who is overjoyed to see that I've finally regained consciousness. With difficulty I manage to ask, "Where am I, and what am I doing here?" She tells me I'm lying in the 502nd MASH (mobile army surgical hospital) of the U.S. Army in Zagreb. After that I lose consciousness again.

Suddenly a doctor is standing over me and apologizing for taking so long to find out what had been ailing me. From my ID card, the staff know only my name and blood type. It seems I had acute appendicitis, which they caught just in time. He assures me that everything will be fine, and prior to leaving he smilingly recommends that I watch *M.A.S.H.* on the U.S. Armed Forces Satellite Television. I have no idea what he's talking about because this famous series with Captain Hawkeye Pierce, Major Margaret Houlihan, and Corporal Radar O'Reilly had yet to make it onto our television sets back home or else I missed the first episodes. I just stare at him but can tell from his hearty laugh that this show is going to be a riot. He points to a television set, winks his eye, and disappears through a hole in the tarpaulin wall. I go back to sleep.

As I begin to recover my strength, I take a keen interest in how the field hospital operates. It stands next to some railroad tracks, a few hundred meters from the terminal at the Zagreb airport. It's surrounded by a barbed-wired fence, and there are sandbags piled up at the entrance to form a defensive wall. I count perhaps a dozen military tents inside the compound, probably bigger and better equipped than those used during the Korean War. The khaki green, however, is the same, and so too is the type of staff: scruffy doctors, attractive nurses, American soldiers, and the military police (MPs) who guard the compound against possible intruders.

You can't compare running a field hospital to doing the same for a city or university hospital. The tents have wooden floorboards, and the beds are cots crammed into one area for a dozen or so patients. The facility is only there to save lives, so everything about it is spartan. That includes the latrine. It was simply a few toilet bowls surrounded by a tarp curtain, with no sound insulation whatsoever. Now anyone who has had abdominal surgery knows how painful it is to empty your bowels and what an embarrassing ordeal it can be. I have to hobble there with the help of nurses, who seat me on the bowl, close the curtain, and wait for me to do my business. Fortunately, the nurses are sympathetic and probably used to this sort of thing. At least they have a good ear for grunts and know when to come in, haul me up and, well, you get the picture.

The road to me ending up in an American field hospital in Zagreb in the first place began in 1984, when I joined the Prague Criminal Investigative Department (CID). I loved the job. With a gun at my side and a badge in my pocket, I chased after criminals all around Prague. But I'm an ambitious type, and in 1992 I jumped at the chance to join the National Central Bureau (NCB) of Interpol in Prague. I couldn't resist the glamour and risk of taking the chase after criminals around the world, in sports cars or helicopters naturally. Only after I walked into my new office did I realize that the Interpol of the movies was nothing like reality.

My office had shiny new furniture and a computer instead of a typewriter; everything about it was high tech, the kind of stuff our CID in 1992 could only wish for. Yet for all that, my job was boring paperwork. From morning till evening, with a gun still at my side and a badge in my pocket, I waded through mounds and mounds of paper. I had no sooner plopped into my comfortable new chair than I couldn't wait to get the hell out of it.

Then one day my brother-in-law asked me if I would like to go off to war in Yugoslavia. He had seen a recruiting flyer on the bulletin board of the office where he worked, so I filled out an application and sent it to a headhunter in London looking for civilians to work for the United Nations Protection Force (UNPROFOR), the United Nations peacekeeping force in the former Yugoslavia.

A month or so later, I was navigating another mountain of paperwork when the phone rang. I answered it with my usual, "NCB Interpol Prague, how can I help you?" The pleasant voice on the other end, with a distinctive British accent, told me that they had received my application and their representative was coming to Prague to conduct interviews with several candidates. Was I still interested in the job? What a dumb question. The rep came, we talked, and he offered me a one-year contract. That's it. I was off to war in the Balkans.

What Happened to Yugoslavia?

For decades the Socialist Federal Republic of Yugoslavia was under the firm grip of Josip Broz Tito. Following his death in 1980, power was divided among representatives of the various republics that comprised Yugoslavia, and no single leader emerged to truly keep this country of many nationalities together as one.

This was not so significant as the Communist Party still controlled everything, but by the beginning of the 1990s, with the first free elections, things began to change. A new group of leaders came to power—Tito's offspring of sorts—the presidents of the six republics that made up the federation. They were Slobodan Milošević of Serbia, Franjo Tuđman of Croatia, Alija Izetbegović of Bosnia and Herzegovina, Kiro Gligorov of Macedonia, Milan Kučan of Slovenia, and Momir Bulatović of Montenegro. Instead of working together to bring Yugoslavia through a deepening economic and political crisis, they began bickering and intriguing among themselves and plunged the federation into further instability, an instability filled by growing nationalism. The country split apart as a result of it, which spelled disaster for the Balkans.

The Slovenes were the first to break their republic away from the federation dominated by the Serbs. Then came the Croats, followed by the Serbs themselves rising up in Croatia, and after that it was Macedonia's turn. Finally, on March 3, 1992, Bosnia and Herzegovina declared independence, and this led to civil war there among the Bosnians, Croats, and Serbs. By the end of the year, the Serbs controlled two-thirds of the territory of Bosnia and more than a third of Croatia.

The United Nations Security Council established by Resolution 743 of February 21, 1992, a peacekeeping force, UNPROFOR, to address the civil war in the very heart of Europe. Starting in 1992 its task was to protect the civilian population by creating "safe havens." UNPROFOR units for the former Yugoslavia were headquartered in Zagreb, Croatia, on the compound of the army base at the intersection of Selska and Ilica Streets. On the sidewalk to the entrance, the families of killed or missing Croatian nationals built a symbolic "Wall of Pain," made out of red bricks and containing the names of their loved ones.

I had been to Croatia only once, back in the days of the former Czechoslovakia. It was June 1982, and I was on my honeymoon. I would never have guessed then that after a dozen years I would be coming back to a country full of smoldering villages, refugee camps, ethnic hatred, and destruction everywhere you looked. And mass grave sites.

When I arrived in Zagreb in February 1994, the only signs that I saw of the conflict around me were soldiers from the peacekeeping force. Zagreb was just a stopover on my way to Bosnia, where I was to assume the post of head of United Nations security for the Sarajevo sector. The few days originally planned for my training ended up becoming two

1. Map of the Socialist Federal Republic of Yugoslavia. (Library of Congress)

months on account of my appendicitis. I don't remember much about going to the local medical clinic, just waking up in the 502nd MASH.

After my discharge from the MASH, I worked a few weeks in the UNPROFOR Security Office in Zagreb with Greg Battley and Matthew Rombough, who both helped me to fully recover and more importantly took me through the induction training.

Greg was the first person who introduced me to the world of war crimes, not to those in the former Yugoslavia, as one might assume, but to the World War II criminal trials at Nuremberg.

Although the legal justifications for the trials, and the procedures they followed were controversial at the time, they are now widely regarded as a milestone toward the establishment of a permanent international court. They set an important precedent for dealing with crimes against humanity.

On April 20, 1942, representatives from nine of the countries that had been occupied by Germany met in London to draft the Inter-Allied Resolution on German War Crimes. Over a series of meetings in Tehran, Yalta, and Potsdam, the four major wartime powers—the United States, the United Kingdom, the Soviet Union, and France—finally agreed in 1945 on how those responsible for war crimes during World War II would be punished. The German Instrument of Surrender defined the legal basis for the jurisdiction of the court, as political authority for Germany rested with the Allied Control Council. This meant that the council had the power to punish violations of international law and the laws of war. The London Charter of the International Military Tribunal established the legal basis for the trials, and this dictated that only major war criminals, civilian or military, of the European Axis countries would be brought before the court.

Over the following years, approximately two hundred German defendants were tried at Nuremberg for war crimes. Those found guilty were sentenced to death or imprisoned in Spandau, in the British Sector of West Berlin. Troops from the four occupying powers guarded Spandau prison on a rotating basis, three months at a time.

The prison was demolished in 1987 after the death of the last surviving Nuremburg prisoner, Rudolf Hess, known as Prisoner Number 7, and rebuilt as a shopping center, to prevent it from becoming a neo-Nazi shrine.

From 1983 through 1986, while serving in the British Army, Greg was regularly assigned to duty in Spandau Prison, and he was the only person I had met who had directly dealt with a World War II war criminal. During long evenings in Zagreb, he told us many stories of the six-hundred-cell prison that for many years was maintained for Rudolf Hess, its only prisoner.

Most of the evenings in Zagreb, however, I spent reading various magazines and watching Croatian television. There was often talk about alleged atrocities in Vukovar, a town in the east of the country. A large group of civilians had been taken from the local hospital, never to be seen again. Word had it that they had been murdered at a nearby pig farm in the village of Ovčara.

I couldn't know it at the time, but this alleged war crime incident would come to dominate my life for the next decade.

The Establishment of the International Tribunal

In 1992 the UN Security Council established a commission of experts to analyze information about violations of the Geneva Conventions and international humanitarian law in the former Yugoslavia. A year later it was clear that something had to be done to make sure those responsible for these violations did not go unpunished. Among those leading this process was Madeleine Albright, who at this time was the permanent representative of the United States at the UN. On February 22, 1993, the UN Security Council unanimously approved a draft resolution on the establishment of the International Criminal Tribunal for the former Yugoslavia (ICTY). The secretary-general was given sixty days to elaborate on its structure and procedures.

On this occasion Mrs. Albright spoke at a press conference: "The Nuremberg principles have been reaffirmed. The lesson that we are all accountable to international law may finally have taken hold in our collective memory." In response to criticism that the Nuremberg trials dealt with justice only insofar as the victorious powers defined it, she added, "This will be no victors' tribunal."

The tribunal was officially established by Security Council Resolution No. 827 on May 25, 1993, but did not begin its activities at its headquarters in The Hague until early 1994. Madeleine Albright recounts: "Well, I think that all of the people that were involved in the establishment—the permanent representatives to the Security Council, the nonpermanent ones and others who were not on the Security Council—were very much aware that we were involved in something new, though discussing the Nuremberg precedents, that this was not a war of victors, that we were really dealing with a situation that was ongoing, that the procedures had to be established that would not only identify individual guilt and expunge the collective guilt but make sure that proper punishment was meted out. And it was in many ways being present at the creation of a brand-new organization. I must say that we ran into a great deal of skepticism. It was easy enough to take the first vote in February to get the tribunal created, but nobody really believed that it would work. There were questions about how the judges would be selected. I must say that especially the women permanent representatives of the United Nations wanted to make sure that there would be women judges because so many of the crimes had been committed against women in terms of rape and horrendous crimes. And so the judges were then selected by the entire UN system. And then the question was how to get a prosecutor. And that was very complicated, and nobody thought that would happen. And then nobody thought that there would ever be a court that actually functioned, that would be set on what the precedents were going to be. And we then in May voted on how the—1993, voted on how the procedure of the tribunal would work. And then still nobody thought it would work. They said that there would never be indictees, and then they said there would never be any trials, and then they said there would never be any convictions, and there would never be any sentencing. And at each part along the way, I would point out that they were wrong. And one of the reasons that I think that it is so important that this procedure is going forward is to show that they were all wrong, that this—that the tribunal is very much a part of the international judicial system that is playing a very essential role, I think, in making sure that this individual guilt is assigned, that punishment is meted out, and that there can be reconciliation. I think that was the whole purpose behind having such a tribunal, so that there could ultimately be the reconciliation of the various people that were innocent."

In July 1994 the Office of the Prosecutor, now staffed with a sufficient number of investigators and lawyers, launched its first investigation. After four months Chief Prosecutor Richard Goldstone issued the first indictment of the International Tribunal. Dragan Nikolić, the

2. International Criminal Tribunal for the former Yugoslavia. (Vladimír Dzuro)

commander of a detention camp in the village of Sušica in Bosnia and
Herzegovina, was accused of war crimes. Two more indictments followed in February 1995 against twenty-one of his cohorts.

My Baptism by War

Civil war had broken out in Bosnia and Herzegovina after it was internationally recognized as an independent state in April 1992. Now a
foreign military force, the Yugoslav People's Army (Jugoslovenska
narodna armija, JNA), began withdrawing, but only to make room
for local Serbian units. On May 20, 1992, the former Second Military
District of the JNA became the base of operations for the newly established Army of Republika Srpska, known by its Serbian acronym as the
VRS (Vojska Republike Srpske). The troops stationed around Sarajevo,
formerly the Fourth Army Corps of the JNA, were transformed into
the Sarajevo-Romanija Corps of the Army of Republika Srpska and
stationed in Lukavica to the southwest of the city.

Sarajevo, the capital and cultural center of Bosnia and Herzegovina, lies on the banks of the Miljacka River in a mountainous valley formed by the massifs of Bjelašnica, Igman, Jahorina, and Trebević. It was once a beautiful and historic place, and it virtually blossomed during the Winter Olympics of 1984. But after violence erupted eight years later, the VRS used its strategic position in the surrounding hills to blockade and bombard the city. Snipers from the Sarajevo-Romanija Corps took aim at marketplaces, trams, funeral processions, and parents walking with their children. They regularly picked off civilians as if they were on a trophy-hunting safari.

When I came to Sarajevo in April 1994, ten years after the Olympics, most of what had been refurbished, upgraded, or newly built now lay in ruins. On the way from the airport, I passed by burned out and destroyed houses and found a city afflicted by hunger and corruption. The Holiday Inn, where I stayed for some time, was hit by a rocket that left a huge gaping hole in the front. To make it possible for people to get around, UNPROFOR lined the roads with shipping containers to provide, as it were, protective walls that at least gave residents the semblance of safety. At other dangerous points in the city, UNPROFOR deployed armored personnel carriers to serve as a steel shield against the bullets of Serbian snipers. Every day was a challenge for the living to get from one part of the city to the next. Reports of civilian deaths became the daily routine.

I flew into the Sarajevo airport on an Antonov cargo plane, which UNPROFOR was using to supply the city and move personnel and humanitarian aid. These UNPROFOR military flights were known as Maybe Airlines. One look around the airport, which was dotted with holes from mortar attacks, and it was clear what had inspired the name. Maybe you landed, maybe you didn't.

Traveling with Maybe Airlines was an adventure not only for me but for any UN employee who had to move between Zagreb and Sarajevo. Sarajevo International Airport remained under the control of the Bosnian authorities throughout the conflict, but only because they had UNPROFOR soldiers there to protect it. There was only one runway,

3. (*top*) Improvised sign warning of possible sniper fire in Sarajevo. (Vladimír Dzuro)

4. (*bottom*) French UNPROFOR soldiers helping protect civilians from sniper fire in Sarajevo. (Vladimír Dzuro)

5. (*top*) Maybe Airlines Sarajevo—a cargo airplane used by UNPROFOR for supplying Sarajevo and transporting UN personnel to and from Sarajevo. (Vladimír Dzuro)

6. (*bottom*) Seal of Maybe Airlines UNPROFOR Sarajevo. (Vladimír Dzuro)

and it ran right through the middle of no-man's land. Civilian flights didn't exist because it was both dangerous and impossible to find an insurance company to insure such flights. Even UNPROFOR flights often came under fire, making landings and takeoffs as frightening as the steepest rollercoaster.

Since these transport aircraft also had to accommodate shipping containers and heavy military equipment, passenger comfort was more or less an afterthought. We had to make do with hard plastic benches running along the sides of the aircraft. We always had to wear a bulletproof vest and a helmet. The more experienced personnel advised us to sit on the vest because we ran a greater risk of getting shot from fire below the plane. One of my superiors, a retired U.S. Army colonel, got hit as his plane was taking off and ended up a paraplegic.

To minimize the time the aircraft was exposed to fire from small arms, the pilots revved the engines to full blast while still at the end of the runway. The plane and cargo shook violently, and the noise inside was deafening. The pilot then released the brakes, added even more juice to the engines, and the plane rocketed off after taxiing only a few hundred meters. The steep angle of takeoff terrified us because it looked as if the containers would snap their ropes at any time and crush us. Once we were out of firing range, the pilots leveled off, and the flight continued completely normally.

Landing in Sarajevo was just the opposite, like a free fall. The pilots released the landing gear, put the aircraft into the same steep angle used for takeoff, and within a few short minutes we were touching down hard on the runway. To the roar of the reverse thrust of the engines, the pilots applied full brakes to slow the plane as quickly as possible to get it away from the runway and to the terminal, which was somehow out of the snipers' reach. It was a miracle that not a single tragic event was connected to the airport operations there.

When I landed in Sarajevo the first time, I was picked up at the terminal as arranged and taken to the headquarters of UNPROFOR. There I saw a long line of cars getting refills of gasoline and diesel from UN stocks. The emergency services and police vehicles I could understand, but the others were civilians helping themselves because fuel in Sarajevo was in short supply and going for as high as fifteen dollars a liter. At the reception desk, I pulled out my ID card and called over a security guard to tell him to write down the license plates of the private cars lined up outside.

I took the list to the office of the military police. After introducing myself, I asked Martin Ronnberg, a young military policeman from Sweden, why the people on the list were helping themselves to UNPROFOR gasoline. He directed me to the commander of the military police, Colonel Miloslav Čech, who, like me, was a Czech national. We discussed the situation in our native language. I had to proceed delicately because the UNPROFOR military staff charged with managing fuel stocks was not under my jurisdiction, but my intervention paid off. When next week rolled around, only police and emergency vehicles were filling up at the station.

Later that week Ronnberg and I conducted a surprise inspection at the PX, a store set up and run by the United Nations for its employees. The manager of the PX was said to be selling alcohol and cigarettes to military staff for half of what regular UNPROFOR staff had to pay for them. I talked to some civilian customers, Martin did the same with soldiers, and in one day we were able to paint a proper picture of what was going on at the Sarajevo PX. We discovered, for example, that members of the French Foreign Legion deployed to Sarajevo received additional goodies such as a wristwatch or other keepsake after completing their mission. When Ronnberg asked the PX manager whether he had created this private welfare program on his own initiative or had been ordered to do so, the questioning came to an abrupt end. The manager stopped speaking in English, looked very indignant, and all we could make out from his torrent of words was the-general-this and the-general-that.

Ronnberg handed over the results of our investigation to Colonel Čech at the military police headquarters in Zagreb. Our surprise inspection led to the immediate dismissal of the manager and to greater uniformity in prices. Selling gasoline and diesel fuel from UNPROFOR

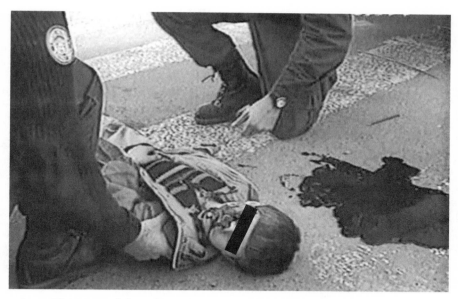

7. A small boy gunned down by a sniper in front of the Holiday Inn hotel in Sarajevo. (Vladimír Dzuro)

stocks and jacking up prices at the PX had been an extremely profitable business for everyone involved. Martin and I joked that if we ended up with a bullet in our heads one day, it wouldn't be clear which side had pulled the trigger.

But the fact was bullets were flying all over the place then, and I still think about one incident in particular. Every morning and evening, a boy of about ten years old would stand out in the open at the entrance to the hotel begging for batteries for his Walkman. One day I found him on the sidewalk outside, shot through the head. To this day I can't understand what went through some sniper's head that prompted him to kill a defenseless boy, but then I suppose it will never be understood or was even meant to be.

Our office was in the city center next to the Bosnian Ministry of Defense. Units of the VRS stationed in the surrounding hills were trying to hit the building with mortar fire, but they mostly struck the buildings nearby. One eventually did hit the rooftop of our building and blew out all the windows. Shards of glass would have flown around the room like shrapnel from a grenade had the windows not been taped over with a special film first.

The task of my little team was to ensure the safety of the civilian personnel of UNPROFOR in the Sarajevo Sector, which was ambitious and laudable but next to impossible. The city was tightly encircled and under daily fire. Keeping check on the situation fell to UNPRO-FOR troops and the Bosnian army. Civilians were dying in the streets, and our people could barely move around the city. My assignment was therefore narrowed down to investigating criminal acts against civilian employees of UNPROFOR and updating our evacuation plans. Security officers Thor Bachmann and Ponnapa Kelapanda worked with me on this impossible task. We all could only pray every day that nothing really serious happened to our staff, since we often could not leave the besieged city to provide needed assistance.

One day I had to go to the town of Split on the coast in Croatia, about a four-hour drive. Sarajevo was still under blockade, and getting past the Serbian checkpoints was always something of a gamble. If the army or police of Republika Srpska decided you weren't getting through, then you weren't. UNPROFOR had the mandate for its free movement, but it did not have the military might to force anybody to back off. That wouldn't change for a few years, not until NATO troops arrived. I came to one of these checkpoints, waited an hour, maybe two, but all in vain and had to turn around and go back.

I tried again another day and got through. It was a sunny, beautiful day, and I finally got to see something other than the ruins of Sarajevo. My thoughts went back to 1982 and the drive through this area on my honeymoon. Maybe this was why, like a complete rookie, I decided it was too hot and uncomfortable to wear my bulletproof vest and helmet. They were on the passenger seat when I arrived in the town of Konjic, about fifty miles southwest of Sarajevo. I drove through the town and stopped at the UNPROFOR checkpoint at the other end. When I asked them about the security situation further south, I was told everything was quiet.

The road wound along Lake Jablanica. There was sky-blue water on my right and hills covered with pine forests on my left, with the narcotic scent of their resin in the air. Who would believe that war had been raging here for several years already? When I reached the turnoff to the village of Ribić, I saw a long bridge and before it another checkpoint. I exchanged greetings with the UNPROFOR soldiers and was told the same thing that I had heard a few kilometers earlier. Everything was fine; all was calm. Great, but just as I reached the bridge, I heard a loud, piercing sound and a frightening explosion. A gigantic geyser of water rose to my right, just a few meters from my car, and rocks were flying everywhere.

I stepped on the gas, but before I could make it to the other side of the bridge, I heard another explosion, this one not far behind me. I headed for a safe zone, stopped the car, and got out. Some soldiers ran up to me and asked if I was okay. I was, but the paint job on the car was a mess, and the rear window was cracked. It was then that I learned from the local UNPROFOR commander that VRS troops kept trying to hit the bridge but had missed so far because they had to shoot over a hill. The bridge could not be closed for the same reason they were trying to hit it: the road was needed to supply Sarajevo. I humbly put on my vest and helmet and didn't take them off until I reached the Adriatic coast in Croatia. I would make many more journeys across that bridge, each time crouched behind the wheel with my foot heavy on the gas.

One day UNPROFOR management decided that the cost of my stay at the Holiday Inn, a luxury hotel long ago but since then extensively damaged, was getting too expensive. I had to relocate, and I was able to find an affordable apartment with everything a tenant could ask for. It had a modern bathroom, a spacious living room, and a balcony that offered spectacular views of the devastated city. More importantly, it was out of reach of sniper fire. The catch? There was no heat or running water inside the apartment, and power outages were common. Summers there were survivable, but the winter I lived in Sarajevo was a long and nasty one. Heavy gray clouds hung over the city, an icy fog rolled through the streets, and the ground was covered in filthy snow. The sleeping bag I crawled into every night grew damp over time because there was no way to dry it. Some mornings I woke up with a sheen of frost on it. For water I had to fill canisters at a supply point and haul them back to the apartment, just enough for some basic washing up and flushing the toilet. There was no relief in my office either, for it was just as cold. The only place I could warm up was inside the squad car.

Not surprisingly home improvement was popular in Sarajevo, especially ideas for improvised heating. The contraption installed by my landlord consisted of a long rubber hose connected to a stove. He stuck a circular piece of steel piping with small holes drilled in it inside the stove, attached the hose, and opened the shutoff valve. As gas hissed out, he struck a match and flames roared forth. The warmth was heavenly. Unfortunately, I couldn't use this makeshift heater through the night because the pressure in the line fluctuated or else dropped off completely. It might then start up again out of nowhere, filling the place with gas that could suffocate me in my sleep. It is needless to say that explosions took place in Sarajevo on a daily basis due to people having to jury-rig their home heating.

In January 1995 I returned to Sarajevo after spending Christmas in Prague, and to no surprise freezing cold was waiting for me in my apartment. I had taken my trousers off to change into my uniform when, for no apparent reason, I decided to start up the heating. I opened the gas valve, heard hissing, and struck a match, but got no spark. During the time I was away, the matches had gotten damp. I tried another one, then a third, and still nothing. Finally, with the gas still hissing merrily away, the fourth match sparked and just about engulfed me in a fireball that singed the hair on my hands, legs, eyebrows, and eyelashes. I was lucky to only get slightly burned—it could have been much worse—but it took forever to rid my apartment of the acrid smell of burnt hair.

On top of the cold and damp, for a long period the only food served in the dining hall at UNPROFOR came from military supplies, the so-called MREs (meals ready to eat). This only added to an already unbearable winter. I have always hated beans but had to make do with them in order to survive. As the fighting around Sarajevo intensified, UNPRO-

FOR was forced to suspend resupply flights, and the convoys of humanitarian aid to the city also dried up. More than a month passed before we received something other than the same parcel of beans, canned meat, chocolate, wafers, paté, jam, tea, and powdered milk. So I began to dine out at a pizzeria and restaurant that served up an expensive but pretty good *ćevapčići*—skinless sausage made of minced meat. I had heard it might be mixed with dog meat, but it was a regular gourmet's delight compared to beans. I still wonder how small children and elderly people survived the blockade of Sarajevo.

In the summer of 1993, an eight-hundred-meter-long tunnel was dug under the airport. It was used to bring food, medicine, and military equipment into the city and evacuate the sick and wounded. The goods that made it in were then sold at ridiculously high prices at markets around the city. One of the biggest markets was located at Markale. In February 1994, prior to my arrival in Sarajevo, it was hit by a mortar attack that left sixty-eight people dead. Shortly after my departure on August 28, 1995, another attack killed forty-three people.

At the Door of the International Tribunal

The friends I met during the war who still have my admiration include former U.S. Marine Joe Binger. He was part of the security detail that flew cash into Sarajevo to keep UNPROFOR liquid. Joe was a mountain of muscle and cartilage and somebody you could always depend on. Today it's nothing special, but in 1994, five years after the fall of the Iron Curtain, a U.S. Marine hitting it off with a policeman from the former Czechoslovakia was a rare sight. One day he told me that he had gotten an offer to work for the tribunal in The Hague and was leaving for the Netherlands in a few days.

My own contract was coming to an end, and the specter of returning to the Interpol office in Prague loomed before me. Since the tribunal was still hiring, I signed up for an interview as an investigator and a security officer. I waited and waited, but nothing, so I called Joe at The Hague to see if he knew anything. He called back a few days later to say that he had found my paperwork under a pile of hundreds of other applications. He took personal charge of mine, and just like that I was invited for an interview at the headquarters of UNPROFOR in Zagreb. Two members of the Office of the Prosecutor grilled me over coffee, focusing on my practical experience with investigations and knowledge of the conflict in the former Yugoslavia. I passed the interview, and soon after returning to my homeland on April 1, 1995, I received the magic envelope with UN written on it. Inside was a contract to work as an investigator in the Office of the Prosecutor for the International Tribunal.

In many jurisdictions investigations are carried out by the police, but the Office of the Prosecutor had its own department of investigations, which was divided into several teams. Each team was led by a senior investigator and consisted of other investigators, lawyers, analysts, interpreters, and other experts as needed. At the time of my arrival, there were nine teams in all; later two more teams were formed. Their individual number and mandate were based on a report compiled by a UN commission of experts. Five teams were focused on crimes committed by Serbs in Croatia and Bosnia and Herzegovina, two teams focused on crimes committed by Croats, one team investigated the Bosniaks, and the rest dealt with members of the Yugoslavian government and crimes committed in Kosovo.

The Office of the Prosecutor

On the morning of April 15, I received my commission from the UN administration and came on board. They took my height and weight, photographed me, recorded my blood type, and noted the color of my eyes. I was issued an ID card and assigned to Team 4, which was led by Jo Limmayog, a police officer from the Philippines. We were charged with investigating war crimes committed by Serbs against Croats in the territory of Croatia.

My colleagues were two British investigators, Kevin Curtis and Dennis Milner; the team lawyer, American John Clint Williamson; a Canadian Russian analyst Serge Krieger; and a French administrative assistant Christine Roumagere, who was later replaced by a Brazilian woman, Dayse de Oliveira.

The team was a happy, collegial group that sometimes slipped and made comments in the office that were not really appropriate in mixed company. Although there was nothing malicious about the remarks, Dayse would take her ruler out of the drawer and suddenly become the schoolmistress, threatening to discipline us if we continued misbehaving in her presence. We always had a great laugh about it, and no one ever took offense.

The countries that came into being after the breakup of Yugoslavia had no interest in cooperating with the tribunal, and when they were forced to, they did so only formally and then always focusing on the crimes committed by the other side in the conflict. In places where there had been bloodshed, no one conducted even a cursory inspection. Areas where civilians had been massacred and buried were either unknown or the international community was denied access to them. The task given to us had probably never been previously encountered by investigators, and frankly we had no idea where to start.

Kevin, Dennis, and I decided to divide up the material the tribunal had received from humanitarian organizations and proceed as in any other investigation. We would read the material, analyze it, formulate an investigative plan, compile a list of potential witnesses and perpetrators, and, with legal support from Clint, set out to disentangle this web of horror. So we sat down at our computers and began to go through the mountains of unsorted documentation.

I envy the way detectives in movies or books always know where to find witnesses and look for evidence. As an ordinary detective, one trod up and down endless staircases and spent countless hours casing various joints, since the key breakthrough in an investigation usually comes down to patience, luck, and coincidence. In the Czech television series *The Sinful People of Prague*, a police inspector exhorts his underlings to never underestimate coincidence: "It's a powerful thing that must be taken seriously in detective work."

It wasn't easy to discern coincidence in the documents before us because many of the interviews with witnesses had been conducted by aid workers who lacked experience in preparing such records and reports. The statements they took were heart-wrenching—desperate mothers and fathers looking for their children or children looking for their parents—but they provided little material evidence to go on.

Yet in the case of Vukovar Hospital, all the testimonies had one thing in common: on November 20, 1991, the JNA took away members of their family, and no one had heard a word from them even as of 1995, when we began our investigation. We had to sort the documents in order of importance because the time and budget allotted us ruled out questioning every witness, many of whom had become scattered throughout Croatia or different parts of Europe and even North America. Our first list numbered nearly 350 people, which we divided into three groups. The main witnesses included those who had survived the alleged massacre and so could provide firsthand testimony: Zdenko Novak, Emil Čakalić, Dragutin Berghofer, Vilim Karlović, Stjepan Gunčević, Vlado Gudaš, and Tihomir Perković. The second largest group consisted of the relatives of the missing, while the third included employees of the hospital, Croatian humanitarian organizations and NGOs, journalists, and employees of ECMM, the European Community Monitoring Mission deployed in Vukovar in November 1991.

One of our eyewitnesses from the monitoring mission was Petr Kypr, an employee of the Ministry of Foreign Affairs of the Czech Republic. In 1991 he and a Danish colleague, physician Jan Schou, were present when Major Veselin Šljivančanin of the JNA prevented the Red Cross from entering Vukovar Hospital. In 1995 Kypr was serving as the Czech ambassador to Slovenia, and Dr. Schou had a medical practice in Norway. I interviewed Ambassador Kypr in Slovenia; it was the only statement I wrote up for the tribunal in Czech, as the normal practice was to record all interviews in English. Kypr had insisted, however, because as a state representative he maintained that he had the right to be questioned in his mother tongue.

8. Argument between Major Veselin Šljivančanin of the JNA and Nicolas Bosinger of the Red Cross on a bridge over Vuka River in Vukovar. (ICTY)

In December 1995 Kevin and I traveled to Tønsberg, Norway, where Dr. Schou had his practice. Since he had time for us only after office hours, we went to have a look around the city. The hotel reception recommended we pay a visit to a place called "The End of the World." There was no way we could get lost because there was only one road to it. It was thirty kilometers away, but it took us nearly an hour to reach it on the narrow asphalt road.

We stopped and looked around in every direction. Steel-gray clouds hung overhead, while a stormy ocean raged below the jagged cliffs, which were barren except for a sheen of anthracite and squawking seagulls making do with what shelter they could find. The feeling of hopelessness and despair was underpinned by an abandoned kiosk and what looked like an ancient well. I told Kevin that, since we were there, we should at least get out of the car and take a few pictures. He reluctantly agreed and opened the door. The arctic blast outside mercilessly hammered us with icy beads whipped up from the rolling waves. After just two minutes, we were frozen to the bone. A couple of photos later, we dashed back to the car and returned to the hotel. After that I was unable to interest Kevin in any more excursions in this part of Norway. We conducted our interview with Dr. Schou, and he promised to testify for us when the time came.

In mid-1994 the Office of the Prosecutor opened a liaison office in Zagreb with Ton Kempenaars as its head. The office assisted the investigative teams to coordinate their activities in Croatia. In June we set out to interview the first eyewitnesses. It was a step into the unknown, as none of us had ever had to use interpreters to question foreigners previously. On average each interview took two days. On the first day, we conducted the interviews, which were recorded; the next day was spent reading each interview back to the witness and making clarifications. Once the witness was satisfied, he or she signed the document, and we left.

After a cold and suspicious start, practically every interview ended in tears, from both women and men. Each had a different breaking point that was impossible to predict beforehand. Often, we had to call in a psychologist to comfort the witnesses. In such instances our interpreters proved to be invaluable because they helped the witnesses deal with their emotions in their mother tongue. Their hard work and ethical behavior were exemplary and often inspiring.

During the next few months, we were more often in the field than in our office in The Hague. We conducted interviews wherever possible. We visited witnesses at their homes, met them in hotels, or they came to us at the police stations in Osijek, Zagreb, Slavonski Brod, as well as in Split, Zadar, and other cities and villages across Croatia. The contrast we noted traveling through this country was remarkable. There was war and destruction, on the one hand, and the beauty of the landscape, on the other. The food and traditions in the interior were very similar to back home in Prague, but the light meals on the Adriatic, consisting primarily of fish, vegetables, and a variety of salads served with delicious Croatian wine, were more reminiscent of Italy and Greece.

But life is made up of not just tragedy but also funny experiences, and our travels were no exception. Our accommodation on one mission was in a hotel in Zagreb. There were ads in the elevator for various services, one of them being massages. The smile of the beautiful young woman in the photograph gave us a pretty good idea of what kind of massages one could expect. Kevin, Dennis, and I goaded one another into going for one of these massages. Our chief, Jo, never expressed an opinion one way or another about it. His habit was always silence. Then one morning at breakfast, he said in broken English: "They tricked me; it's a scam." We looked at each other puzzled, so I asked him what was up. "There was a guy there," he said. All right, we still had no clue, so I tried once more. "Jo, what are you talking about?" Finally, we learned that he had fallen for one of those ads in the elevator and went for a massage in the wellness center of the hotel. But instead of a smiling young woman waiting for him with open arms, it was some bearded man.

Then there was Kevin's personal story. His interpreter was Andrea Čačić; mine at the time was Dolores Bakica. After several days of conducting interviews together in Osijek, I had to leave for Budapest. Kevin and I agreed to call every evening to keep each other informed about events. Dolores and I got to Budapest late in the afternoon. After checking into the hotel, we went for dinner and had only just sat down in a restaurant when my phone rang.

It was Kevin, and his first few words and the tone of his voice were a clear indication that something had happened. He was an Englishman used to driving on the left but had mastered driving on the right side after a couple of weeks in Croatia. He had no idea, however, whether cars or trams had the right of way at an intersection. To cut a long story short, the tram plowed neatly into the passenger side door of his vw Golf. Both he and Andrea suffered only minor bruises, but the impact of the crash had sent her flying into his lap. Several years later, when the two of them got married, I mischievously recalled the story of how they first got close to each other during their wedding reception. For some people it's about expressing their feelings, for others buying flowers or presents, but for Kevin and Andrea, it was about getting hit by a tram.

Propaganda as an Instrument of War

Joseph Goebbels, the propaganda minister for Adolf Hitler, was known for his energetic verbosity and his ability to manipulate a crowd. He allegedly once remarked, "If you tell a big lie and repeat it long enough, people will believe it's true." Whether or not Goebbels actually said that, I did see with my own eyes how the big lies of wartime propaganda make it possible to achieve military and political objectives.

At the end of the 1980s, Slobodan Milošević assumed control of the media in Serbia as part of achieving his territorial goals in Croatia and Bosnia. The loud, repetitive, and constant theme of the Serb propaganda was the Croat atrocities during the World War II. The atrocities were real and horrendous, but Milošević's propaganda strove to present the World War II atrocities as closely connected to the Croat independence aspirations in 1990s. Television, radio, and newspapers were also used to glorify Milošević's "farsighted" policies and to attack the stooges of the Western powers.

As the battle of Vukovar intensified, military propaganda deliberately spread lies and half-truths about what was happening in the city and in particular at the hospital, which was under the direction of a Croatian doctor, Vesna Bosanac. The hospital itself had not been spared from shelling and aerial bombardment by the JNA. The conditions there were grueling. There were power outages, rationed water, shortages of medicine and dressing materials, and too many wounded for the hospital to cope with even during peacetime. The staff of the hospital was not exclusively Croatian but included Serb doctors and nurses as well.

During the most intense fighting, between August and November 1991, the Serbian propaganda machine began spreading misinformation that Dr. Bosanac and her Croatian staff had committed war crimes against wounded Serb civilians and paramilitaries by denying them treatment. It was claimed that local Serbs were forced to donate blood and that doctors in the hospital had removed body organs from

9. (*top*) Dr. Vesna Bosanac testifying before the tribunal. (ICTY)

10. (*bottom*) Vukovar Hospital in November 1991. (ICTY)

the Serbs to save the lives of Croatian patients. On top of all that, the whole Serb population was deemed at risk of being liquidated in Vukovar. After occupying the hospital, the JNA arrested the director, Dr. Bosanac, and interrogated her for days, but were unable to prove any wrongdoing.

Just before the end of the siege, the propaganda was ratcheted up to include an allegation guaranteed to incite hatred. After the surrender Serbian media published reports that Croats in Vukovar had slit the throats of more than forty Serb children. The reputable Reuters organization repeated the claim on November 20, 1991. Its source was Goran Mikić, who had told Radio-Television Serbia that he had counted forty-one children aged five to seven years old who had been murdered at the school in Borovo Naselje. Afterward their bodies were dumped in a cellar. Mikić also said that members of the JNA had told him that they had seen Serb children murdered by Croatian soldiers.

The following is an extract from Goran Mikić's interview for the Serbian media:

Goran Mikić: "We saw plastic bags full of little dead bodies. I managed to creep up to about twenty meters distance. It was plain to see that they were children between five and seven years of age. Their throats were slit. There was a lot of blood around their heads. It was so sickening, even the soldiers wept, and so even at the cost of our lives we wanted to . . ."

Editor: "Do you have an estimate for the number of dead bodies that could be called children's?"

Goran Mikić: "It was all a big pile. They were putting heads and bodies together. It was all so horrible. There must have been around forty according to their count, but it was impossible to be more accurate."

Editor: "You had a camera. Did you try to take pictures?"

Goran Mikić: "I did. I got up. However, bullets were whistling all around me. A soldier pointed his rifle at me and ordered me to lie down because otherwise I would have been killed."

Editor: "You were explicitly forbidden to take pictures? Do you have any idea whether anyone took some pictures?"

Goran Mikić: "Well, I don't know. I assume the army did. That could be reasonable, and those pictures needed to be taken."

Reuters retracted its report the next day when Mikić admitted that he had neither seen nor counted any children. The JNA also disassociated itself, and Radio-Television Serbia published an apology, stating that Mikić had been hallucinating. But the damage had been done. Despite the disclaimers, the Belgrade daily *Politika* made these "murdered" Serb children its headline as late as November 22.

People later tried by the tribunal for war crimes, including Milan Babić, the first president of the Republic of Serbian Krajina (RSK), confirmed the impact of this propaganda on them. Babić pleaded guilty to the crimes for which he was charged, saying that at the start of his political career he had been strongly influenced and misled by Serbian propaganda, which repeatedly talked about the genocide of Serbs committed by the Croatian regime. This atmosphere deliberately provoked fear and hatred of Croats in their Serb neighbors.

False or unverified information had invariably influenced the thinking of the Serbs who took control of Vukovar on November 19, 1991. This inevitably led to their exacting revenge on the Croatian population, whether on those remaining in the hospital or in Velepromet, a local factory complex located on the outskirts of Vukovar, where Croats were waiting for evacuation. The massacre at Ovčara was an outcome of this effective manipulation of the media and public opinion.

What Happened at Ovčara

In 1991 Vukovar and its surroundings had more than eighty-four thousand inhabitants, 44 percent of whom were Croats and 37 percent Serbs. The remainder consisted of ethnic minorities, among them a considerable number of Czechs and Slovaks who had settled there before the Second World War, when the Czech-based Bata shoe company opened a large factory in the Vukovar suburb of Borovo Naselje. These Czechs and Slovaks lived not only in the local Bata settlement but also in Vukovar itself and surrounding villages.

11. (*top*) The battle of Vukovar. The city was practically destroyed by JNA shelling. (Vladimír Dzuro)

12. (*bottom*) View from the Vukovar water tower in the direction of the suburb of Mitnica. (Vladimír Dzuro)

After the declaration of independence, Croatian policy began to focus on building national unity, and in early May 1991, the first serious clashes between Serb and Croat inhabitants broke out in Eastern Slavonia. Often each expelled the other from the communities where they were in the majority. In August the JNA began operating along this eastern edge of Croatia. The first shelling of Vukovar took place on August 25, together with an especially hard-fought battle for the armory and its arsenal of heavy weapons. Teaming up with the local Serbian Territorial Defense Force, the JNA gained control of the entire territory, with the exception of Vukovar. They launched an assault on the city on the pretext of protecting the Serb population, but the Croats repelled it. By September 25 the battle of Vukovar was well under way. A weeklong offensive in October succeeded in encircling the city, and the defenders were gradually hemmed in. On November 18 the last bulwark was breached and the city captured. The JNA and Serbian paramilitaries like the "volunteer guard" took control of the entire city. The prisoners were transported to camps inside Serbia.

After three months of fighting, Vukovar was in ruins. Several thousand men, women, and children had taken shelter in the hospital, and on the day of the surrender, the JNA and the Croatian government agreed that they should be evacuated under the supervision of international organizations. Colonel Mrkšić, who was in charge of the military operation, assigned this task to Major Šljivančanin. The next day, November 19, Mrkšić and Šljivančanin were informed that paramilitaries had tortured and executed some non-Serbian inhabitants of Vukovar at the factory complex in Velepromet.

In the early morning hours of November 20, Šljivančanin blocked Red Cross and ECMM representatives from accessing the hospital and ordered the hospital staff to assemble for a meeting with JNA officers. There they were held in a room while soldiers under the command of Captain Radić led approximately three hundred civilians from the hospital to buses waiting outside. These people were secretly transported to the JNA garrison south of Vukovar, where they were detained under armed guard for about two hours. Another order from Šljivančanin

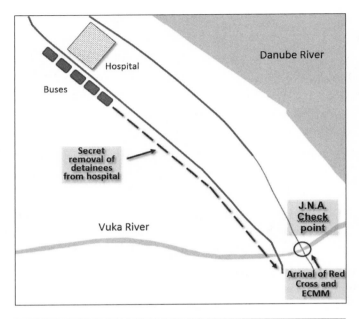

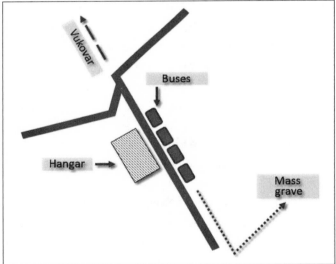

13. (*top*) Diagram depicting secret removal of detained people from the Vukovar Hospital. (Vladimír Dzuro)

14. (*bottom*) Diagram of buses with prisoners parked in front of a hangar at Ovčara. (Vladimír Dzuro)

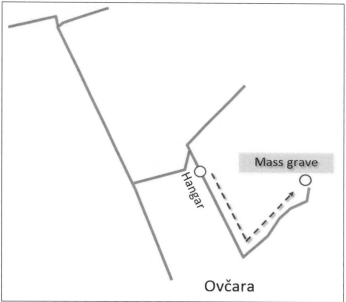

Mass grave

Hangar

Ovčara

15. (*top*) Hangar at Ovčara used for detentions of non-Serbs in November 1991. (Ralph J. Hartley)

16. (*bottom*) Transport of the detained from the hangar to the execution site. (Vladimír Dzuro)

then arrived to take about fifteen of them, mostly medical staff, back to the hospital. The rest were driven to a pig farm at Ovčara.

The convoy of buses stopped in front of a hangar at the farm. The people were dragged out and searched, had their personal belongings taken from them, and were forced to run a gauntlet of soldiers and irregulars into the hangar. They were mercilessly beaten during this run, and the cruelty continued once they were inside the building. Several Croats were eventually spared after they were recognized as neighbors or acquaintances of the soldiers from before the war. They were removed from the hangar and taken back to Vukovar.

Inside, the inhuman treatment continued even while JNA soldiers drew up a list of the detainees, who included two women. When evening arrived, Colonel Mrkšić sent an order for his unit to withdraw from Ovčara, and that sealed the fate of these 264 people. The irregulars herded them in groups of twenty onto a covered flatbed truck, which was hitched to a tractor. They were driven about one kilometer south of Ovčara to an area that before the war had served as a disposal ground for pig remains.

A huge pit, dug with an excavator, was waiting for them. The prisoners were ordered to stand at the edge, and then they were shot by the irregulars with short bursts of machine-gun fire. Most of them tumbled backward into the pit, but a few fell to the side and had to be thrown in. The killers covered up the site with the excavator and left before dawn on November 21, 1991.

The Discovery of the Mass Grave

The crucial role in discovering the mass grave was played by a Croat of alleged Czech ancestry named Zdenko Novak. He had been in one of the groups of twenty who, having survived their ordeal so far, now found themselves being driven off into the dark.

He recounted the ordeal: "The canvas covering the truck had a slit in it, so I could see they were taking us toward the village of Grabovo. After about a kilometer, I saw a long ravine lined with trees and bushes. The tractor veered off to the left and headed onto a dirt road. Some of us were saying we should try to escape, because no one was guarding us then. But Željko Jurela was against it, saying, 'If we try to escape, they will kill us.' But at that moment I decided to make a jump for it. Something urged me on, I couldn't stand it anymore. I didn't tell anyone. I just pulled the canvas back and jumped. I landed on my knees, but was all right. I could see from the lights on the tractor where they were going. A moment later I heard several shots. I ran as quickly as possible toward Vukovar, through a cornfield and then a wood. After about two hours, I reached the village of Čerić, where I was stopped at a Serbian checkpoint. I managed to convince the soldiers there that I was a Serb. That saved my life."

Reading through the statement Novak later gave, you get a sense of not just his courage but also the fear he must have endured. Running through the cornfield in the dark, stumbling over the sharp edges of stalks protruding from the ground, while the air reverberated with gunfire. Breathless, sweating, his body covered in dirt and blood, and scared to death, he still managed to talk his way past a checkpoint.

I noted in Novak's statement that he had already talked about his experience at Ovčara several times. One of those he confided in was Clyde Snow, a renowned forensic anthropologist who, it was said, was the model for a famous movie figure Indiana Jones. Snow had gained his reputation by inspecting the mummy of King Tutankhamen, doing forensic work on different aspects of the murder of President Kennedy, investigating the Oklahoma bombing site, and identifying Nazi murderer Josef Mengele. In October 1992 Snow was sent to the former Yugoslavia as a member of the Mazowiecky Commission, tasked with locating mass grave sites. He flew to Zagreb and met Dr. Ivica Kostović, the dean of Zagreb Medical School and head of Croatia's own commission. They discussed several cases of presumed mass graves and gave the existence of one at Ovčara top priority. It was then that Snow learned about Zdenko Novak. Three days later Novak walked into his hotel room.

"When I met the witness in Zagreb," Snow recalled, "we looked at a map of the terrain near the hangar at Ovčara. We agreed there was only a single place they could have turned off from the road, at a ravine. I can tell you from living in Texas and Oklahoma that the end of a ravine is often chosen as a landfill, if for no other reason than that no good farmer would dig a grave in the middle of a fertile field."

None of us believed that a bunch of murderers would care about the fertility of soil in the Danube basin, but he was right. He pointed to a place on the map where the grave was likely to be found. A meeting took place at UNPROFOR command for Eastern Slavonia in Erdut with Staff Sergeant Larry Moore of the Royal Canadian Mounted Police. He had served there for several months and mapped out the area around Vukovar in detail. The team left for Ovčara the next day, October 18, 1992, accompanied by Colonel Peeters, the commander of the Belgian battalion in Sector East.

They parked just before the turnoff onto a dirt road and walked along the ravine to the end of it, just as Novak had described. Even from a distance, they could see a skull and part of a human skeleton in the soil. After examining it Snow said it was the remains of a young man whose skull showed the typical signs of a gunshot wound. Another skeleton was unearthed whose bones had traces of being gnawed on by animals. Next to the remains lay a pendant with a cross; the inscription said in the Croatian language, "God and Croats." An examination of the surrounding tree trunks showed that they had been damaged by bullets, and a large number of spent cartridges were scattered about. Because the site was not secure, Snow took several pictures and went back to the base. UNPROFOR ordered the Russian battalion, RUSBAT, to guard the area until further notice.

Around mid-December 1992 Snow returned to Ovčara. This time he was accompanied by Eric Stover, the director of Physicians for Human Rights (PHR) and anthropologist Rebecca Saunders. They were there to conduct a test examination of the scene. While assessing the size of the grave, Saunders found visible traces that a bulldozer had been used on the site. With considerable assistance from the Russian soldiers, the team of experts began a controlled test excavation. The remains of at least eleven other victims were discovered at a shallow

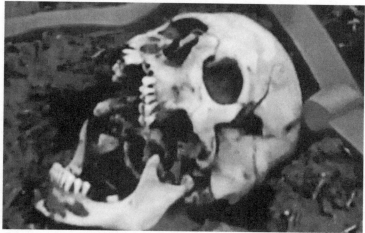

17. (*top*) Human skull and bones found by Clyde Snow at Ovčara in
1992. (Ralph J. Hartley)

18. (*bottom*) Detail of the human skull found at Ovčara by Clyde Snow in
1992. (Ralph J. Hartley)

depth beneath the surface. Snow estimated that the bodies had been
lying in the earth for six to eighteen months.

Before leaving the site, they covered the remains with a black plastic foil and carefully filled in the excavated part. They wanted every-

19. (*top*) A necklace with a Catholic cross and a tag found at Ovčara in 1992. (Ralph J. Hartley)

20. (*bottom*) Initial inspection of the alleged mass grave at Ovčara in 1992—digging a test trench. (Ralph J. Hartley)

21. (*opposite top*) Area where the Ovčara mass grave was located. (Ralph J. Hartley)

22. (*opposite bottom*) Initial examination of the mass grave at Ovčara in 1992. (Ralph J. Hartley)

Grave Site

23. (*top*) The Ovčara mass grave in December 1992. (Ralph J. Hartley)

24. (*bottom*) Diagram depicting the initial examination by Clyde Snow and his team in December 1992. (Ralph J. Hartley)

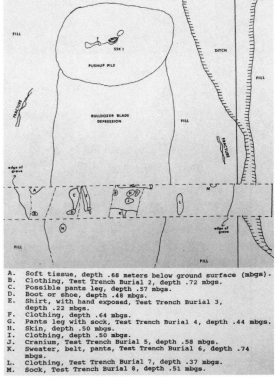

A. Soft tissue, depth .68 meters below ground surface (mbgs).
B. Clothing, Test Trench Burial 2, depth .72 mbgs.
C. Possible pants leg, depth .57 mbgs.
D. Boot or shoe, depth .48 mbgs.
E. Shirt, with hand exposed, Test Trench Burial 3, depth .22 mbgs.
F. Clothing, depth .64 mbgs.
G. Pants leg with sock, Test Trench Burial 4, depth .44 mbgs.
H. Skin, depth .50 mbgs.
I. Clothing, depth .50 mbgs.
J. Cranium, Test Trench Burial 5, depth .58 mbgs.
K. Sweater, belt, pants, Test Trench Burial 6, depth .74 mbgs.
L. Clothing, Test Trench Burial 7, depth .37 mbgs.
M. Sock, Test Trench Burial 8, depth .51 mbgs.

25. Members of Snow's team placing a black plastic foil in the test trench in December 1992. (Ralph J. Hartley)

thing reverted to its original state until they could return to perform a complete exhumation.

The Mazowiecky Commission planned to launch an investigation into the massacre the following year. At this time they would carry out the exhumation, obtain evidence, transport the bodies to a morgue, and conduct autopsies to identify the victims. Managing the logistics and hiring a sufficient number of experts proved no problem, but a lack of political will brought everything to a standstill.

In order to reach a political agreement to initiate the exhumation, members of the commission visited Zagreb and Belgrade and then also Knin and Erdut, where the government and parliamentary institutions of the breakaway "Republic of Serbian Krajina" were located. On October 19, 1993, international teams left Zagreb to begin preparatory work. But literally at the last moment the parliament of Serbian Krajina decided to suspend all activities related to the exhumation until the question of the status of the Serbs living in Croatia was resolved.

The Mazowiecky Commission again tried to get permission to start work, but to no avail, and the teams had to pull back to Zagreb with their equipment before the end of October. In April 1994 the commission completed its mandate and handed all documentation over to the newly appointed tribunal in The Hague.

The Indictment of the Vukovar Three

Meanwhile, the investigators questioned witnesses and obtained evidence, which Serge Krieger pored over. Clint Williamson worked hard on the form of the first indictment, which he finished in early October 1995. Lawyers from other teams took on the role of defense attorneys for a mock hearing to spot weaknesses in our work. The consultation process paid off. On October 26, 1995, Chief Prosecutor Richard Goldstone signed the indictment. The defendants were three officers from the First Guards Motorized Brigade of the JNA:

Colonel Mile Mrkšić, commander

Major Veselin Šljivančanin, counterintelligence officer

Captain Miroslav Radić, of special forces affiliated with the
brigade.

They were charged with grave breaches of the Geneva Conventions, with violations of the laws and customs of war, and crimes against humanity related to beatings, torture, and murder of at least 260 men and 2 women abducted from Vukovar and taken to Ovčara. The indictment purposely included the names of all the victims who we knew with sufficient certainty went missing after they were taken away from

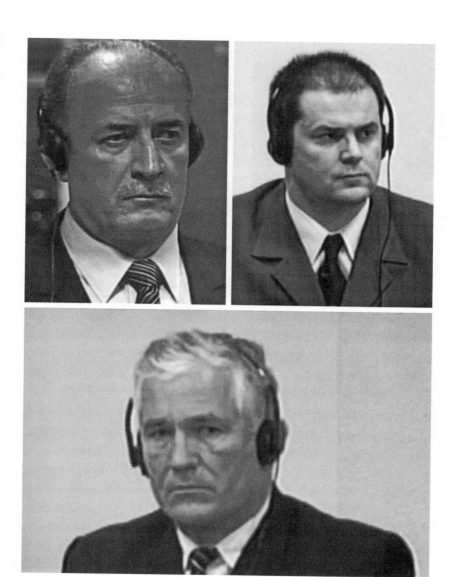

26. The Vukovar Three: Colonel Mile Mrkšić, Major Veselin Šljivančanin, Captain Miroslav Radić. (ICTY)

27. Dragutin Berghofer testifying before the tribunal. (ICTY)

28. Emil Čakalić testifying before the tribunal. (ICTY)

the hospital on the morning of November 20, 1991. At that time we knew from witnesses that Slavko Dokmanović, the mayor of Vukovar, was also involved in the atrocity at Ovčara, but we did not as yet have enough evidence to include him in the indictment.

Trial in Absentia and Adding Dokmanović to the Indictment

At this point the tribunal still faced the problem of not having any indicted people to try. By late 1995 the situation had become critical. According to Chief Prosecutor Louise Arbour, several judges of the tribunal had become so frustrated that they pushed to conduct Rule 61 hearings, effectively trials in absentia and known by the provision in the tribunal's rules of procedure, which allowed for these proceedings as an alternative way of moving cases forward when no defendants were in custody. In early March 1996, during a closed session, Judge Fouad Riad noted that more than enough time had passed since the indictment of the Vukovar Three.

The prosecutor had made every effort to notify Colonel Mrkšić, Major Šljivančanin, and Captain Radić of the indictment against them and had sent warrants to the Federal Republic of Yugoslavia for their arrest. Justice Riad therefore ordered the judicial proceedings to go forward in accordance with Rule 61. The hearing, chaired by French judge Claude Jorda, was held March 20–28, 1996. Clint Williamson, representing the prosecution, summoned eleven witnesses.

The first to appear was Emil Čakalić, a Croat born in 1934, who was the sanitary inspector at Vukovar Hospital. The following testimony is taken from the transcript:

Williamson: "What did you see at Ovčara when you arrived there?"

Čakalić: "There were many civilian cars parked on the right side of the road all the way up to the hangar. The bus approached, stopped there and we got out, one after the other. Then a JNA captain who I thought was a reservist frisked us. He took my glasses. He put them on, and when he couldn't see with them, he threw them down and stomped on them. We then had to run between two rows of Serbs who beat us. Before I reached the hangar, someone called out my name. 'Emil, what are you doing here?' I turned and saw Slavko Dokmanović. I told him that I was doing what the others here were doing. Dokmanović called me 'Inspector,' so the ones who were beating me thought I was a Croatian police inspector and so they beat me even more. When I got inside the hangar, I saw Dokmanović kicking my friend. His name was Dado. At that moment, a Vukovar Serb named Miloš Bulić came up to me and hit me on the back of the head with a wooden crutch."

Williamson: "How do you know Mr. Dokmanović?"

Čakalić: "He worked in the same institution as me. He was an agricultural consultant and mayor of Vukovar."

Williamson: "What was your relationship before you met on November 20?"

Čakalić: "Friendly. We saw each other occasionally in June 1991."

The second witness was likewise a Croat, Dragutin Berghofer, born in 1940. He also testified to the presence of Dokmanović at Ovčara:

"I put my hands up to my head to protect myself from their blows. I was already covered in blood before I reached the hangar. Emil Čakalić got there just after me. He was also beaten but I didn't see it. Once in the hangar, I saw his injuries. I have known Emil for many years. We are both fans of the Dinamo Zagreb football club. Emil was the sanitary inspector and I would see him at work. I saw Slavko Dokmanović

29. Colonel Ivan Grujić (*left*) and Dr. Davor Strinović (*right*) testifying before the tribunal. (ICTY)

there, who I knew was a reservist and the mayor of Vukovar. He came up to us and asked Emil, 'You're here too, Inspector?' and then they beat Emil again. Dokmanović kept going back and forth across the hangar. They were beating us without mercy, and I got the impression that he was the one in charge, but I didn't hear him give any specific orders. One young man named Vladimir Djukić was sitting crouched up against the wall because they injured his leg. Dokmanović went up to him and kicked him in the face."

At the conclusion of the hearing, the Appeals Chamber resolved that the indictment as presented had been proven, that the beatings and executions linked to the three accused had been committed in a manner characteristic of crimes against humanity. The chamber also stated that there was a reasonable suspicion that Mrkšić, Radić, and Šljivančanin were culpable and therefore fell under the jurisdiction of the tribunal. International warrants for their arrest were sent to all member countries of the UN, as well as to NATO troops under IFOR command in Bosnia. It was further announced that the failure to turn the men over would be considered a refusal by the Federal Republic of Yugoslavia to cooperate with the tribunal. The Security Council issued several resolutions calling on Serbia to act, yet not one of the Vukovar Three was taken into custody.

The new development, however, was that we had the evidence to include the former mayor of Vukovar, Slavko Dokmanović, in the indictment as well. On March 26, 1996, his name was added but kept secret at the request of Chief Prosecutor Richard Goldstone.

The Exhumation at Ovčara—from My Notebook

By April 1996 we had obtained sufficient evidence and issued indictments and international arrest warrants for the Vukovar Three, but we did not have the bodies of the victims buried at Ovčara, and without bodies we could not prosecute anyone. Our efforts therefore had to be focused on getting permission to carry out the exhumation. We would need a team of specialists not only to carry it out but also to give evidence about our work in proceedings before the tribunal.

Our key figure for the planned exhumation was General Jacques Paul Klein. He had joined the U.S. State Department in 1971, worked for the Pentagon, and was a reservist in the air force with the rank of major general. In 1993 he became a political adviser to the commander of U.S. forces in Europe. He was serving in that position when UN Secretary-General Boutros Boutros-Ghali appointed him as the head of the United Nations Transitional Administration for Eastern Slavonia, known as UNTAES, with the position of under-secretary-general.

I knew nothing about General Klein until Clint came back from Brussels, where he had met with him at the U.S. embassy as Klein stopped over for consultations with NATO officials en route to his new posting in Croatia. During that meeting Clint talked to Klein and complained to him about the problems with the exhumation at Ovčara. Klein promised he would look into it as a priority and also indicated that he would be willing to arrest indicted suspects who happened to be in the territory under his jurisdiction—a willingness that would come to have a significant impact on the ICTY in the months ahead. Clint subsequently also took up the problem of commencing the exhumation at Ovčara with the Croatian authorities in Zagreb.

Meanwhile, Kevin, Dennis, and I crisscrossed Croatia, Hungary, and Austria in search of witnesses to question. Sometime at the end of July

1996, Clint called me to say I was going to be the principal investigator at the site at Ovčara, adding that I should not count on going home anytime soon. Clint and Thomas Osorio, our operations officer at the Zagreb office, were waiting for me in Erdut when I arrived on August 30. We had a beer in a military bar while they debriefed me about the exact plans for the exhumation.

We chose the military camp of the Belgian battalion, BELBAT in Erdut, as our base of operations. We slept in containers that UNTAES used for the Belgian soldiers. They were like small bungalows in both size and appearance. The commander, Major General Schoups, treated us like VIPs, which meant we got one container for two persons, whereas the soldiers normally got one for four people. That's where the privileges ended, because everything was spartan. The scene consisted of rickety doors, two small windows, one white fluorescent bulb hanging from the ceiling, scuffed linoleum, clothes hanging from the wall, and two iron-frame beds separated by a narrow aisle. Sagging mattresses, starchy sheets, and foam pillows were also part of the picture. We had to do a complete inspection in order to report that everything we had received from the command was in order. The army does pride itself on order.

DAY ONE

It was in the early hours of the morning that we set off in a convoy under the protection of UNTAES military police, the first of many fifty-kilometer treks between Erdut and Ovčara. It may have been a hundred kilometers there and back, but there simply wasn't a safe place for our entire team anywhere around Vukovar. We arrived at Ovčara with mixed feelings. We stopped in front of the hangar and could almost see the suffering inflicted on those unfortunate people playing out before us on a large screen. Everything we had read or heard during our investigation was happening again, right here in front of us, the shouting and beating, the victims receiving blows from all sides as they ran the gauntlet into the hangar, its doors wide open. Blood and pain culminated in death for most of them in the end.

The narrative alone makes it hard to imagine just how far the buildings and the execution site were from each other. The Vupik pig farm consists of several large sheds, equipment, two or three hangars, and various homes scattered along a narrow asphalt road. At first glance everything looks deserted, but we knew there were Serbs still living in these homes. They could be either important witnesses or a serious threat. We had no idea whether any of them had participated in the massacre, and if they had, then our successful recovery of the bodies was not in their interest.

From the hangar we retraced the route recalled by Zdenko Novak. The narrow and poorly maintained asphalt road, full of potholes and lined with ditches full of trash, led us from the hangar toward Grabovo. When we reached the wooded ravine, we turned left across a makeshift bridge and continued along a recently restored dirt road that meandered along the overgrown ravine to where the mass grave had been found. There I discovered that the site was no longer guarded by Russian soldiers but rather by Jordanians from JORDBAT. We got out of the car and looked around.

We were standing in a cornfield halfway through the harvest. The Vukovar water tower rose in the distance like a beacon in a sea of green. At the end of the ravine, on our left, stood a provisional military camp about the size of a football field. It was surrounded by a fence made from planks covered with tarp and reinforced by three rows of barbed wire. The entrance was guarded by a watchtower for JORDBAT, with two soldiers at the top manning a machine gun. The blue flag of the UN flew above the roof. The residential containers of the garrison stood nearby. Through the open gates, I saw several refrigerated transport containers, a makeshift hall, and another container probably used as an office. The entrance was blocked by an armored personnel carrier.

A television crew arrived after us. They had permission to film the exhumation under the condition that they would hand the film over to the prosecution, free of charge, and in return they would receive exclusive rights to broadcast it in a documentary called *True Stories: The Grave.*

30. (*top*) End of the wooded ravine at Ovčara showing the provisionally fenced-off area guarded by UNPROFOR. (Vladimír Dzuro)

31. (*bottom*) Beginning of the exhumation at the Ovčara site. (Vladimír Dzuro)

The JORDBAT unit was commanded by Captain Hassan, who was especially chosen for this task because of his good knowledge of English. This good knowledge turned out to be roughly two hundred words, and that would lead to many problems and misunderstandings. Hassan carefully checked our identity cards and led us inside the compound, where we almost had a stroke. Someone wanted to prove to us that the order to "prepare everything for the exhumation" had been fulfilled to the letter and so had ordered the UNTAES engineering unit to thoroughly clean up the area. The engineers had come in with their heavy equipment, cleared away shrubs, and cut down the bullet-riddled trees, all part of our evidence. They had then leveled the terrain so that the site was neat and orderly, but nobody could say exactly where the grave was located.

The team of specialists was led by forensic anthropologist William Haglund, accompanied by archaeologist Douglas D. Scott and forensic anthropologists Rebecca Saunders, Ralph J. Hartley, Melissa A. Connor, and Clea Koff. Scott, Hartley, and Saunders had been part of the team that worked at Ovčara in 1992 with Clyde Snow, and it was only thanks to their sense of orientation and good memory that we were able to roughly determine the location of the grave site.

A major exhumation presents formidable logistical challenges, but Thomas Osorio, operations officer from our Zagreb Liaison Office, proved that he was more than up to it. The body bags were plain white ones from the United Kingdom or premium green ones from the United States. There were rubber and textile gloves, soap, cloth and paper towels, shovels, picks, hoes, paint brushes, plastic raincoats, rubber boots, brooms, buckets, detergents, disinfectants, and two refrigerated containers for storing the bodies before transporting them to Zagreb. Everything was in place and ready. The exhumation could begin.

We carried out our first inspection of the site later that afternoon. It was decided that we would perform a test excavation perpendicular to the one dug by Clyde Snow and his team in 1992. The reason was obvious. We were looking for a black plastic foil that Snow had earlier buried at the bottom of his test trench. If we found it, we would be certain that the grave had not been relocated. So we all set about digging.

In Croatia, meanwhile, there were rumors that the Russian troops of UNTAES had helped the Serbs dig up the grave and move the bodies to another place. Croatian government officials were convinced that we wouldn't find anything there and the Serbs were hoping this was the case. Conspiracy theories abounded, the nervousness of family and survivors grew, and with it the political instability of the region.

The first day we found nothing. Around five o'clock we had to leave the camp because it began to rain. Rain would continually plague us throughout the exhumation. Vukovar lies in the fertile Danube basin, formed by silt, and when the rain starts, the soil quickly turns into a heavy, sticky mud.

DAY TWO

The next morning we accompanied the team to Ovčara, and then Clint and I left to show the television crew the places in Vukovar directly linked to the tragedy: the hospital, JNA barracks, Velepromet, and the bridge over the River Vuka, where Major Šljivančanin had prevented Red Cross workers from entering the hospital. The situation hadn't changed when we returned to Ovčara in the afternoon. The excavation work continued, but there were no signs of either bodies or the black plastic foil. The site, however, was littered with dozens of spent casings, undoubtedly fired from Kalashnikov AK-47 assault rifles. Each casing was documented, photographed, and stored. It was time consuming, but we had to manage a large crime scene that had been tampered with by the engineers and their bulldozer. Darkness fell, and still nothing had been found. A shadow of doubt began to creep into our thoughts on our way back to Erdut.

DAY THREE

On September 2 the black plastic foil was finally uncovered in the trench. That discovery told us that we were in the right place and the grave had not been disturbed since 1992. It was the end of all our fears

32. (*top*) Exhumation work on the test trench at Ovčara. (Ralph J. Hartley)

33. (*bottom*) Collecting evidence from the grave—spent AK-47 ammunition. (Vladimír Dzuro)

and doubts. We could now fully concentrate on determining whether we had found one mass grave site or Snow had in fact found only the bodies of several individuals that had been thrown into a landfill for animal waste.

We watched closely as Rebecca Saunders skillfully examined the trench walls. She was able to demarcate the borders of the grave at the point where the intact, compact ground began.

We knew that one cubic meter of burial space can hold approximately eight human bodies. We estimated that the size of the grave was approximately thirty square meters, but we did not know its depth.

Once Saunders had established the entire periphery, we lined it with stakes and enclosed the area with tape. From that moment on, anything relevant found within that location was surveyed by Ralph Hartley and Douglas Scott using a leveling instrument and photographed. The discovery of a skull was always critical, since it later allowed us to visually display the position of bodies in the grave. These detailed measurements made it possible to determine the order in which the detainees were executed.

Clint informed the Croatian government and representatives of the Serbian authorities about the discovery of the grave. We returned to Erdut that evening and guzzled some excellent Belgian beer in the container bar. For security reasons we were confined to the BELBAT camp, where the routine was the same every day: shower, dinner in the military canteen, followed by one or two beers and sleep, then wake-up call in the morning, breakfast, getting into the convoy, and heading back to Ovčara.

Because Clint and I lacked the experience of anthropologists and archaeologists, moving in close proximity to a place where hundreds of people lay buried was initially difficult. We had to get used to the sickly sweet smell of decaying human flesh, the mud, to morning and evening chills, and swarms of tiresome flies. Since logistical and hygienic reasons made it impossible for us to dine at the UNTAES mess hall in Vukovar, we were provisioned with MREs, which were the canned food rations that the U.S. Army supplied its soldiers on missions.

34. Removal of the soil from the grave at Ovčara by the PHR team. (Ralph J. Hartley)

35. Exhumation at Ovčara closely observed by Colonel Grujić (*first from the left*).
(Ralph J. Hartley)

The film-encased food was actually quite good and had sufficient nutritional value for surviving under difficult conditions, but after a while there was grumbling, particularly from our specialists, for a regular meal. When it became clear that we would not finish the exhumation in the originally planned three weeks, there were signs of rebellion, so we worked out an agreement with General Klein to have UNTAES bring in cooked meals from headquarters. It was a welcome step. A bowl of hot soup or stew with pasta managed to perk up the team and instill new vigor in our efforts.

DAY FOUR

On September 3 the Croatian observers Colonel Grujić, head of the Croatian government office for missing persons and detainees, and Davor Strinović, head of the Institute of Forensic Pathology at the University of Zagreb, arrived at Ovčara.

They were followed by the Serbian observer Časlav Niksić. We agreed that they would have access to the area every Monday, Wednesday, and Friday, but only when the exhumation team was there. In our absence no one was permitted on location. On this day a delegation also arrived from ECMM. We allowed them to observe the exhumation for a period of time, but only from designated points outside the demarcated area. The same applied to the Croatian and Serbian observers, none of whom had access to the grave itself. We had to absolutely guard against any allegations that someone might have planted or removed something from the site.

DAY FIVE

Slovak soldiers from SLOVBAT arrived with a mini JCB excavator. This greatly accelerated our work in removing the soil from around the grave. I was fascinated by the interplay between two of the workers, one an Indian from our team and a Slovak soldier. They didn't understand each other at all until they got to work; then everything was perfectly clear. In their spare time, they started seeing who could dig up a bigger piece of dirt with the excavator bucket or close a box of matches intact with the monstrous bucket. Everything was secretly filmed by the television crew.

DAY SIX

On September 5 the head of the specialists, William Haglund, arrived from Bosnia. He surveyed the exhumation site, questioned his team, and then left with Clint and me for UNTAES headquarters in Vukovar for our first press conference. The press center was completely packed, not just with journalists from the former Yugoslavia but also with reporters from major world media outlets. I was there to watch and observe in the event I had to substitute for Clint some day. Both men talked about the commencement of the exhumation and the present situation on site. They answered some questions, and then we went back. Around three o'clock that afternoon, we had to suspend all activity because it started raining again. We returned to Erdut but had no idea what might await us in Ovčara in the morning.

William Haglund was a forensic anthropologist and true expert, but he appeared to have a great talent for offending and upsetting anyone he came across. Clint and I heard some gossip from his PHR colleagues indicating that he planned his trips from the exhumations in Bosnia to Ovčara to coincide precisely with the press conferences.

That we could live with, but the first thing Haglund did after arriving at Ovčara was to eject Lieutenant Montesara from the exhumation site. Montesara was Captain Hassan's deputy, and Haglund insulted him by treating him in this manner. Not a good thing to do to the people with guns providing us security at Ovčara. Haglund couldn't seem to understand that the exhumation was being done not for scientific purposes but rather for building our case at the tribunal. His job was to lead the forensic aspects of the exhumation; everything else fell under Clint's authority.

DAYS SEVEN THROUGH TWELVE

When we arrived at Ovčara on the morning of September 6, the entrance was blocked by an armored carrier with two angry-looking

Jordanian soldiers leveling their machine gun at us. Captain Hassan approached our convoy and, clearly upset, began explaining something in his incomprehensible English. The only thing we understood was that the exhumation site was off-limits to us. Clint tried to negotiate, but he had to call Major Neel, the special assistant to General Schoups, the UNTAES military commander, for help. While we waited in our vehicles, Hassan's troops, who were supposed to be guarding us, now surrounded us. That's the way it remained until Neel arrived. He brought along an interpreter, and we finally learned about the offense taken by Montesara. Hassan's deputy received an apology, the gate was unblocked, and we could finally get on with our work. Captain Hassan invited us to a lunch prepared by his soldiers as a gesture of friendship.

Lunch was *mansaf* chicken in yogurt sauce with rice. The yogurt was watery enough to drink. It confirmed our fears about preparing and serving food next to a mass grave. Flies darted on and off our meals, the same flies hovering over the bodies. There was nothing we could do about it, however. We simply couldn't afford to convey another insult.

Captain Hassan invited us to his command container. Incongruously there was a picture of Princess Diana hanging on the container wall, and several magazines with photos of her were lying about on the table. In his broken English, Hassan excitedly explained that Diana was a real lady, but Prince Charles was a mean, no-good liar. Hassan's excessive admiration for her seemed ridiculous, but of course none of us laughed. We appreciated the gesture of reconciliation. Clint, Thomas, and I later returned the favor later by scouring up some local lamb for the Jordanian soldiers, which they enjoyed. That sealed our friendship with Hassan and his troops.

It rained practically every day, and puddles and mud were everywhere. The only thing we could do about it was dig a drainage ditch around the entire grave. Every night we covered the exhumation site with heavy tarpaulins made of a rubberized fabric and photographed it. This precaution was necessary to ensure the credibility of the evidence concealed underneath. Although the site was guarded by the

36. First body exhumed from the Ovčara mass grave marked as OCV 001.
(Ralph J. Hartley)

military, we didn't underestimate attempts to disrupt the exhumation.
A truce was in effect, but the war was still not over.

Our specialists removed the soil from the grave and its surroundings with detailed perseverance. Like a scene from a horror movie, the bodies of these murder victims emerged centimeter by centimeter from the earth.

The sheer number of body parts spoke of a massacre manifesting unspeakable depravity. There was no order to the torsos found in the upper part of the grave, proving they had just been dumped there. They were in a late stage of decomposition, so we put only skeletal remains and residual clothing and footwear into the bags.

As we dug deeper, the bodies were less decayed and in some semblance of order. They were usually on their backs, feet pointing upward. The victims were undoubtedly standing at the edge of the hole facing their executioners before falling backward into the trench. The bodies at the bottom of the grave were preserved enough to identify face features, scars, and tattoos. We immediately took pictures for fear

37. William
Haglund and
Clea Koff
discussing work
progress. (Ralph
J. Hartley)

that exposure to the air could degrade the tattoos. We were looking for
anything that could aid identification, and tattoos or scars were very
helpful. We photographed and described every single body, sealed it
in a bag, and tagged it with a number beginning with ovc-001.

We were unable to bring the remains of the victims up in meaningful
numerical order. We would find a skull and immediately mark it with
the next number, but that didn't mean the body it belonged to was the

38. (*top*) PHR team working inside the grave. (Ralph J. Hartley)

39. (*bottom*) A member of the PHR team, David Del Pino, removing dirt from the bodies. (Ralph J. Hartley)

next thing to come out of the grave. It was nonetheless important to cause as little damage as possible when retrieving each corpse from the grave, to keep the remains together as much as possible.

Like the sword of Damocles, the approaching winter was hanging over the success of our work. Rain showers increasingly tormented us. They interrupted our work, forced us to cover up the grave again and again with tarpaulin and wait in the tent until the bad weather passed. During these moments an almost total silence permeated the site, with the thumping and echo of rain drops acting as an eerie reminder of that salvo of machine-gun fire back in November 1991.

DAY THIRTEEN

On the morning of September 12, Major Neel was waiting for us with a message from Captain Hassan. He reported that after we had left the previous evening, the Serbian observer Časlav Nikšić came back and tried to bribe the guards into letting him into the exhumation site, saying he only wanted to take pictures of the mass grave.

Because Nikšić could have either intentionally or recklessly disturbed a crime scene, the incident was reported to General Klein. He had Nikšić informed by telephone that he was immediately revoking his access to Ovčara. He then called the local Serbian authorities and told them that if they wanted to continue having their own observer participate in the exhumation, they had to choose someone with more integrity. Major Neel was then sent back to Ovčara with the announcement for Captain Hassan that General Klein and his team would arrive the following day to map out the site.

DAY FOURTEEN

It rained again on September 13. The slight drizzle had turned into a heavy shower when we spotted the convoy of several SUVs, which included General Klein with a military escort. A member of the security detail opened the heavy door of the armored SUV, and Klein slowly got out and looked around. As always he looked imposing. Tall, wearing a leather flight jacket with a blue UN baseball cap on his head, holding a lit cigar in his hand, he had the appearance of someone who had just bought the property and was now thinking about what to build there. Clint and I were of the opinion that Klein looked like a conqueror who had come to watch his army make a victory parade.

In the tent Clint filled him in on the progress of the exhumation, on the logistical problems, and the considerable delay on account of the rain every day. Then we led him directly by the mass grave. Despite the sheets of rain pouring from the clouds, he stared with fascination at the forsaken mound of human bodies partially covered by the black tarpaulins. After a while he turned to us and asked if there was anything he could do. We answered in unison. "We need a Rubb Hall to cover the exhumation site." A Rubb Hall is a large tentlike structure made of aluminum frames and polyester water-proof skin. It would allow us to work on the exhumation regardless of the weather conditions.

Klein wasted no time. He said, "Give me the phone. I'll get it for you." The rest of that afternoon and all the next day the phone rang constantly as several dozen employees of UNTAES tried to figure out exactly what we needed. In spite of this carousel, the first attempt failed. The tent they brought didn't cover even a third of the area required. It became clear to everybody that we did not need a tent but a rather large Rubb Hall.

Before the general left, we noticed how one woman who accompanied him kept observing the mound of bodies from a safe distance. She was a Serb from Vukovar who had refused to believe that such a mass grave really existed. For years the Serbian media had spread misinformation that it was just Croatian propaganda. But on that day at Ovčara, as the expression on her face alternated between stunned and horrified, the bitter truth caught up with her.

DAY NINETEEN

On the morning of September 18, the Slovak engineers arrived again and constructed a steel frame for the tent before Clint and I got back from another press conference. By evening the heavy rubberized can-

40. Exposed top layer of bodies at the Ovčara mass grave. (Dr. Ralph J. Hartley)

vas had been stretched across the site, and we finally had some decent shelter. We could do our work regardless of the weather.

DAY TWENTY-ONE

On September 20 Clint, Thomas Osorio, and I went to the Čepin airport in Osijek to pick up Louise Arbour, the incoming chief prosecutor, and Clyde Snow. We drove them to Ovčara. For Arbour it was her first glimpse of the ghastly sight of mud, rotting tissue, rain, and cold. A group in blue overalls was carefully moving around a pile of bodies doing tedious, painstaking work with brushes, shovels, and buckets.

On our way back to the airport, we drove through Vukovar to show Arbour and Snow the now-infamous places directly related to the tragedy.

Over a local beer at a ramshackle kiosk, Arbour asked about evidence and legal issues regarding the exhumation and identification of the bodies. After dropping her off at the airport, we drove on to Zagreb since Clint had to return to The Hague. Snow not only turned out to be

41. (*top*) PHR team working on the exhumation after the grave was covered by the Rubb Hall. (Ralph J. Hartley)

42. (*bottom*) William Haglund working on the Ovčara exhumation. (Ralph J. Hartley)

43. Visit by Chief Prosecutor Louise Arbour and Clyde Snow at the Ovčara exhumation. (Ralph J. Hartley)

a great anthropologist but also a good storyteller, and I quietly did a couple of extra circuits around the streets of Zagreb just to hear more.

The following morning Clint and I talked over breakfast about what needed to happen at Ovčara, in Zagreb, and back in The Hague before the exhumation was over. I dropped Clint at the airport, we shook hands, and he left. I stayed behind to handle the exhumation on behalf of the tribunal.

DAY TWENTY-FOUR

On September 23 I had a meeting with Major Neel. He was the classic example of an army officer working in intelligence—cold, precise, and suspicious. We spent several hours discussing how to safely transport the exhumed bodies. The Serbian side was decidedly unhelpful in getting them to Zagreb. In Croatia there was the concern that various nongovernmental organizations might trigger demonstrations or block roads, which could lead to someone opening the sealed containers. That would contaminate evidence and play right into the hands of

44. Damaged Vukovar water tower—view from a distance.
(Vladimír Dzuro)

lawyers for the accused. The secret operation therefore got the very original code name "Confidential."

Another difficulty was protecting the convoy. There were police and military units of the United Nations in territory administered by UNTAES, but once we crossed into territory controlled by the Croatian government, the safety of the convoy would be the responsibility of the Croatian police. To minimize complications at that critical point of handover, we opted for two routes. Route A led from Ovčara to the village of Lipovac and then on to the Zagreb-Belgrade highway. Route B went through Vukovar to Osijek. We had already decided which one to take, but we wouldn't inform the Croatian side until we actually left Ovčara.

DAY TWENTY-FIVE

On September 24 we found the first identification card, bearing the name Ivan Plavšić. I grabbed our copy of the indictment and spotted his name on the list of the missing. This did not as yet mean anything because we first had to identify the bodies, but we were now all sure we were on the right track.

I immediately called Clint in The Hague. He told me that the deputy chief prosecutor, Graham Blewitt, agreed that it was going to be my job to speak at the next press conference. I was not to mention any specific names, not to comment on any plans of the prosecution, and stay strictly on the subject of the exhumation. I got a lump in my throat but gave no sign of it. I spent part of the evening thinking about what to say and what not to say, but then figured it was better to sleep on it, so I went to the container bar for a pint of dark Belgian beer.

DAY TWENTY-SIX

On September 25 I held my first solo press conference. I arrived a little early at the UNTAES center in Vukovar so I could discuss it beforehand with the UNTAES spokesperson. As we left our meeting, the journalists were already waiting. I introduced myself, made an opening statement, and went through all the information that I felt would interest the press corps. At the end I took some questions in the time remaining. I heaved a sigh of relief when the red lights of the cameras went off. We went back to Ovčara, and in the evening I had to pick up my boss, Jo, and colleague Evangeline Candia at the local UNTAES airport. They had come to help with the transport of the bodies to Zagreb.

DAY TWENTY-EIGHT

On September 27 I convened another meeting at the logistics base in Klisa. I invited Major Neel; the logistics manager, Kevin Stork; and Peter Tripp, the chief inspector of the UNTAES civilian police. We went over the last details of the transport. The first convoy was set to depart at exactly 6:30 a.m. on September 30.

DAY THIRTY

On September 29 I met with Colonel Grujić to coordinate the logistics of the transfer. I couldn't tell him the route of the convoy we had planned, but I did mention it would be easier to move heavy trucks on the highway than somewhere through the countryside. Grujić understood completely. By evening we had loaded sixty-five bags into the refrigerated container. We locked the door, affixed it with seals, and put the keys in an envelope, which I kept on me.

DAY THIRTY-ONE

It was September 30, and we were all in our positions at six in the morning. Two heavy trucks arrived. The container was hitched to the first one, while the second one drove behind it as a backup. The convoy was ready and left Ovčara at exactly half past six. An armored personnel carrier was in the lead, followed by an SUV from the civilian police force under the command of Tomas Knutsson of Sweden. Behind it was the truck with the container and a Land Rover belonging to the tribunal. It was driven by Jo, whose assignment was to keep his eyes on the container all the way. Jo also had a sealed envelope with the keys. After him came the spare truck, then me, and then Major Neel. Bringing up the rear of the convoy was another armored personnel carrier. Security on the territory under UNTAES was provided by a platoon from the Belgian Battalion and two helicopters from the Belgian Air Force that had been deployed to UNTAES.

I called Colonel Grujić to confirm that we were taking Route A toward Lipovac, and then to the highway to Zagreb. We arrived at the meet-

45. (*top*) First convoy with bodies from Ovčara crossing UNTAES checkpoint to Croatia. (Vladimír Dzuro)

46. (*bottom*) Dropping off the container with bodies from Ovčara at the Šalata hospital in Zagreb. (Vladimír Dzuro)

ing point at a quarter to nine. Grujić was waiting for us along with a strong contingent of Croatian police. There were no unnecessary delays with the handover. The protocol was signed, and the convoy continued to Zagreb. The escort helicopters returned to the airport, and I went back to Ovčara to continue the exhumation. At seven o'clock that evening, I went to Zagreb to evaluate the transport of the bodies. Serge Krieger told me that the container had been placed in a safe location, inspected, and handed over to Snow, who would undertake the examination of the bodies to determine their identification and the cause of death.

DAY THIRTY-TWO

In the morning I went to the Department of Forensic Medicine at the University of Zagreb, where the autopsies would be carried out. It was absolutely forbidden for family members to attend, but since we had no power to stop them, I arranged with the Croatian authorities to set up a 24/7 police patrol around the building. Before I left Zagreb, I met with Grujić to discuss logistics for the second convoy.

After returning to Ovčara, I called a press conference at UNTAES and announced the transport of the first sixty-five bodies. Journalists and TV crews again showed intense interest at the conference. We continuously monitored the media in Croatia and Serbia. Their reporting on the Ovčara exhumation could, without doubt, influence the security situation in the region, and we had to be ready to evacuate our forensic team before things got out of hand.

DAY THIRTY-FIVE

On October 4, at two o'clock in the afternoon, we exhumed the last body from the mass grave. For the two hundredth time, the PHR experts opened up a bag, put a body inside it, and tagged it with an identification number; Hartley then photographed it, zipped the bag up, sealed it, and put it with the others in the refrigerated container. Now all that remained was to clean up the site and hand it back over to UNTAES.

DAY THIRTY-EIGHT

On October 7, at nine o'clock in the morning, the second convoy left Ovčara. The same security measures were taken, as UNTAES didn't want to underestimate the risks. A platoon of soldiers from BELBAT, two helicopters, personnel carriers, and military police were ordered to secure the convoy. The meeting with Croatian police and Colonel Grujić occurred in the same place at ten o'clock in the morning. We handed over the container, signed the protocol, and with that, the exhumation at Ovčara came to an end. My assignment was finished.

I made the announcement at the final press conference: "On behalf of the International Tribunal and team of forensic specialists, I would like to report that the exhumation of the mass grave at Ovčara was completed today. The team led by Professor Haglund pulled the last body out of the grave at two o'clock in the afternoon on the fourth of October. The total number of exhumed bodies at Ovčara reached two hundred."

We said goodbye to our UNTAES colleagues and left Vukovar for Zagreb. Before I went to my hotel, I briefly stopped at the morgue to ensure that the second container had arrived and was secured.

Once in my room, I got into a tub filled with hot water. In the evening we held a farewell dinner. My thirty-fifth birthday was the next day, so there were two reasons to celebrate. The completion of the exhumation was a huge success for us. All two hundred bodies had been transported to Zagreb, and nobody got hurt.

DAY THIRTY-NINE

When I got into my staff car in the morning, a surprise was waiting for me. My windshield had been shot at four times. I called our security detail, and they in turn called the Croatian police. Local television and radio stations and the print media were reporting extensively on the conclusion of the exhumation at Ovčara. The next morning, in the very center of Zagreb, the person who announced the conclusion also found four bullet holes in his car. Neither the tribunal nor the Croatian

47. (*top*) Final press conference at the UNTAES press center in Vukovar. (Vladimír Dzuro)

48. (*bottom*) ICTY and PHR team that exhumed the Ovčara mass grave together with the Croatian and Serbian observers. (Vladimír Dzuro)

49. ICTY vehicle with four bullet holes in the windshield. (Vladimír Dzuro)

authorities wanted media to get involved in the shooting incident. The police investigated but failed to determine who was behind it so the case was put on ice.

DAY FORTY

On October 9 I went back to Ovčara for the last time and handed Kevin Stork the material we had used during the exhumation. I said goodbye to Captain Hassan and then handed over our keys to the residential container to Major Jacobs from BELBAT in Erdut. I thanked Major General Schoups on behalf of the tribunal for all the help and support given to us by BELBAT throughout the operation.

Finally, I went to see General Klein. He was in a meeting but immediately told everyone to clear out while I made my report on the conclusion of the exhumation and transfer of bodies. Back in Zagreb Serge and I collected from our specialists the evidence obtained during the exhumation. It consisted of personal belongings of the victims such as wristwatches and identification cards, but also a considerable number of bullets, which had been secured from the exhumed bodies. After registering and sealing these items in plastic boxes, I signed my final handover protocol, thus bringing my mission in Ovčara to an end.

In the afternoon my interpreter, Vlatka Leko, and I stopped for a hamburger at McDonald's. As we walked outside, she asked me if I had heard what the two men standing behind us in line were talking about. I hadn't paid attention, but apparently they were complaining about the smell inside the place, how the waste disposal system in that McDonald's must have been broken. But I knew that wasn't it. The culprit was my clothes, and the stench I was unable to get out of them.

The three weeks originally set aside for the exhumation turned out to be nearly seven. Not until October 12 did I fly back to The Hague. As I entered my apartment, I was greeted by these words: "Take off all your clothes, throw them on the balcony, and take a shower!"

Identification of the Bodies Found at Ovčara— the Confrontation with Reality

Just before the start of the exhumation on August 28, 1996, Clint Williamson had a meeting in Zagreb with the very influential nongovernmental group Mothers of Vukovar. We worked very closely with this organization during the investigation, but their public meeting in front of the press had been a stormy one with Clint in the hot seat. It would seem that the survivors and families of the missing, still waiting for good news after all these years, had become panic-stricken when Clint announced that we were about to start the exhumation at Ovčara. Dr. Ivica Kostović, who was one of the deputy prime ministers, had to intervene until passions subsided.

Now, with our having announced at the press conference that two hundred bodies had been recovered at Ovčara, it was clear that many of the mothers from Vukovar were seeing their worst fears come true. Croatian government representatives knew what a painful and emotional process this was going to be. It was essential at this critical juncture to identify the bodies, ensure we had conclusive evidence, and try not to upset the emotions of those waiting for news of what had happened to their loved ones.

The government had modernized the morgue in the Šalata district of Zagreb, but it was simply too small to accommodate two hundred exhumed bodies. Therefore, we had to keep them in refrigerated containers outside the building until autopsies could be performed. Serge stayed behind in the pathology unit for several weeks to assist in identifying the victims and determining their cause of death.

Nobody on the team was better suited for the task. Serge had a certain quality we investigators lacked. A librarian and analyst, his mind worked like a Rolodex. You might search in vain for a file for two hours, then go to him and say, "Hey, Serge, do you remember such-and-such? It had two or three pages, with two, maybe three photos on the last one. Any idea where we put it?" He would say, "Give me a minute," and disappear. When he reappeared, lo and behold, your desired file was in his hands.

The exhumation and identification of the bodies put him in completely new territory. His sterile, benign world of paper and computer programs suddenly became filled with human remains, anthropologists, pathologists, and morgue technicians, the worlds of Clyde Snow. The evidence at the morgue in Zagreb had to be collected and documented, requiring an orderly mind for sure, but also someone with the stamina for it day after day, victim after victim, and Serge turned out to clearly be the man.

Everything proceeded as instructed by Snow. A bag would be removed from the refrigerated container and x-rayed as required, then examined, and the cause of death determined. After DNA samples were taken and decomposed flesh removed, all that remained of the bodies was thoroughly cleaned bones. They were then assembled on a table into the shape of a skeleton and photographed in detail. All pieces of clothing were washed and documented, along with all objects found on or close to the body.

The medical records of the persons missing from Vukovar Hospital were provided by Croatian institutions. The information was

50. (*top*) Collecting evidence—discovery of an identification card. (ICTY)

51. (*bottom*) Collecting evidence—discovery of a wedding ring. (ICTY)

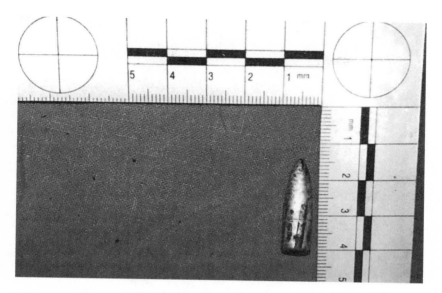

52. (*top*) A bullet found in the Ovčara mass grave. (ICTY)

53. (*bottom*) Collecting evidence—taking DNA samples. (ICTY)

54. Identification of victims from the Ovčara mass grave. (ICTY)

entered into a computer database and the records compared to the data obtained from the autopsies. Clyde Snow also had objects found on-site and pieces of clothing entered in the database as well so that the records were complete.

Dr. Strinović, the head of the Forensic Medicine Department in Zagreb, called in the families of the missing to assist in the final identification. Those who agreed to come forward and confirm the iden-

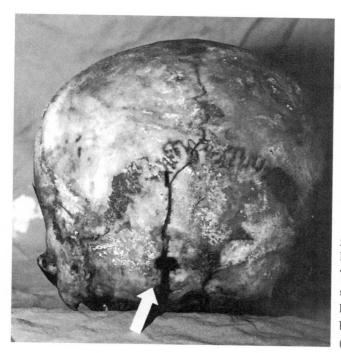

55. Damaged
human skull.
The arrow
shows the
location of the
bullet impact.
(ICTY)

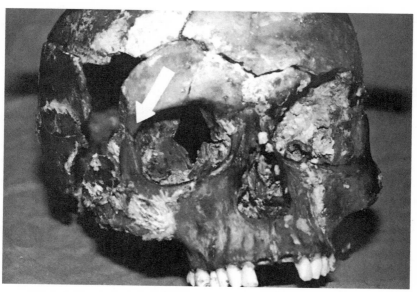

56. Damaged human skull. The arrow shows the location of the trauma. (ICTY)

tity of their loved one could take home their remains. In cases where relatives refused to cooperate or were unable to confirm the identity, identification was made using DNA, a still uncommon and very expensive form of analysis in 1996. Of the 198 men and 2 women exhumed, 193 people were eventually identified.

Our Team 4 had made significant progress. We now had the bodies of the victims to support the indictment of the Vukovar Three and Slavko Dokmanović. All we lacked were the indictees so that we could begin proceedings against them. The prison in Scheveningen was still empty. Until its doors started swinging shut, the situation for the tribunal and the international community would remain untenable.

2

Operation Little Flower

The Powerlessness of the International Community

The three and a half years of interethnic conflict in Bosnia and Herzegovina was brought to an end with the signing of the Dayton Accords on December 14, 1995. Implementation Force (IFOR) units from NATO were deployed on December 20 and replaced a year later by another NATO mission called Stabilization Force (SFOR). The accords, however, did not help in apprehending war criminals in the least.

NATO left nothing to chance in Bosnia and Herzegovina and opted to keep the hostile camps separated by creating a demilitarized zone with checkpoints every few kilometers. The paramilitaries who had robbed and massacred civilians when the poorly armed UNPROFOR was still in control now retreated into the background. But even in this quickly stabilizing situation, the various military commanders did not take any action to arrest the accused—and despite the fact that both IFOR and SFOR had received international arrest warrants from the tribunal, together with photographs and information on where the indictees might be hiding. Arresting them was simply not an IFOR or SFOR priority. Their soldiers had strict orders to arrest accused war criminals only in the event that they came into contact with them in the course of their normal duties. This basically meant they might never be caught.

The reason for this cautious approach lay in a recent event elsewhere. In October 1993, as part of a humanitarian mission in

Somalia, U.S. Rangers, Delta Force soldiers, and Navy SEALs were dispatched to Mogadishu with orders to arrest members of the Mohamed Aidid gang. The operation was a complete fiasco. The insurgents brought down two Black Hawk helicopters, killing nineteen soldiers and wounding another twenty-three. It was the bloodiest deployment of U.S. troops since the Vietnam War, and the footage of dead Americans being dragged through the streets of Mogadishu, broadcast around the world, haunted not only the generals in the Pentagon but also the political elite in Washington.

This Mogadishu Syndrome came to signify nonintervention, and it had an impact on solving the crisis in the Balkans. American generals came to believe that achieving zero losses and earning promotion because of it were far more important than catching a few criminals whom most Americans had never heard of. Not until after the reelection of Bill Clinton as president did a turning point in this policy occur. According to information later made public, Clinton convened a meeting at the White House attended by the chairman of the Joint Chiefs of Staff General John Shalikashvili, Secretary of Defense William Cohen, and CIA director John Deutsch. Despite their counsel to continue the gun-shy approach, Clinton declared that the United States had a moral obligation to seek out and arrest war criminals. So in early February 1997, David Scheffer, the first U.S. ambassador-at-large for war crime issues, arrived in Europe to persuade allies of the need to start making arrests. His efforts, however, met with a cool response, and the French for one did not change their opinion until after Madeleine Albright visited Paris at the end of that month.

As a result a commission composed of representatives of the United States, Great Britain, France, Germany, and the Netherlands was set up in The Hague under Dutch leadership. The commission began meeting under the strictest secrecy to begin planning Operation Amber Star, but from the outset there were disagreements over the legal basis for using alliance troops to apprehend war criminals. The military planning was far more robust and straightforward. The command center for Amber Star was set up at the European headquarters of the U.S.

Special Operations Command near Stuttgart, Germany. The personnel consisted of special forces of the military, police, and intelligence services from the five countries represented on the commission. The first and biggest catch was to be Radovan Karadžić, the president of Republika Srpska, but nothing came of it.

The greatest blow to Amber Star was dealt by French major Hervé Gourmelon, who was assigned by SFOR to infiltrate the Serbian leadership in Pale. Gourmelon won the favor of Serbs and Serbian politicians and was moving freely between Sarajevo and Pale. He even came into direct contact with Karadžić. American intelligence received information that Gourmelon might be slipping reports to the Serbs. The commander of U.S. and NATO forces in Europe, General Wesley Clark, passed along this information to his French colleagues. Major Gourmelon was recalled to Paris, but the French authorities expressed their complete confidence and sent him back to Sarajevo. This incident led to a deep freeze in the intelligence shared between France and the United States, and the work of Amber Star was paralyzed as a result. It was clear no arrests were going to be made in this atmosphere of lack of cooperation.

Secret Indictments

It has often been claimed that the preparation of secret indictments was begun by Chief Prosecutor Louise Arbour, but it was in fact the work of her predecessor, Richard Goldstone. He was faced with the unpleasant situation of having teams of investigators and lawyers working hard at producing indictments under his direction, yet the prison in Scheveningen was empty. Goldstone made a public statement about the problem: "The credibility of the tribunal could be mortally wounded if, for any appreciable time further, it becomes manifest that the tribunal is not able to do the job for which it was created." He was looking for a starting point, and using secret indictments was one of the ways forward.

Goldstone took up the post of chief prosecutor on August 15, 1994. Louise Arbour was named as his replacement on February 29, 1996, by order of UN Security Council Resolution 1047. But Goldstone did not relinquish the office until October 1. It was on his watch that Slavko Dokmanović was added to the indictment, on March 26, 1996, during the Rule 61 trial of the Vukovar Three. The indictment was signed by Goldstone and confirmed by Judge Riad on April 3. Judge Riad agreed to the prosecutor's request to keep the indictment sealed to facilitate the arrest of the accused.

Louise Arbour was the third chief prosecutor of the International Tribunal for the former Yugoslavia. Her key role in bringing newfound relevance to this body was not in formulating the secret indictments but in ordering the first arrests based on them. That's what got the ball rolling.

The Idea That Changed the Fate of the Tribunal

It all started off rather unexpectedly. In December 1996 Serge and I were having a cup of coffee with a French colleague. She was working in the Belgrade office on a team investigating crimes committed against Serbs in Croatia. We were talking about our lives and work when she casually mentioned that in October she had met Slavko Dokmanović and had agreed to hear testimony from him sometime after New Year's. This revelation meant the secret indictment was working. The colleague had no clue that we were after him. We asked her whether she had his telephone number. We didn't betray any excitement when she said yes and gave it to us.

After mulling over the information for a few days, I devised a plan and told Clint. In the beginning he was very skeptical: "You want to lure Slavko Dokmanović to Eastern Slavonia under the pretext of questioning him as a witness?" Sure. Since the area was under UN control, we would be within our legal rights to have him arrested and transferred to The Hague. Clint's interest grew the more I kept on about it, but he didn't see any way around the hurdle that mattered most, namely, where to get Dokmanović's contact information. He was all but inviting me to play my trump card, only I pulled it not out of my sleeve but rather out of my pocket. I told him about my conversation

57. Chief Prosecutor Louise Arbour (*center*) and Deputy Chief Prosecutor Graham Blewitt (*right*). (ICTY)

with Serge and the colleague and showed him the card with the address and telephone number of one of our most-wanted. Clint leapt up from his chair and took me to see John Ralston, one of the commanders in the Office of the Prosecutor, and then to the legal coordinator, Terree Bowers. Together, we all went to see Cees Hendriks, the chief of investigations. After some vigorous discussion, we all agreed that, with a little luck, we could pull it off. So we went to the office of Chief Prosecutor Arbour.

Her visit to the exhumation site at Ovčara in September 1996 had left her deeply shaken, and our proposal to nab one of the people responsible for this massacre got her immediate attention. There were risks involved, naturally, and Clint told her flat out that our plan to arrest Dokmanović could leave him injured or dead, not to mention the same for anyone on the team taking part in the arrest. That would certainly create an international furor.

Except for the hum of the air conditioning, the room was quiet. We sat still around the table, looking at each other, waiting for a decision. Then the chief prosecutor lifted her gaze, looked each of us firmly in the eye, and said it was worth the risk. She felt the way the rest of us did, that the successful arrest of Dokmanović could force NATO to act. She observed, "If we put the ball in their court, they will have no choice but to follow." She would be able to go up to NATO commanders and say, "We apprehended this man in Vukovar with the help of poorly armed UNTAES troops. You, with your sixty thousand troops on the ground, should be able to do the same in Bosnia." She concluded by saying, "Fortune has given us this chance to arrest Slavko Dokmanović. It's only the beginning."

Out in the hallway, John Ralston summed it up in his thick Australian accent: "That woman's got guts!"

To ensure the secrecy of our plan, we had to come up with a code name. A couple of suggestions were floating around, including one that was perhaps too revealing, "Operation Mayor," since Slavko Dokmanović used to be the mayor of Vukovar. Eventually Clint suggested a reference to another mayor: Fiorello La Guardia, who had been mayor of New York City in the 1930s and 1940s and who was nicknamed the "Little Flower" (Fiorello literally means "little flower" in Italian). That would be the code name of our operation.

Two days after our meeting with the chief prosecutor, Clint and I flew to Croatia to meet with General Klein. Thanks to the very strong mandate that the UN member states had given UNTAES, Klein was something of a temporary dictator in the war-ravaged eastern part of the country, a fact that had been instrumental in bringing about the exhumation at Ovčara. But Klein had more than just a mandate. He also had the courage and the will to get things done.

We stayed at the Lady M hotel in the town of Vinkovci, which was just a few kilometers from Vukovar in the free part of Croatian territory. We always stayed at this family-run hotel when we were working in Eastern Slavonia. It was owned by a married couple named Josip and Marija, who considered us something akin to newfound sons.

Later that day we went to Vukovar for our meeting with General Klein. He received us in his enormous office, where Souren Seraydarian, Jacci Johnson, and several members of his senior staff were present. He sat in a massive leather chair behind a huge desk with a glass of fine cognac in front of him. The equally huge cigar in his hand was just another prop that made him an unusual UN official. The kudos he received for ensuring the successful completion of the exhumation at Ovčara had whetted his appetite for more collaboration.

In broad terms we outlined our plan to lure a certain war criminal into territory controlled by UNTAES. The units based there would then take this person into custody and escort him to The Hague. We didn't say who it was specifically, just that this person was connected to Vukovar and hiding out in Serbia.

We concluded our meeting with a framework agreement that UNTAES would take part in the arrest in coordination with the tribunal. The way was now open for us to begin planning Operation Little Flower. As we were about to leave, Klein ordered his colleagues out of the office and asked us to give him the name of the person we were after. We had no reason to keep it secret from him; Klein knew Dokmanović well and had often met him when he was the mayor of Vukovar. Hearing his name Klein nodded his head, munched on his cigar, and said that if the former mayor had indeed had a hand in it, then he was a "son of a bitch" and deserved to go to The Hague.

In the euphoria of our planning that followed, we set an overly ambitious goal of slapping cuffs on Dokmanović by the end of January 1997. In Vukovar we met with U.S. Army major David Jones, who worked for UNTAES as Klein's special assistant and had experience in military intelligence. The general appointed him as our liaison, tasked with coordinating and planning the actual arrest. Because we were doing something completely unprecedented here, neither Klein nor Jones was sure whether UNTAES actually had the authority to carry it out. Klein had a simple way of putting it: "We'd better make sure before we go in there. I hate stepping in dog shit." Clint said that Arbour herself was sure that their authority to arrest the accused on territories under the control of the United Nations, such as Eastern Slavonia, fell within that jurisdiction.

Arbour's position was supported by UN Resolution 1037. Passed on January 15, 1996, it said in no uncertain terms that UNTAES had the duty to cooperate with the tribunal in matters covered by its mandate, and that included protecting personnel involved in investigations. Article 16 gave the prosecutor full authority to pursue and prosecute persons responsible for committing grievous violations of international humanitarian law, and Section 19 within it said that a judge may act on a request of the prosecutor to issue orders for the arrest, detention, and extradition of such persons.

Although the office of the prosecutor was not conceived as a police force to hunt down war criminals, the chief herself was adamant that the law was on her side and so was determined to act. Klein, on the other hand, was a stickler for the proverb "trust but verify," and at a meeting with UN secretary-general Kofi Annan asked him about the scope of his powers.

"Kofi, Arbour and her people are telling me I have the mandate to arrest war criminals. What do you think?"

His reply was unequivocal. "Jacques Paul, you not only have the mandate to do it; you have the duty to work with the tribunal."

Preparing the Trap

We had no idea whether Slavko Dokmanović was willing to set foot on territory controlled by UNTAES or how much support he might still enjoy in Eastern Slavonia. Another problem was how to put together a multinational force under UNTAES without compromising our planning and the operation itself. UNTAES had military and police units from Belgium, Jordan, Pakistan, Poland, Russia, and Ukraine. Save for the last two, none of them shared a mutually intelligible language. Their leaders all spoke English, but an intervention of this type made it absolutely necessary that the soldiers and policemen also be able to communicate with one another.

Putting together this multinational team became more unrealistic as the deadline for the operation approached. In the end General Klein entrusted the intervention to one of two special police units from Poland, JW GROM. GROM was providing protection for UNTAES headquarters in Vukovar, as well as personal protection for Klein, so it got the nod. GROM had been secretly formed in July 1990, but only after another four years, when it was deployed to Haiti, would its existence become known. It was similar to the U.S. Army Delta Force, Navy SEAL Team Six, and the British SAS. Candidates wishing to become a member of GROM had to undergo a "truth test," the idea being to exclude individuals who might crack under extreme pressure. Members of GROM were specially trained in ways to apprehend and neutralize perpetrators.

The First Attempt Ends in Failure

Once the green light was given, Major Jones and Major Jacek Kita, the commander of GROM at UNTAES, went about planning the arrest and conducting exercises for it. Back at The Hague, we were working on the second part of the plan, to gain the trust of Slavko Dokmanović so he would enter UNTAES-controlled territory of his own accord. Kevin Curtis and his interpreter, Thomas Osorio, were executing the deception. Kevin would pretend to be investigating cases of crimes committed by Croats against Serbs. On January 23, 1997, Kevin and Thomas dialed the number my French colleague had given me in December. After several failed attempts, Dokmanović picked up the phone in his home in Sombor. Serving as the interpreter for Kevin, Thomas knew his task was to keep Dokmanović on the phone as long as possible. Kevin explained that as the mayor of Vukovar, Dokmanović had valuable information for our team about the crimes committed by Croats. Dokmanović refused to come to Vukovar, not only because he was afraid to but also because he had ongoing disputes with the Serbs who had remained in Vukovar after he fled. But he could be persuaded to come to the city of Beli Manastir, which was under UNTAES control. The call ended with an agreement that Thomas could call again the next morning to determine the precise location and time to meet.

Thomas called as agreed, but nobody picked up. When Dokmanović finally answered in the evening, he said he had changed his mind and would not to come to Beli Manastir. In fact he absolutely refused to go to Croatia at all. We couldn't figure out what had caused his change of attitude. Dokmanović invited the team to come see him in Sombor instead, which was out of the question for our team because of the security situation in Serbia, which was still ruled by Slobodan Milošević, a number one person on our target list.

Before saying goodbye, Thomas promised to be back in touch. Afterward, we admitted to ourselves that expecting Dokmanović to walk into our trap the first time around was naive. We lost that round, but we were not about to give up.

Laying a New Trap

Major Jones arrived in The Hague in May to report on the various scenarios worked out by GROM. The unit needed new, specific information for the arrest in order to complete its training and to make other necessary preparations. Upon returning to Vukovar, Jones gave Klein and Kita the final plan of operation. Major Kita was given four weeks to be ready. In Vukovar only two people, Klein and Jones, knew the name of our target. The success of the operation depended on complete secrecy because UNTAES was riddled with informers from Croatian and Serbian intelligence services.

It was clear that any chance of luring Dokmanović from his home was going to require Kevin and Thomas to visit him in Sombor, a city of about fifty thousand in the Serbian region of Vojvodina. Sombor was just twenty-five kilometers from the borders of both Croatia and Hungary but well within the Federal Republic of Yugoslavia. Conducting a covert operation to arrest a war criminal on the territory of a sovereign country was a new element in the work of the tribunal and therefore a further step into the unknown.

We convened a meeting to consider what was legally acceptable and where we might find ourselves on thin ice. We even considered the possibility of our being handcuffed and hauled away to a prison in Belgrade. It was finally agreed that Clint and I would fly to Belgrade, rent an ordinary car, and drive to Sombor. We would pretend to be Czech and American tourists on our way to Vojvodina, making a random stop in the picturesque town of Sombor. Naturally, we hid our intention to map out the area around Dokmanović's house and to pinpoint the location of the local police station, army base, and hospital. We would analyze this information to determine the most feasible entry and departure routes.

We arrived in Belgrade on June 15 and headed for Sombor. We had lunch in the town, checked out the National Museum, then drove through Dokmanović's neighborhood. The home he had been living in since fleeing Croatia was on a typical street. The trees and bushes that lined the sidewalk prevented us from casing his home from afar, but we found a small café with an outdoor garden that gave us a pretty decent view. After we got back to Croatia, Thomas picked up the phone again, dialed the number implanted in his head, and arranged to meet Dokmanović at his home on June 24.

One week prior to this meeting, our team met at GROM headquarters in Erdut. In the command room, Major Kita gave us a briefing describing various possible scenarios: "Slavko Dokmanović arrives in a car with Kevin and Thomas. We set up a roadblock, force the car to make a left leading into our camp; we stop the car and arrest Dokmanović. If someone pulls out a gun or other weapon, we shoot him. The next scenario is Slavko Dokmanović arrives in a vehicle provided by GROM, which we send to him at the border. Again, we block the road, force the vehicle to the left into our camp, stop the car, and arrest Dokmanović. If he or anyone pulls out a gun, we shoot him."

There was a third, similar scenario that ended in the same possible bloodshed. Dennis Milner could no longer hold back and said: "Major, you can't just shoot him." Dennis was proving to be a true British policeman, one who had never held a gun in his hand.

58. Colonel Jacek Kita, commander of the GROM arrest team. (Col. David S. Jones [Ret.])

Kita looked at him and said in the same monotone voice that accompanied his scenarios: "Sir, you must understand one thing. This is no game. My first priority is to protect your lives; my second priority is to protect the lives of my men. If Mr. Dokmanović or someone with him will be so stupid as to pull out a gun during this operation, we will shoot him." And just so there was no misunderstanding, he added, "There will be no operation unless I get a written order from General Klein giving me permission to use lethal force if there is danger to life."

After the briefing broke up, we went out to watch Kevin practice ramming a Land Rover into a wall, part of the scenario where he arrives with Dokmanović and crashes the car into a barrier composed of sandbags. The impact was meant to throw Dokmanović against the front seats, causing him to lose his balance and orientation, and at that moment GROM would enter the car and arrest him. Then came the exciting part where Kevin had to jump out of the car and roll under it to avoid getting hit by any gunfire.

At first it was impossible for Kevin to hit the wall at full speed; his instincts naturally caused him to hit the brakes before the crash. This was unacceptable to Major Kita. It took several attempts before he was satisfied with the impact. Kevin, of course, survived all these dry runs, but the front end of the robust Land Rover got smashed up pretty badly. The real problem, it turned out, was his inability to roll under the car in James Bond style. Kevin simply couldn't manage this with his, let's say, less than athletic frame. All he could do was promise to do everything in his power to save his own skin. With a little luck, he would survive too.

After completing the training, Clint, Jones, and I went to Klein to report on the progress of the preparations. His reaction to Dennis's concerns about guns going off was typical. He leaned back in his massive chair, puffed on his cigar, and stared at the ceiling: "Of course. Shoot the son of a bitch, dump his ass in a pit, and hang a sign over him that says, 'Don't f**k with the tribunal.'"

He then grew serious and assured us that he would issue a written order for Major Kita before he hopped on a flight to New York for some UN thing. The end of the order read as follows: "Should the life or health of members of UNTAES or the International Tribunal be at risk, I authorize the use of deadly force." It was signed Ambassador Jacques Paul Klein, UNTAES Administrator.

On the morning of June 23, we all gathered again in Erdut to go over the final details of the operation. We received confirmation that a plane from the Belgian Air Force would be on standby at the Čepin airport near Osijek to transport Dokmanović to The Hague. There would also be a doctor on hand to ensure he was ready to fly after his arrest.

The plan called for Kevin and Thomas to enter Serbia in a Toyota provided by UNTAES and drive to Sombor. They were supposed to convince Dokmanović to go with them to Vukovar so they could show him the sites where alleged crimes were committed. Once they had crossed the border and entered Erdut, GROM would pounce and arrest him in line with one of the scenarios.

My job was to go to Budapest and fly from there to Belgrade, where I would rent a car. The next day I would drive to Sombor and observe the house and surroundings from an inconspicuous location. Kevin and Thomas were supposed to park in front of Dokmanović's house with the front end of their car sticking out of the bushes growing along the side of the road to make it easier for me. Basically, I was there for any unforeseen circumstance that might lead to Kevin and Thomas getting arrested by the local police or worse. Once—we hoped—Dokmanović got into the car, my job was then to follow them and inform GROM the minute they crossed the border.

Prior to things kicking off, Major Jones reported that General Klein had consulted with the secretary-general about Operation Little Flower and got the green light. The U.S. State Department was not directly involved in the case, but Madeline Albright conveyed her support to Klein just the same.

Thomas drove me to the airport in Budapest, wished me luck, and returned to Vukovar. I called Clint before getting on the flight, then turned my cell phone off, took out the battery, and flew to Belgrade. I rented the car as planned and drove to a hotel. I tried to sleep but tossed and turned instead, going over and over what could happen tomorrow if someone had betrayed our plans and Dokmanović was expecting us. I got up and went to the hotel bar for a glass of white wine. Within an hour I was fast asleep.

I made sure no one was following me as I hit the road for Sombor, some 160 kilometers northwest. I was there and watching Dokmanović house from a nearby vantage point when Kevin and Thomas arrived and parked as planned. They rang the doorbell, and Dokmanović appeared, but to my dismay, he gestured for to them to drive farther up his driveway. He then closed the gate. Since this was not according to the plan, I had to hang out somewhere close to the house. I went to the same café I had visited on my earlier trip and ordered coffee. As time dragged on, I grew more and more nervous. I paid, crossed the road, and came back. After doing this a couple of times, the pretty young waitress asked me if I was waiting for someone. I had to quickly make something up.

"I'm supposed to meet this girl here. I met her in Prague, where she was a refugee from Croatia. She moved to Sombor, so I've come here to meet her."

Two hours and a half dozen cups of coffee later, the waitress must have guessed that I had been stood up. Suddenly I saw Kevin and Thomas going out into the yard, saying goodbye, and leaving for the border. It was while overtaking them on the road that Kevin made a sign to me that Dokmanović had still refused to go to Vukovar. I turned on my phone and told Clint that they were coming alone. No package. I parked my car at an agreed-upon location and waited for someone from UNTAES to pick me up and take me back to Erdut.

A Change of Plans Necessary

At an operational meeting in Erdut, Kevin and Thomas filled us in on what had happened inside Dokmanović's house after he closed the gate. They got out of the car and were greeted by him and a pair of huge Rottweilers he kept for protection. He invited them inside for the traditional cup of coffee. Not even one minute into it, and our whole grand plan began to fall apart. Dokmanović pointedly announced that he would not cross the border into Croatia at any price but would be happy to describe what the Croats had done and who he believed was responsible. He explained his decision by saying that the Croatian authorities had partial control over border crossings under an agreement that unified Croatian territory currently under temporary UNTAES administration. He was worried the Croatian police would arrest him if he even tried to cross the border. Dokmanović was afraid of being arrested not by the Tribunal but by the Croats. It occurred to Kevin what a wise decision it had been to keep the indictment sealed.

Kevin did not register his disappointment and spent several hours interviewing Dokmanović as a witness. To gain his trust, he offered to photograph the sites he described and return to verify the photos and complete his testimony. It was clear that Kevin was the right negotiator for this job. Apparently coming from Shakespeare's Stratford-upon-Avon had imbued him with a talent to play his role to the hilt.

As they were leaving, Dokmanović's daughter and granddaughter entered the room. He introduced them to Kevin and Thomas, and for a while they talked about life before the war in Vukovar and in Trpinja, where Dokmanović had lived before fleeing Croatia and where he still had a house that he could neither use nor sell. At that moment a brilliant idea occurred to Kevin. He asked Dokmanović if he knew General Klein, the administrator for Eastern Slavonia. Dokmanović said he had interacted with him quite a lot when he was the mayor of Vukovar. Kevin suggested that he might arrange a meeting with Klein, where Dokmanović could discuss not only his house but also the problems faced by the Serb population in Eastern Slavonia. Dokmanović liked the idea, but he was still afraid of being arrested by the Croatian police. And what if Klein gave his personal guarantee of a safe conduct to Vukovar and that he would not be arrested by the Croats?

We realized that without Klein's name, everything would have ground to a halt. We called him in New York, where he was just then discussing the budget for UNTAES. He readily agreed to go this route and had his chief of staff, Michael Hryshchyshyn, call Dokmanović to arrange a meeting in Vukovar. Clint suggested that Kevin and Thomas return to Sombor the next day to tell Dokmanović about this plan in person and mediate the telephone conversation with Hryshchyshyn. We had every reason not to linger. Not only could Dokmanović learn from the TV or newspapers that Klein wasn't even in Vukovar at that moment, but in July 1997 Croatia was set to assume full control over its borders. That would seriously tie our hands in getting Dokmanović across.

Thus on the morning of June 25, Kevin and Thomas went back to Sombor. Since there was still the danger of the local police getting involved, I had to get there first to scope out the situation. A UNTAES driver took me over the border to a point close to where I had left the rental car, and I arrived there in good time. I found everything to my liking, with no sign of shady individuals inside police or unmarked cars.

The situation unfolded in the same way as the previous day. Kevin parked in the yard, and I went back to the café across the street. It was a repeat of the same coffee and the same story to the same waitress.

I had decided to give this beautiful girl one more chance to show up. I had lots of time, and maybe something had held her up yesterday. Besides, their coffee was great.

The wait was much shorter this time. After about an hour, Kevin and Thomas drove out of the gate and headed for the border. We crossed without any problem and the entire team again assembled at GROM headquarters in Erdut. Kevin told us what had happened in Sombor: "I told Dokmanović that Klein had agreed to meet him and gave me a list of telephone numbers for him to call Hryshchyshyn for the details. He took the paper without looking at it and went to make the customary cup of coffee. When he came back, I told him that Hryshchyshyn was waiting with an interpreter for the call, but he was happy to continue our interview. As we drank the coffee, I was frantically trying to work out my next move while he sat there like he had all the time in the world.

"Finally, we had to leave and I needed another excuse to come back to Sombor. Since I was having some photos developed to show him, I asked, 'Shall I come back on Friday with the photos, say around 2:00 p.m.?' Dokmanović quietly replied, 'I am meeting Klein at three.'

"I was relieved to hear that, but I still wanted to make sure our arrangements appeared genuine to him. I suggested I would return to Sombor at 7:00 p.m. on Friday after his meeting with Klein, so that I can show him the photographs and finalize his statement. Dokmanović smiled and said, 'My wife will prepare dinner for you.'"

Clint confirmed to us that Dokmanović had indeed called Hryshchyshyn, and they had arranged for Dokmanović to cross the border at the Bogojevo bridge at precisely three o'clock in the afternoon of June 27. A VIP escort would be waiting to escort him to his meeting with Klein. The trap was set, and now all we could do was wait.

Until the decisive moment of 3:00 p.m. arrived, time truly seemed to stand still for us. Every minute felt like an hour, every hour a day, and it seemed like the day itself would never dawn. Everything was planned, talked about endlessly, repeatedly rehearsed. As the one designated to make the official arrest, I had to memorize the ICTY's version of the Miranda rights of the accused. No stone had been left unturned. All we could do was wait patiently to see if Dokmanović would really arrive at the appointed time and place.

During the wait I remembered the words of John Rhys-Davies, a charismatic Welsh actor, known for his role, among others, as the excavator Sallah in the Indiana Jones movies. He said, on the theme of heroism: "In the film world, we can all be heroes. In the real world, where heroism can cost you your life or the life of the ones you love, people aren't so willing to make those sacrifices." A similar comment on the theme of bravery and heroism by the Czech actor and writer Jan Werich seemed apt for the situation in which we found ourselves, something to the effect that a person had to be pretty brave to do something big, but that didn't necessarily make him a hero. In Werich's mind, they were completely different things. Heroism involved a singular moment, where the hero could be anybody at random, even somebody acting out of stupidity, desperation, or the desire to be famous. Cemeteries are full of these heroes. But we have no desire to emulate them because people only speak of heroism when success is the result. When it's not, people shake their heads and say what a fool the person was, and none of us likes to be thought of as a fool.

Bravery, on the other hand, suggests a certain amount of self-awareness, of a person wanting to do something, of believing in it and having the discipline to achieve it. Equally important this person has the ability to pull back in time, because a misstep is a misstep and then there's no going back. Supposedly, all people have the capacity for both heroism and bravery in them and can choose to use these qualities whenever they want. We reached a crossroad and had to make that call.

I dare say we had something of this bravery in us because we were about to do something that no one had tried before. It was well thought out, and all we needed was a little luck to pull it off, and not just for our own personal success but more so for the victims at Ovčara.

Arresting a War Criminal

Our interpreter, Zvezdan, arrived during the evening of June 26 and had breakfast with Kevin, Clint, and me the following morning. He didn't have a clue about what was going on; he just knew that something big was about to go down. The most he learned at breakfast was that he would be informed about things in time. We all knew Zvezdan very well, he had interpreted for us several times already, but there was no point in subjecting him to needless stress.

We spent the final hours holed up in one of the containers that formed a bunker for General Klein in case armed conflict broke out in Vukovar. It had food, drink, TV, but above all air conditioning, because it was hotter than hell that day. It was there that Zvezdan was let in on the operation. He looked as if he was going to have a stroke. He was worried not only about what could happen during the arrest but also about himself and his Serbian family in Bosnia. Zvezdan was a brave man. He could have turned around and left—nobody could force him to stay—but he, without hesitation, went along with us right into this risky operation.

Zvezdan and I closed ourselves away in a room and rehearsed the reading of the charges and the Miranda rights of the accused. We didn't want to leave anything to chance. The arrest had to be absolutely perfect, not just to ensure it stuck but also to serve as the textbook example for NATO should it get the nerve to make an arrest.

At 1:30 p.m. two armored SUVs pulled up to take our team to Erdut. It was all done very secretly, and we stayed out of sight when we got there. All that talk about a minute feeling like an hour had disappeared. Now it felt like a week, and the air seemed to reverberate with the ticking of a clock as the hour approached. We didn't even want to think about what was going to happen on the Bogojevo bridge. At half past two, Major Kita arrived, shook hands with us, and wished us luck. The next thing we heard was the rumbling of the SUVs as they departed to meet Slavko Dokmanović.

We were all huddled around the radio in the communications center. The heat was unbearable, but I dared not loosen my tie, even as the sweat poured down my back. The first report we got was that the convoy had reached its destination. It was followed by the same static that preceded it. We stared at the clock and followed the second hand. Nobody said a word because there was nothing to say.

Then, at exactly 2:55 p.m., the radio crackled: "The target has entered our vehicle; Operation Little Flower is on."

There is no way to describe the feeling of relief that comes after more than half a year of hard work, uncertainty, mistrust, and doubt about whether the plan was even going to work. Relief mixed with tension, because it wasn't over yet. There was still the grand finale to go.

We were concealed behind a container, which was protected by a wall of sandbags. In the distance we heard, in turn, the sound of approaching vehicles, squealing brakes, the opening of the gate to the base, and the screeching of two armored SUVs coming to a halt inside the compound. A GROM member barking commands in Polish burst onto the scene. We appeared from our location and watched how the elite unit opened the rear door of the vehicle and pulled out an individual who was trying to put his jacket on. It was Slavko Dokmanović. They pulled another man out from the other side of the vehicle, but we didn't know or care who he was at that moment.

The Polish officers took the unknown man to the side and searched him, but led Dokmanović to stand by the container, where he was handcuffed. The GROM team leader who went by the name of Gajowy took Dokmanović's leather shoulder bag from him, quickly searched it, and stowed it in the vehicle. The GROM soldiers then frisked Dokmanović and removed all his personal effects. Clint handed them to Kevin, telling him that they were his responsibility now. Major Kita then announced that GROM had the situation fully under control.

Everything was caught on video. With the camcorder still running, Zvezdan and I walked up to Dokmanović. This was the first time since the Nuremberg trials that an accused war criminal was being arrested on the orders of an international tribunal. It was up to me to read out the charges and his rights. Zvezdan translated everything into Serbian for him.

"Mr. Dokmanović, my name is Vladimír Dzuro. I am an investigator with the Office of the Prosecutor of the International Criminal Tribunal for the former Yugoslavia. You are charged in an indictment, and your name appears in an arrest warrant issued by the tribunal. You are charged with grave breaches of the Geneva Conventions, crimes

59. (*top*) Arrest of Slavko Dokmanović. (Col. David S. Jones [Ret.]

60. (*bottom*) Vladimír Dzuro reads the charges and the ICTY version of the Miranda rights to Slavko Dokmanović. (Col. David S. Jones [Ret.])

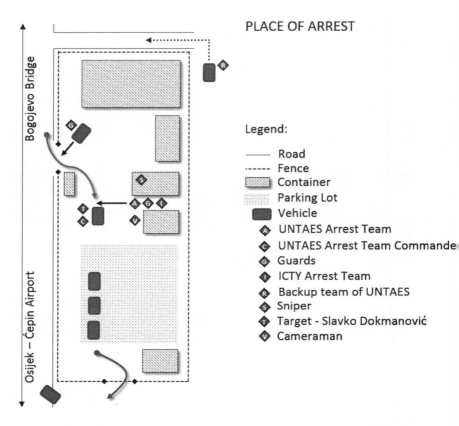

61. Erdut, the location where Slavko Dokmanović was arrested. (Vladimír Dzuro)

against humanity, and violations of the laws and customs of war, for your role in the beatings and killings that occurred at Ovčara farm near Vukovar on the twentieth of November 1991. Do you understand?"

"I understand," he said, "but it's not true."

I then read him his rights, such as the right to remain silent and the right to have an interpreter at his disposal. At the end of this part of the arrest, the Polish officers threw a black hood over his head and put him into the back seat of the SUV. The driver, Clint, and a GROM member were already inside. I got in behind Dokmanović and held up a microphone to record anything he might say between his arrest

62. Slavko Dokmanović at the Čepin airport. (Col. David S. Jones [Ret.])

and transfer to the prison in Scheveningen. It would be our proof to refute any complaints that we did something illegal during the process.

Major Jones informed air traffic control at the Čepin airport to prepare the Merlin twin-engine turboprop from the Belgian Air Force for immediate flight. Departure clearance had been arranged in advance despite the Croatian authorities not knowing the names of the passengers or the destination.

The Incident at the Čepin Airport

We covered the forty-three kilometers to the airport in half an hour. Since Dokmanović still had the black hood over his head, there was no risk of him being recognized by the Croatian police stationed at the numerous checkpoints between Erdut and Čepin. Our convoy stopped next to the airplane, and Clint and Major Jones got out to discuss the departure with the captain. GROM members immediately locked the car and surrounded it in a defensive position. We couldn't hear anything through the bulletproof windows. There was just the hum of the air conditioner and engine and the occasional crackle of the radio.

After another long wait, a doctor assigned to GROM approached to see whether Dokmanović was fit to fly. Team members unlocked the car, opened the door, and helped our prisoner onto the tarmac. The examination revealed that Dokmanović had an irregular heartbeat but was otherwise uninjured. The doctor gave him some medication and pronounced him fit to travel. Clint signed the transfer protocol for Major Jones, thereby accepting responsibility for Dokmanović on behalf of the tribunal. Dokmanović was escorted inside the plane with me just behind him.

Once inside the plane, Kevin went over to Dokmanović and removed his hood. Dokmanović looked at Kevin and said in English, "Thank you, Mr. Curtis." He then continued in Serbian, "My wife is preparing dinner for you." Kevin looked back at him straight in the eye. "I'm sorry, Mr. Dokmanović, but you have been indicted as a war criminal, and we are going to The Hague." Dokmanović sat in his seat, and I sat down behind him with the audio recorder still on.

Suddenly, we saw several Croatian police vehicles roar up, followed by the pilot telling us that our permission to take off had been revoked. Quite rightly, they wanted to know the identities of the handcuffed person with the hood over his head and the foreigners accompanying him who were planning to leave the Čepin airport. They told us to submit a passenger manifest.

The air inside the plane grew stuffy because the air conditioner wasn't working, and the situation on the tarmac looked tense. The plane was surrounded by armed members of GROM, now facing a group of lightly armed Croatian policemen. Since the Čepin airport was under Croatian jurisdiction, the police were in a good legal position to snatch the hated mayor of Vukovar from our grasp. In an instant our successful operation would become a debacle. President Tuđman of Croatia would parade Dokmanović around as a political triumph, while the Serbian authorities, still under the control of Slobodan Milošević, would accuse the International Tribunal of playing into the hands of the Croats. The arrest was supposed to herald a new phase in the existence and operation of the tribunal, but unless we got Dokmanović

63. (*top*) Medical examination of Slavko Dokmanović at the Čepin airport. (Col. David S. Jones [Ret.])

64. (*bottom*) Preparation for takeoff at the Čepin airport. (Col. David S. Jones [Ret.])

out of there fast, we would have to cede the initiative to NATO, which meant no initiative at all.

Nothing was happening. The captain informed us that flight control was still insisting on the manifest with all our names on it. Standing on the hot tarmac, Clint spelled out our names to a Croatian police officer until finally he said, "And one more person."

There was a pause.

"One more person?" asked the officer.

"Yes," said Clint. "One more person."

"One more person you say?"

"Yes, one more person."

Another pause.

"You say one more person?"

"Yes."

"We need his name!"

The inane exchange between Clint and the policeman went on indefinitely, and the police officer finally said that he would have to call Zagreb to get their authorization for us to fly. Then Clint telephoned and asked for help from Croatian deputy prime minister Kostović, who had been his interlocutor from the Croatian government during the period of the exhumation at Ovčara and back as early as 1994, when Clint had undertaken the first contacts on behalf of the ICTY with the Zagreb government. The policeman jumped into his car and quickly drove back to the airport offices. A couple of minutes later, he returned to say that Kostović had given us authorization to depart.

And like that, it was a whole new ballgame. Within minutes the pilot received permission to start; Clint then shook hands with Major Jones and the police commander and ran up the steps to the plane. The copilot slammed the cabin door shut, and GROM relaxed the perimeter around the plane.

We took off with a steep climb and several sharp banks to the left and right. Nobody said a word. The heat and stress had taken their toll. The loudspeaker broke the tension as we heard what we had all been holding our breaths for: "We have just left the airspace of Croatia."

That was it. Now we were sure we would make it to the Netherlands without any problems. None of us had the slightest suspicion of how close we had actually come to the opposite scenario.

The Surprise in the Shoulder Bag

As soon as we left Croatian airspace, Clint had the indictment read out to Dokmanović in Serbian to allow him to become familiar with its contents. At the end Dokmanović asked for his shoulder bag so that he could put the document inside. Going by the book, Clint forbade it, saying he would do it for him. A while later Dokmanović again repeated his request for his shoulder bag; his cigarettes were inside it and he needed to smoke. Although the pilot allowed smoking in this exceptional case, his request was again denied. Kevin offered him one of his own out of goodwill, but Dokmanović refused it. He insisted on his cigarettes from his bag. Both Clint and Kevin remained adamant. Eventually, Dokmanović took the cigarette that Kevin offered him.

After landing at the Valkenburg Royal Dutch Navy airbase near The Hague, we handed Dokmanović over to the Dutch police and left together for the tribunal's detention center at Scheveningen prison. Meanwhile Clint went to meet Chief Prosecutor Arbour and briefed her on the execution of the arrest.

Upon our arrival at the detention center, we all underwent a security check of belongings before entering the cell area. We were then led to a room where we made the formal transfer of Slavko Dokmanović to the authorized representatives of the tribunal.

As in any detention procedure, we had to register all his personal belongings and hand them over to the custody of the prison authorities. Kevin began with the things GROM removed during the arrest, until finally it came to opening the shoulder bag that Dokmanović was so eager to get his hands on. He reached inside it and, to our astonishment, pulled out a handgun. Kevin, who had never held a gun in all his life, turned to me and asked, "How should I handle it?"

"Put it on the table!" I said.

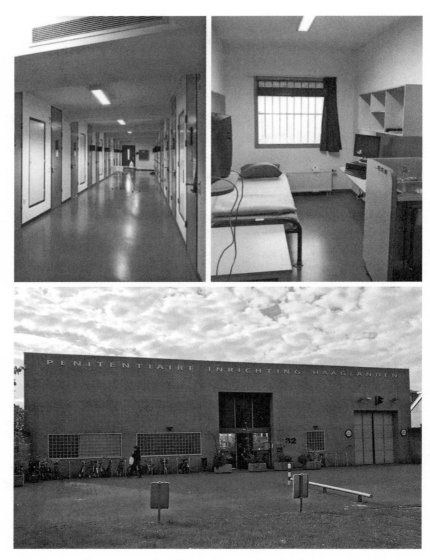

65. UN Detention Centre—the Scheveningen Prison in The Hague. (ICTY)

Prison staff immediately seized the weapon. It was a Zastava 357 Magnum revolver, and it was fully loaded. We could just imagine what would have happened had Clint or Kevin given Dokmanović his bag during the flight. He would go from being our prisoner to the only armed individual on board. We may have survived the flight in the end, but we certainly wouldn't have landed in Valkenburg. For all that, however, Slavko Dokmanović was sitting in a prison cell. We could finally sit back and take in the sweet smell of Little Flower.

Wrapping Up Operations in Vukovar

There was always concern that our operation might lead to unrest in the Serb-populated areas of Croatia. General Klein rushed back from New York to Vukovar to monitor the situation from an UNTAES helicopter, to be ready to personally intervene at a moment's notice in Erdut or at the airport in Čepin, if something went badly wrong. In the end there was just a single incident in territory controlled by UNTAES. A hand grenade exploded near its headquarters in Vukovar, but an investigation revealed that it had been part of a raucous wedding celebration.

After we left Čepin, Majors Jones and Kita returned to Erdut to resolve the tricky affair with Milan Knežević, the man who had accompanied Dokmanović on his fateful ride. General Klein ordered him released and taken back to Serbia, but not before he swore not to breathe a word about the arrest to the press. Of course he broke his word and started giving interviews to Serbian newspapers and other media. Slavko Dokmanović had been violently abducted from the sovereign territory of the Federal Republic of Yugoslavia, he declared. Klein was again forced to act in order to maintain peace and security in the area controlled by UNTAES.

First, he called Knežević and bluntly told him that because he had decided to break their nondisclosure agreement, he was preparing an open letter thanking him for helping UNTAES in this action. He even read him a draft of it that concluded with the statement: "Without you, we could never have arrested Slavko Dokmanović. You have our eternal thanks." It must have sent shivers down Knežević's spine. He knew that Klein, by threatening to denounce him as a traitor to the Serbs, was all but holding a knife to his throat. He started screaming into the phone. "You can't do that! You will kill me!" Klein's reply was ice cold. "No, Mr. Knežević, I won't kill you. They will." Knežević shut up after that and spoke not another word to journalists about the arrest.

A few days later, General Klein was summoned to a meeting with President Milošević, still the most powerful man in areas controlled by the Serbs. He was furious about the arrest. When Klein was led into his office, Milošević lifted his head and with clenched teeth snapped in English, "General, I'm not going to tolerate this shit!"

The question of the sovereignty and territorial integrity of Yugoslavia has always been a very sensitive matter. Klein rightly suspected, however, that Milošević was getting his information largely from Serbian media, so he had brought along photos clearly showing Dokmanović and Knežević walking across the bridge and getting into the parked suvs supplied by UNTAES of their own volition. After examining the photos, Milošević looked up in amazement and asked, "He crossed the border on his own free will?" General Klein just nodded. Milošević brushed the photo off the table: "Well, in that case, he's an idiot!"

Congratulations, but Still Gnashing Our Teeth

The plan worked out between Clint and Chief Prosecutor Arbour called for a three-hour delay before issuing the announcement of the arrest. This measure made sure we got Dokmanović to The Hague safely (with no thoughts about any hidden firearms). It was Klein himself who informed the senior management of the United Nations in New York, as well as the governments of the former Yugoslavia, United States, the Netherlands, NATO and SFOR authorities, UN headquarters in Sarajevo, and other organizations whose activities might feel the impact because of the arrest.

Arbour made the following press statement: "First, I would like to confirm that on Friday, June 27, at about 15.00, the accused Slavko Dokmanović was arrested in Eastern Slavonia during a joint operation

66. General Jacques Paul Klein and Slobodan Milošević. (REUTERS / Alamy Stock Photo)

between UNTAES and my office. . . . The arrest of the accused Slavko Dokmanović has confirmed the existence of secret indictments. This was my strategy. The whole world knows that the International Tribunal has seventy-four persons under indictment. With just a few exceptions, countries that have the legal obligation and responsibility under the Dayton Accords to cooperate with the tribunal are guilty for failing to arrest and extradite these accused. The Federal Republic of Yugoslavia has the obligation to arrest and hand over the other three persons who stand accused with Dokmanović."

On June 27 President Clinton said in his statement: "We welcome the news that accused war criminal Slavko Dokmanović was arrested by investigators of the International Tribunal for the Former Yugoslavia in cooperation with the UNTAES administration. We congratulate you on successfully arresting him. The United States continues to support the work of the tribunal to bring indicted war criminals to justice."

NATO secretary general Javier Solana was not going to remain on the sidelines. He also congratulated the tribunal on the success of the mission, but in truth NATO officials were less than thrilled by it. Indeed, they were seething beneath the surface of their official congratulations. General Klein told us how shortly after Little Flower he got a call from an American general in SFOR in Bosnia, who irritably asked: "What the hell do you think you're doing?" NATO forces were worried about possible losses resulting from the arrest of war criminals, and here was General Klein, one of their own, taking part in a guerrilla operation behind their backs, making them look ridiculous in the process.

Neither Klein nor Kita had asked their governments for explicit approval before carrying out the operation. Had it failed, it would have meant the untimely end of their careers. Supposedly Major Kita's superior found out about GROM's involvement at a diplomatic reception hosted by the American military attaché. It was said that GROM got a glowing tribute from Klein in his report to Washington, and this helped facilitate Poland's accession to NATO. A different outcome would have left Kita with a lot of explaining to do. As it was, he was promoted to lieutenant colonel, and General Klein, now reputed to be a man not afraid of getting things done, became a megastar at the United Nations. And Arbour gained the reputation of being the prosecutor whose daring had forced the international community to change its attitude toward arresting war criminals.

As a trial attorney, Clint had access to the political infighting surrounding the tribunal. After one meeting he told us how Arbour had been relentless in reminding NATO and SFOR troops in Bosnia of their obligation to bring in the accused. Her argument was the same one that motivated us in the first place. Surely their sixty thousand fully armed soldiers could accomplish what her one little white-collar office had done. Finally out of excuses, NATO knew it was either act now or risk a dent in its reputation. First up were the Prijedor Three: Milan Kovačević, Simo Drljača, and Milomir Stakić. They had been secretly indicted on March 13, 1997. Drljača was the police chief in Prijedor

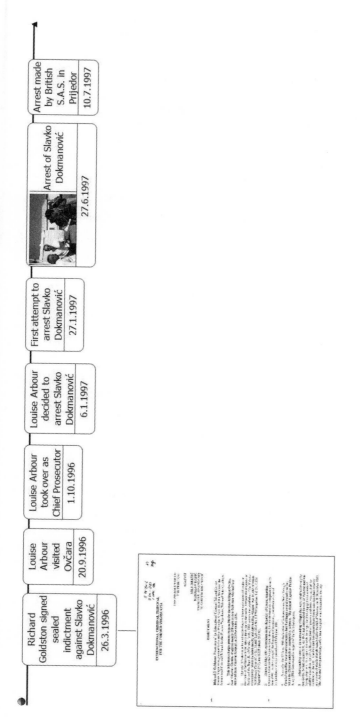

67. Timeline depicting approval of the indictment of Slavko Dokmanović from his arrest to the first NATO-SAS arrest operation in Bosnia. (Vladimír Dzuro)

in 1992, when some of the most heinous war crimes in Bosnia and Herzegovina were committed, and Kovačević was Drljača's superior in Banja Luka. Both were accused of genocide. Stakić, the last of the trio, was a doctor and chairman of the crisis staff in Prijedor. For his conduct he was charged with genocide and crimes against humanity in western Bosnia.

On July 10, 1997, British SAS special forces in Prijedor went into action. They apprehended Kovačević without resistance, but Drljača put up a fight and was killed in a gun battle with the SAS. Stakić got lucky that day and managed to escape. He would spend four years hiding out in Serbia before local authorities swooped in and handed him over to the tribunal.

The worry had always been that such dramatic interventions, ending variously in the arrest, killing, or escape of the accused, would provoke a wave of outrage in Bosnia and permanently damage the Dayton Accords, thus creating a nightmare for more than just NATO. With the exception of some sporadic protests in a few cities, however, nothing serious materialized. In Prijedor itself most Serbs were relieved to see the three criminals go. SFOR had proven to itself that it could be done and quickly followed up with more arrests.

Of the 161 persons indicted by the tribunal, 10 died before they could be arrested, and the charges against 20 others were dropped. Of the remaining 131, 65 were tracked down and arrested sometime after the Dokmanović arrest; the others were apprehended in later years, after the countries of the former Yugoslavia began cooperating with the tribunal and began handing indictees over. In an interview with Radio UN in New York in 2016, Serge Brammertz, the last ICTY chief prosecutor, laid out the significance of the arrest of Slavko Dokmanović:

> It was very important because it was the first one made on the basis of a secret indictment.
>
> It gave legitimacy to the tribunal and credibility to the legal procedures established by the Security Council.

It gave hope to victims, because the tribunal acquitted itself for the first time in their eyes.

It made clear to the other defendants that if the political will was there, then justice was coming after them.

General Jacques Paul Klein Recounts

One of the most personally rewarding accomplishments of my tour as the United Nations Transitional Administrator for Eastern Slavonia (UNTAES), Baranja, and Western Srijem was the planning and carrying out of the first apprehension of an indicted war criminal in the former Yugoslavia. Having exhumed, in conjunction with the ICTY, the war crimes site at Ovčara, where 260 wounded military and civilian personnel from the Vukovar Hospital were murdered, I found it gratifying to apprehend and transport to The Hague at least one of the principal perpetrators indicted for this crime against humanity.

Vladimír Dzuro, the leading Czech investigator, and his ICTY colleagues Clint Williamson and Kevin Curtis deserve great credit for their dogged determination and high level of professionalism in bringing Slavko Dokmanović and the other indicted war criminals on the ICTY prosecutors' list of war criminals to justice. Our principal concern in planning the operation was for the safety and welfare of the seven hundred United Nations personnel residing on the economy or living in Serb homes in Eastern Slavonia. We had to continually factor in this major security issue throughout the planning phase.

However, my faith in the ICTY team, the UNTAES Planning Cell, and our military personnel was not misplaced. Their superb operational planning, the repeated rehearsals, and the flawless execution of the operation by all concerned ensured success. The UNTAES and the ICTY staffs, as well as the assigned military personnel demonstrated such a remarkably high level of professionalism that any threats of violence in the region were minimized. The operation went far to dispel the notion that war criminals could not be apprehended and that the international community did not have the resolve to do so. We succeeded, and other arrests have followed.

Our failure to act would have been unconscionable and would have put into doubt the very reason for our presence in the former Yugoslavia. This was the most difficult war of all: a war between neighbors and friends, and war between people who had lived together in a functioning community for centuries. We know that the physical wounds of war often heal faster than the psychological ones. Bringing to justice those who perpetrated such heinous crimes, we hope, will go far to heal the psychological wounds as well.

3

The Tribulations of Slavko Dokmanović

Was Dokmanović Lawfully Apprehended or Kidnapped from Serbia?

On July 4, 1997, Slavko Dokmanović entered the courtroom with his defense lawyer, Toma Fila, from Belgrade. This was the arraignment part of the procedure, where the charges against him were read out, and he was allowed to plead guilty or not guilty to them. He pleaded "not guilty" to all counts.

A total of five hearings were held in July, September, and November solely to discuss the legality of the arrest. Fila lodged a complaint that Dokmanović had in fact been kidnapped from the Federal Republic of Yugoslavia, and therefore our arrest was illegal. The defense and the prosecution summoned several witnesses. One witness for the defense was Knežević, the friend who made the mistake of letting Dokmanović persuade him into accompanying him to the meeting with General Klein.

Milan Knežević testified: "On June 26, 1997, Slavko called to ask me to come as soon as possible. I decided to go because I wanted to help him. He was having coffee at home with two friends. I joined them, and we talked about the freedom of thought, about sports and politics. After about half an hour, Slavko turned to me and said, 'Milan, I have something I want you to do.' He asked me to go with him the next day to Vukovar. I said I didn't trust the Croatian authorities or police or the people from UNTAES. But Slavko was really optimistic and convinced me to go. He boasted that he had assurances from Hryshchyshyn, the chief of staff for General Klein, and mentioned the name of Kevin Curtis. I had never heard of him, but he said that Mr. Curtis guaranteed his safe passage and there would be no problems. He and Mr. Curtis were going to Vukovar and back under the protection of UNTAES. He also told me that General Klein was returning from New York to Zagreb to meet President Tuđman in order to talk with him about protecting the property of Serbs. I said that if we could help in some way, why not go to Vukovar. General Klein is one of the most honest men I know. I myself participated in two meetings with him in Zagreb.

"On June 27 at 14:15, Slavko picked me up and it took us about thirty to forty minutes to get to the border at the Bogojevo bridge. On the way we talked about how dangerous it was going to be for us in Croatia because the day before a Croatian court had sentenced an innocent Serb to five years in prison. But Slavko had trusted General Klein and believed he would protect him.

"When we got to the bridge, it was seven minutes to three. Our friend drove Slavko's car back to safety; we went through customs and exchanged a few words with our police and customs officers. At about five minutes to three, we got to the bridge and at a distance of approximately thirty meters saw two parked UN vehicles. There was a smartly dressed man holding an identification card; he greeted us and asked if one of us was Mr. Dokmanović. Slavko nodded his head, and this man handed him the identification card, which turned out to be from UNTAES, and Slavko put it in his pocket. The man then asked who I was, and we both answered together that I was Slavko's friend. The man only nodded and opened the car door for us. After a minute or two, we drove over the bridge and headed toward Vukovar with an armed escort. I was sitting behind the driver. The window was open, and because the wind bothered me, I tried to close it but couldn't. That's when I began to suspect that something was wrong.

"We crossed the other side of the bridge and approached Croatian customs. The cars began to slow down because other ones were arriving at that moment. I had gone through this border crossing at least two hundred times, only this was the first time that I noticed everyone was saluting us. I thought it was because the cars belonged to General Klein. We then drove off at high speed to the UNTAES checkpoint, which was about four kilometers from the border. We slowed down because there was a truck parked on the side of the road marked with the UN emblem. As we approached, it suddenly took off and partially blocked our way. I panicked because I thought we were going to hit him, but our driver dodged it and swerved off the road into the UNTAES compound, which was located on the left side, and braked so hard that we came to an immediate stop. I would guess it was about five minutes after three."

Grant Niemann, who was representing the prosecution, next summoned Kevin Curtis. During the cross-examination, defense attorney Fila was hoping to catch him in a lie.

Fila: "When you went to visit Mr. Dokmanović, did you have any intentions with him?"

Curtis: "My intention was to gain his trust in order to bring him to territory controlled by UNTAES, so he could be arrested there."

Fila: "Did Mr. Dokmanović ask you at any time during your two meetings for guarantees that he would not be arrested?"

Curtis: "The only guarantee he asked me for was not to come into contact with any Croatian authorities."

Fila: "What did you say to that?"

Curtis: "I told him that I would tell UNTAES representatives about it when I spoke to them."

Since Kevin candidly told the court about his plans with Dokmanović, Fila was unable to call his credibility into question. Another important part of the complaint that Fila presented to the court was the argument that the place where Dokmanović was arrested was on a bridge over the Danube, behind the border checkpoint of the Federal Republic of Yugoslavia (FRY). According to Fila the arrest took place the moment Dokmanović got into the UNTAES vehicles, which were still on FRY territory. But the argument was moot because the border between Croatia and Yugoslavia was and is in the middle of the Danube. To our surprise Fila called Dokmanović as a witness, which Clint Williamson marked down as a gross mistake on the part of the defense. Clint conducted the cross-examination.

Williamson: "You believed that on June 27 you were going directly to a meeting with General Klein and then back?"

Dokmanović: "Yes."

Williamson: "Up until that time, you trusted General Klein?"

Dokmanović: "I trusted him."

Williamson: "Did you have any reason not to trust him?"

Dokmanović: "No."

Williamson: "Up until the time you were pulled out of the car, you still believed you were on your way to a meeting with General Klein. Is that true?"

Dokmanović: "Yes."

This brief exchange was crucial for the prosecution's argument that the arrest did not take place until Erdut, meaning after Dokmanović was pulled out of the car by GROM. During the hearing the prosecution submitted our video record to the court. It clearly showed that although Dokmanović had been lured to the scene of the arrest under false pretext, he had been informed of all his rights after the handcuffs were slapped on him.

On October 22 the Trial Chamber chaired by Gabrielle Kirk McDonald issued its decision that the accused had been arrested on Croatian territory, as administered by UNTAES, with the participation of the prosecutor's office, and that UNTAES carried out a lawful arrest. Regarding the question of the means used to make the arrest, it was ruled that UNTAES did not violate the principles of international law or the sovereignty of the Federal Republic of Yugoslavia.

This ruling is still considered crucial today and not only in the work of international tribunals. Carefully devised entrapment became a legitimate and viable means to arrest indicted war criminals, especially in cases where there are concerns about safety and local authorities refuse to cooperate.

68. (*top*) Kevin Curtis and Toma Fila in the courtroom during Curtis's testimony. (ICTY)

69. (*bottom*) Clint Williamson and Slavko Dokmanović in the courtroom during Dokmanović's testimony. (ICTY)

IV. DISPOSITION

For the foregoing reasons, **THE TRIAL CHAMBER** being seised of the Preliminary Motions challenging the legality of the arrest of the accused, Slavko Dokmanović, filed by the Defence,

PURSUANT TO RULE 72,

HEREBY DENIES the Motions for the Release of the accused.

Done in both English and French, the English text being authoritative.

Gabrielle Kirk McDonald
Presiding Judge

70. (*top*) Justice Gabrielle Kirk McDonald. (ICTY)

71. (*bottom*) Extract from the decision by Justice McDonald to deny motion for the release of Slavko Dokmanović. (ICTY)

The Insider

Two more lawyers joined the team to prepare the evidence for the Ovčara massacre. The investigators were given the task of ensuring that it was complete and that all the witnesses were still alive and willing to testify before the tribunal. We were in the middle of this hectic activity in early November 1997, when Clint called to say the evidence was convincing and the team of lawyers working on it were confident of that fact. In his opinion no major problems were expected at the trial. But he knew from his own experience that a positive outcome against Dokmanović and after him the Vukovar Three might very well depend on the testimony of an insider from among the Serbs involved in the massacre at Ovčara.

Getting such testimony was easier said than done. You have to find somebody who was actually there and willing to cooperate but isn't directly implicated in the killings. We had the names of several members of the death squad at Ovčara, but even if we were sure of their location at that moment, there was no way we could bring a mass murderer into court and present him as a credible witness for the prosecution. Yet we had to keep all options on the table.

While looking through the statements again, I stumbled on something we had either overlooked or didn't consider important at the time. Several witnesses stated in their testimony that their survival was thanks to a young Serb whose father was one of the leading citizens of Vukovar. In pursuing this lead, I would have to change his name to prevent exposing him and his family to danger. I called him Jovan.

I started collecting all available information about him and his father that was available in the tribunal's database and also from my contacts in Croatia. I learned that Jovan's father never left Vukovar and still worked there for the same institution where he had been employed before the war. After consulting Kevin, Dennis, and Clint, I packed my bags and flew to Croatia. The next morning I picked up my interpreter, Vlatka Leko, and drove to Vukovar. We went to Klein's office to arrange some cover in the event of trouble, but the general wasn't in Vukovar. The UNTAES security chief agreed to have his men on call.

We had no idea what to expect when we rang the bell to the apartment of Jovan's father. A pleasant-looking, gray-haired man answered the door. We introduced ourselves, showed our ID cards, and asked for ten minutes of his time. He invited us in, and I got right to the point, namely, if we might talk to his son about the events at Ovčara in November 1991. His face grew worried and sad, but he promised to speak to his son about it. We arranged to meet at ten o'clock the next morning. Neither Vlatka nor I were under any illusions, but to our great surprise, Jovan agreed to talk. His father gave us his phone number, and Vlatka immediately set up a meeting with him at one o'clock. I informed UNTAES, and it dispatched an armed patrol to be within sight of the house in the event we needed help. After a quick lunch, we met up with the patrol. They gave us walkie-talkies and wished us luck. Then we walked up to the door and rang the bell.

A pleasant young woman greeted us at the door and invited us into the living room, where a very sullen man was waiting for us. He had a close-cropped beard, tousled hair, and was slightly overweight. After introductions he snapped at Vlatka to ask whether she was Serb or Croat. Taken aback Vlatka said she was a Croat from Zagreb. To our amazement Jovan's face lit up. He invited us to sit down and quickly explained his initial brusqueness. He said that he would have to throw us out if Vlatka had been a local Serb from Vukovar. His neighbors and friends would call him a traitor, which would subject him and his family to death threats. The arrest of Dokmanović had made the tribunal look more suspicious than ever in the eyes of the local Serb population.

I came right out and told Jovan why we were looking for him. At first he was evasive; then he asked if he could go talk with his wife. We could hear them arguing through the closed door, or rather she was the one doing the arguing. Jovan reappeared to negotiate the best possible deal. If he and his family got new identities, he would tell everything he knew about Ovčara. I made him understand that it was going to work another way: he had to provide testimony, and only after we established the truth behind it would he and his family receive witness protection.

Jovan confided his fears to us. Serbs never forget a betrayal, and he would never be safe. On the other hand, giving his testimony in The Hague would not protect him from the Croatian authorities once they learned that he was present on that fateful day at Ovčara. So what if he helped save the lives of several Croatian civilians? There was no way to prove he didn't pull one of the triggers on others.

We agreed to give him time to think it over. We said goodbye and left him and his wife to consider what the future had in store for them. I immediately telephoned Clint, and he called back that same evening to say he had discussed everything with Arbour and her deputy, Graham Blewitt. Should Jovan cooperate fully, they would offer witness protection for him and his family. The next day we called on Jovan with the security detail again in place. The only change was the calmer atmosphere in the house. Jovan agreed to testify and promised to tell only the truth. We agreed on the arrangements for our next meeting and left Vukovar.

Clint decided to come to Croatia immediately so that he could personally meet Jovan. He wanted to judge for himself the veracity of the information Jovan promised to provide. The meeting took place on December 9, 1997, in Vukovar. Clint was satisfied with the names of those he claimed to have rescued, so they agreed on the terms of his testimony, and Clint flew back to The Hague. I stayed in Vukovar and interviewed Jovan over the next six days. We pieced together a mosaic of his story from the beginning of the war to the Ovčara massacre. His testimony allowed us to confirm not just the names of the many who were killed at Ovčara but also those who did the killing. For the first time, we were confronted with the actual details of the horrors and inhumanity unleashed on the evening of November 20, in a place no one had ever heard of before.

"I remember seeing there one woman who was about thirty or thirty-five years old and 165 cm tall," Jovan recalled. "She had dark hair, about medium in length. I didn't know who she was, but the others told me she was the wife of the biggest Croatian nationalist in Vukovar, a man who allegedly killed many Serb children. I heard that she was pregnant. I saw Stanko Vujanović and Petar Ćirić, who was known by the name 'Pero Cigan,' drag this woman out of the hangar. I was sure they killed her, but I didn't see it. A few days later, I heard Vujanović tell someone how he and Cigan had really enjoyed themselves. Apparently, after dragging her out, Cigan ordered her to strip naked and then told Vujanović to grab her by the arms. Vujanović thought he was going to rape her, so he did what he was told. But Cigan stuck the point of his AK-47 assault rifle into her private part and pulled the trigger. Later that evening in the hangar at Ovčara, some of the Serbs made fun of Vujanović, calling him a 'pussy' because some tissue from the murdered woman's genitals stuck to his face. I had noticed that Vujanović had something on his face, but I didn't understand what it meant until I heard him describe what they did."

After his exhaustive testimony was complete, Jovan read and signed it and said goodbye to his family. We secretly took him to Budapest for his flight to The Hague because the airports in Zagreb and Belgrade would be too dangerous for him to use. He was issued a visa and off we went, but I later returned to Vukovar to verify his testimony as much as possible. In the case against Dokmanović, Jovan was given a code name, and he would testify in other cases, including against the Vukovar Three.

The Trial Opens

Before his case came to trial, we tried to get Dokmanović to plea bargain to a reduced sentence in exchange for him testifying against the Vukovar Three. But his stay in prison yielded nothing. Dennis and I spent several hours with him, but neither Dokmanović nor his lawyer, Fila, was interested in cooperating with the prosecution.

On January 19, 1998, the case of the *Prosecutor versus Slavko Dokmanović*, docket number IT-95-13a, was commenced by the president of the tribunal, Judge Antonio Cassese, assisted by Judge Richard May and Judge Florence Mumba. Dokmanović was charged with crimes against humanity, violations of the laws and customs of war, and grave breaches of the Geneva Conventions. The prosecutor summoned a total of forty-three witnesses and the defense forty-two. With no material evidence that Dokmanović was physically present at Ovčara and only the testimony of Emil Čakalić and Dragutin Berghofer to go on, we had to prove that he had actually participated in the massacre.

Defense lawyer Toma Fila decided to gamble everything on a single item, namely, a videocassette he designated as evidence D-2. In his opinion it validated Dokmanović's alibi that he was not at Ovčara during the incriminating period. Fila was taking a big risk because he would have to call Dokmanović to the stand as a witness again. If he had surprised us by calling him during the preliminary hearing on the legality of his arrest, then doing it during the actual trial left us speechless. Before coming to the tribunal, Clint had worked as a prosecutor in the organized crime section of the U.S. Department of Justice. He shook his head in amazement at this development and kept repeating that Fila was either a very bad lawyer or irresponsible. Perhaps he didn't understand the work of the tribunal enough, or he wasn't defending Dokmanović so much as someone else. Or it could have been that he had some absolutely foolproof evidence of Dokmanović's innocence, so that he wasn't afraid to expose him to more cross-examination, which gave us an unpleasant feeling in our stomachs. All we could do was wait and see what he might have up his sleeve.

D-2, Evidence for the Defense

When Clint received the video recording labeled D-2 from the defense, he called the team together not only to watch but also to scrutinize it. It wasn't clear during the first viewing what Fila hoped to prove with it. And then it hit us. If the recording was authentic and the time on it had not been tampered with, then Dokmanović could not have been at Ovčara on November 20 during the incriminating time. After playing it several times, Clint took the tape out and handed it to me. "Unless we can prove this tape is a phony, we're going to have big problems. So forget whatever you're doing and worry only about this. Our whole case could crumble because of this tape." So I handed my work on preparing witnesses over to Dennis and Kevin and went home to work on the cassette.

I spent the whole weekend watching the damn thing, rewinding and playing it endlessly as I looked for clues to determine precisely where the video was shot. On Monday morning I told Clint I needed to do three things. First, I needed to try to improve the quality of the video. Second, I needed to capture images from the video, something that is easy to do today on a computer but was a technical problem in 1997. Third, I needed to go to Vukovar to make a full discovery of the route shown in the video.

The next day I took the tape to a Dutch police laboratory near Utrecht and asked the technicians to try to clean it up, but the poor quality of the copy made any improvement negligible. They were, however, able to make me a full set of images from it. I had these images with me when I landed in Zagreb on Thursday afternoon. I picked up a car, collected my interpreter, Vlatka, and headed for Vukovar.

We spent Friday morning crisscrossing the city with photos in one hand, a camera in the other, and a camcorder slung around my neck. We were looking for all the points that appear in the D-2 video. It was a lot of going back and forth because Vukovar had changed quite a lot since 1991. But by evening we had at least established the most essential point, namely, the sequence of images did not reflect traveling south from the center of Vukovar as indicated in the video. The second to the last shot shows a severely damaged tree and a road sign marking the boundary of Vukovar. The time stamp on it was 15:36. The next shot comes six minutes later at 15:42, which should have put us in the village of Negoslavci as the video suggests, yet the images still show Vukovar, as if the person with the camera had suddenly turned around and sped back to the city. The sequence clearly seemed to have been tampered with, but we couldn't figure out why Fila was so sure of its authenticity.

In the evening I called Clint, and we agreed that I should record everything on video and take new pictures of the places captured on D-2 so we could compare them. On Monday I was back in The Hague and presenting the outcome of my investigation to the team. You might call it warm-up for the time when I would have to convince the judges just what exactly was on this tape.

At the trial Fila called Zoran Jevtović, Jovan Cvetković, Vukosav Tomašević, Nebojša Lazarević, and Mirko Dragišić to the stand, all friends of Dokmanović who were with him in Vukovar and appear in the video. All testified that on the afternoon of November 20 they left Vukovar, didn't stop or turn around, just kept going straight until they reached Negoslavci six minutes later. Dokmanović therefore could not have been in Ovčara at that time. He cannot be seen in the video at the critical time of 15:42, but his voice could be heard, and it was validated by witnesses.

Only by challenging their testimony could we prove that the alibi was a lie, and Clint went for the jugular in his cross-examination of the men. But they never once swayed from the script: "We never stopped, never turned off the road, never turned around."

If we could prove that the last frame was from Vukovar and not Negoslavci, Clint could ask the court to throw their testimony out. To play it safe, he decided I was going to have to testify to bolster our chances of proving that these men were committing perjury.

As fate would have it, we had a young Dutch lawyer named Jan Vos as an intern on our team. At one meeting he surmised that it was going to take a dendrologist, or expert on trees, to get our case back on track. I for one didn't know such experts existed. We got a good laugh out of it before realizing that it might well prove to be a stroke of genius. By looking at the trees captured in the video, this dendrologist could determine the exact location of each segment of the film.

First, we had to find such an expert, then take him to Vukovar, prepare him for questioning, and summon him as a witness. Since testimony of this kind was unique in criminal cases, we decided our expert had to come from one of the home countries of the judges on the tribunal panel. We figured that they, like everyone else, would be more inclined to trust a fellow countryman than a foreigner. It came down to either Italy (Judge Casesse) or the United Kingdom (Judge May). Assuming an Italian witness might lead to some problems communicating in English, we decided to narrow our search for a dendrologist to the United Kingdom.

After calling several organizations, Kevin traveled to Surrey to meet with an official from the forestry commission. He was still waiting in the commission's office when Paul Tabbush walked in by chance. Kevin told him why he was there. The professor offered to go to Vukovar and take a look for himself. Since I was the only one on our crew who could identify the footage in the video, it was only natural that I should accompany Tabbush. We met up at the airport and caught a plane to Zagreb.

I familiarized the professor with our problem during the flight. I showed him the photographs captured from the D-2 video along with the ones I had taken from the exact same spots. Only the most basic of comparisons could be made under the circumstances—foldout table, overhead light—but according to Tabbush, everything looked in order.

We reached Vukovar in the afternoon, and the professor went right to work surveying the trees as we made our way south toward Negoslavci. I followed him intently, if only out of curiosity about the way in which a dendrologist does research by looking at things the rest of us cannot see. He was finished well before nightfall, and we were back in Zagreb that evening. In the morning we were at the airport, and he was telling me, "See you in court."

The only thing left to do was to authenticate the video recording itself. For this we turned to the FBI, not just for the allure of its initials but also because its agents had lots of experience with courtroom testimony and English was their first language. Clint used his contacts at the Justice Department to get the FBI laboratory in Quantico, Virginia, to agree to take a good look at the recording.

On June 1, 1998, I boarded a flight in Amsterdam and flew across the Atlantic to Dulles International Airport near Washington DC. My spirits were high as I went down to breakfast at the hotel the next morning. Here I was, a detective from Prague CID, about to work side-by-side with the FBI. The sentry at Quantico knew all about my coming and had an ID card waiting for me. He directed me to Building C in the gigantic complex, which was surrounded by a thick forest. Inevitably, I got lost. By the time I got there, the special agent assigned to our case looked a little cross. He was probably thinking, "Who does this Czech chump think he is making me wait like this?"

We had plucked the name of Noel Herold off the list of proposed experts because of his specialization in the synchronization and authenticity of audio and video recordings. I explained our problem to him over a cup of percolated coffee, emphasizing how important the cassette was. I handed him the original copy and spent the rest of the week commuting to Quantico to consult with him about his findings. I dispatched a detailed report of his progress every morning to The Hague.

The legendary FBI Academy was located somewhere within the Quantico complex, and I was curious to have a look inside it, especially the tactical training facility known as Hogan's Alley. Agent Herold was kind enough to give me a tour. It was a long street with a bank, post office, the Dogwood Inn, a dry-cleaners, a barber shop, a casino, apartment buildings, shops, you name it. At first glance it all looks very real, but then it has to because it is where agents from the FBI, the ATF (Bureau of Alcohol, Tobacco, Firearms, and Explosives), the DEA (Drug Enforcement Administration), and other such agencies and bureaus do their training. Using professional actors in the roles of hostages, bank clerks, and sales people, they practice raids, negotiate with kidnappers, and arrest offenders. I was utterly amazed and had to admit that I had never seen anything approaching the same sophistication in all my training as a law enforcement officer.

On Thursday of that week, Clint flew in, and together we met with Agent Herold for one final meeting. Using the information I had been sending him all week, we conducted a mock cross-examination of Herold and prepared an official report for the tribunal. Prior to leaving I had to make one more stop at another laboratory, this one in Washington DC, at the ATF. This lab was conducting ballistics tests on the hundreds of cartridges and projectiles found by our team of specialists at the exhumation site in Ovčara and during the autopsies in Zagreb.

I was met by the ATF deputy director for science and technology, Jack Huntered, a specialist who had already worked for the tribunal as an expert in Bosnia. It was a courtesy visit but nevertheless important because the ATF was doing this work for free as a matter of prestige. Later that day I went to its laboratory in Rockville, Maryland, where ballistic experts had found that a total of eighteen different weapons, all of them AK-47 Kalashnikov automatic assault rifles, had been used to fire the 435 cartridges retrieved from Ovčara. From this we could assume that eighteen people took part in the murders.

The Testimony of Slavko Dokmanović

We were now ready to demolish the fabricated alibi, and Fila had no inkling of it when he smugly called Dokmanović to the stand. He asked him to relate all the events that had occurred on November 20, 1991, focusing in particular on Dokmanović's departure from Vukovar. He wanted to prove that the defendant was unable to go to Ovčara and then on to the village of Negoslavci in the time frame shown in the video. If he succeeded, it would completely undermine the testimony of our witnesses who had said they saw him taking part in the beating of civilians at Ovčara. Dokmanović could well go free.

Clint got up to conduct the cross-examination. He systematically reviewed the defendant's testimony with him, all the while zeroing in on the evidence that supposedly proved his alibi.

Williamson: "At any point between the time you left the center of Vukovar and the time you stopped on account of the buses we see in the video, did you turn around or change your direction of travel at all?"

Dokmanović: "No."

Williamson: "You continued straight in the direction of the village of Negoslavci, which is south of Vukovar?"

Dokmanović: "We drove south to Negoslavci, and when we reached the village, we drove past those buses you see on the video."

Williamson: "And where exactly was that in Negoslavci, do you remember?"

Dokmanović: "I only know that it was somewhere in the village, where exactly, I can't remember. But it was in Negoslavci."

Williamson: "Mr. Dokmanović, the place you identified as being in Negoslavci is really somewhere else. The video was tampered with, was it not?"

Dokmanović: "That's not true."

Williamson: "I would furthermore argue that the houses seen on the video at 15:36 are on the southern outskirts of Vukovar, on the road leading to Negoslavci. Six minutes later, at 15:42, the recording shows a site 370 meters to the north, meaning back toward the center of Vukovar and not to Negoslavci as you claim. You did a 180-degree turn and headed back to Vukovar, from where you had left."

Dokmanović: "That's not true! We did not go back!"

Williamson: "Would you agree that the person who shot the video was standing outside the car?"

Dokmanović: "It's in Negoslavci. You can see for yourself it's a village. There is no mistake about it."

After Clint concluded his cross-examination, Judge May had some further questions.

May: "As I understand it, the prosecutor is arguing that sometime after the defendant left the center of Vukovar, he went to Ovčara. Is that correct?"

Williamson: "Exactly, Your Honor."

May: "The prosecution is arguing that the defendant did not go straight from Vukovar to Negoslavci. Is that correct?"

Williamson: "Exactly, Your Honor. The prosecution will submit extensive evidence to show that the scene shown at time 15:42 on the video is to the north of the scene shown at time 15:36. It could not have been in Negoslavci as claimed by the defense."

May: "Mr. Williamson, perhaps you should ask the defendant how he got to Ovčara instead."

Williamson: "All right, Your Honor. Mr. Dokmanović, isn't it true that after you left the center of Vukovar, you turned off the road that runs between Vukovar and Negoslavci and headed in the direction of Ovčara?"

Dokmanović: "It's not true."

My colleagues and I were sitting in the gallery, closely following the questioning. When Clint announced to the court that we had evidence to show that the defense's alibi was bogus, I looked at Fila to see the reaction on his face. As an experienced courtroom lawyer, he tried to conceal his emotions, but from that point on he knew his case was lost. He wasn't about to give up, but in the face of Clint's confidence and self-assurance, he began making schoolboy errors that were indicative of a lawyer under pressure.

The Alibi

While I was having a go at the D-2 videocassette, Kevin and Dennis were charged with interviewing all witnesses concerned with Dokmanović's alibi. Several of them lived in Bačka Palanka, a town on the east bank of the Danube in the Serbian province of Vojvodina. Kevin knew he was taking a chance venturing into Serbia, where the police could well arrest him on charges of kidnapping Dokmanović. He and Dennis landed in Belgrade, picked up their interpreters, and headed to Bačka Palanka. They split up, with Dennis meeting one witness while Kevin went to see the mayor, Ljubomir Novaković. He expected and received a frosty reception, but the atmosphere was much friendlier by the time he left. Novaković even pulled out a bottle of the local brandy called *rakia*, but Kevin explained there was no drinking on the job. Of course, the job came to an end after the interview, so once Kevin got up to leave, he could raise a glass with Novaković. The mayor even organized a dinner for them that evening at a restaurant on the River Danube.

Much to the surprise of Kevin and Dennis, a whole delegation of officials was waiting to greet them. They sat at a long table and enjoyed an evening of warm and pleasant conversation, despite none of their hosts understanding any English. The mayor got it into his head to try to drink this pair of Englishmen under the table. As they had to drive to Belgrade, it was quickly decided that Dennis and one of the interpreters would abstain. But Kevin was all up for the challenge when Novaković ordered brandy and wine in quick succession. Shot for shot he had no problem keeping up with the mayor, who had no idea what he had gotten himself into. After about an hour, the poor guy staggered toward the bathroom. Dennis went to look for him and reported that his head was ingloriously buried inside a toilet bowl. When Novaković finally reappeared, he sat slumped in a chair next to Kevin, his face greener than a bowl of wasabi. Kevin went for the kill and asked if he might not want to do one final shot of brandy before they called it an evening. All the green suddenly flushed out of Novaković's face. It was his way of saying, "No thank you."

The sequel to all these hijinks was played out in the courtroom, where the prosecution presented its own interviews conducted with witnesses for the defense, including Novaković. During these sessions Fila must have been horrified, finding Novaković to be poorly coached or perhaps saying something he shouldn't have. Fila tried to discredit Novaković by saying he was uttering half-truths and fake information. The course of the trial was in fact showing that if anyone knew about half-truths and fake information, it was Fila himself.

He called Kevin to the stand as a hostile witness and accused him of consuming alcohol during the course of his interview with Novaković. Since Kevin was British, Fila naturally assumed that it was whiskey he was drinking. So he accused Kevin of drinking a whole bottle of Scotch with the mayor during the interview. To argue from an assumption is always a tricky thing in court, and it would take a much better lawyer than Fila to come out of it without looking like a fool. Even Dokmanović had to come to that conclusion when Kevin said he never drank whiskey. I could've told Fila that myself. I was with Kevin several times when he was offered a glass of Scotch, but he never drank it, even when it would have suited the occasion for him to take at least a sip.

Fila: "Did Mr. Novaković's secretary bring you any alcoholic beverages?"

Curtis: "Some alcohol was offered at the beginning and end of our interview. It was a glass of *rakia*."

Fila: "Wasn't it a bottle of whiskey, which was full at the beginning of the interrogation and empty at the end?"

Curtis: "No, it was *rakia*, and nothing at all was drunk during my interview with Mr. Novaković."

Fila: "Mr. Curtis, I didn't say you were drinking alcohol."

Curtis: "That's what you are implying. Again, no alcohol was drunk during the interview, and I don't drink whiskey in any case. Ask anyone who knows me."

Fila: "I asked you if there was a full bottle of whiskey in the room at the beginning of the interrogation and if it was empty at the end of the interrogation."

Curtis: "And I'm telling you that from what I saw there was no bottle of whiskey in the room during my interview with Ljubomir Novaković."

Fila: "If I call witnesses like Mr. Novaković's secretary, who will testify that you are not telling the truth, won't that mean you have lied under oath?"

Williamson: "Your Honor, I object. Mr. Fila is asking questions about potential future witnesses. Mr. Curtis cannot possibly answer such speculation."

Judge Cassese: "The court concurs. Objection sustained."

Fila: "I will reformulate the question. If I bring in a witness who will confirm that your testimony before the court is not true . . ."

Williamson: "Objection, Your Honor."

Judge Cassese: "Sustained."

Fila: "Fine. Mr. Curtis, would you say that Mr. Novaković was completely sober during the entire interrogation and drank no alcohol?"

Curtis: "He looked completely sober and drank no alcohol in my presence during the interview."

Fila: "So he drank nothing?"

Curtis: "Coffee, juice, whatever was offered us, that yes, but no alcohol."

Fila: "That is exactly what I asked. In June I will bring witnesses who will prove you are not telling the truth."

Williamson: "Objection, Your Honor. Mr. Fila is merely arguing in front of the witness. This is unacceptable courtroom manner."

Judge Cassese: "Objection sustained. Mr. Fila, the court understands that you plan to summon further witnesses. That's fine, but it has nothing to do with questioning this witness."

Fila: "I have no further questions."

Clint knew that he had to put an end to this whole ridiculous line of questioning immediately, else a cloud might well hang over Kevin's testimony. He knew from Kevin what had gone down in Bačka Palanka, so he needed to ask him some follow-up questions.

Williamson: "Your Honor, with your permission, I'd like to ask the witness a few questions?"

Judge Cassese: "Proceed."

Williamson: "Just briefly, Mr. Curtis, did you not accompany Mr. Novaković to dinner at his invitation after your interview was complete?"

Curtis: "Yes. During the interview I asked Mr. Novaković if it would be possible to have a look at the bridge across the River Danube that connects Bačka Palanka and Ilok. This bridge was important for our investigation, but we hadn't had an opportunity to see it before then. Mr. Novaković called someone into the office and arranged it. We drove to the restaurant, which was about three hundred meters from the bridge. We had a look at it, took photos of it, and then went to dinner."

Williamson: "And was alcohol served at the dinner?"

Curtis: "Yes."

Williamson: "And would you say, in your judgment, that Mr. Novaković got himself into an inebriated state?"

Curtis: "Yes. He wanted to show off, acting macho and all that, but couldn't handle his liquor and ended up completely drunk."

Williamson: "Just to clarify, the dinner took place after your interview with him had ended, is that correct?"

Curtis: "Yes."

Williamson: "No further questions, Your Honor."

That did the trick. Fila never made good his threat to summon witnesses to undermine Kevin's testimony. The closest he came to it was calling his own investigator to the stand right before the end

72. (*top*) Clint Williamson during the testimony of investigator Vladimír Dzuro. (ICTY)

73. (*bottom*) Investigator Vladimír Dzuro during his testimony on the alibi of Slavko Dokmanović. (ICTY)

of the trial, but all that man did was testify that the secretary confirmed she had brought whiskey into the room. She did not see for herself whether Kevin or Novaković drank it. It was hearsay at best. By then the defense attorney realized that the fate of his client was going to depend on more than whether an Englishman had drunk a bit of whiskey or not.

Prior to my own testimony, Clint and the other lawyers from our team subjected me to a mock grilling. They threw everything at me and dissected everything I said down to the smallest detail. It was an ordeal sitting there under the glare of lights, cameras all around me, and my colleague staring at me as if to suggest I had muffed everything up, so there was no sense in calling Special Agent Herold or Paul Tabbush to the stand afterward.

On June 17, 1998, Clint and I were standing right before the door to the courtroom. "Remember this," he said, "regardless of what happens, just tell the truth. No matter what it is, it's something we can work with in the end. But let them catch you in even the most insignificant lie, and that's it. Our whole case is doomed. Got it?" I told him I got it and entered the courtroom.

The first thing I did on the stand was explain how I conducted the field examination of the D-2 videocassette. I gave a lengthy and detailed narration of where the individual scenes caught on film were actually located and how the key time of 15:42 did not show the village of Negoslavci, as the defense claimed, but rather north of the scene given at 15:36. I then submitted the photos captured from the 1991 recording and compared them with photos I had taken myself in 1998. For example a traffic sign in the 1991 photo is missing in 1998. I described how my interpreter Vlatka found that it had been wrenched out of the ground and tossed into a ditch, where it was hidden by overgrown grass. We picked it up, stuck it back into its original hole, and took a snap of it against the background.

I particularly emphasized a description of the trees that appear in D-2 and those in my photos. In one shot at 15:42, we see a bus moving along the road, and behind it is a house with a fully mature walnut tree. The bare branches of the tree are partially touching the rooftop. This tree was the key element for Tabbush, and my job was to establish its location before he talked about it in his testimony.

I then told the court that according to my investigation, whoever took the video in 1991 had to have turned around at 15:36 and headed back to Vukovar. I added that the recording at time 15:42 shows a spe-

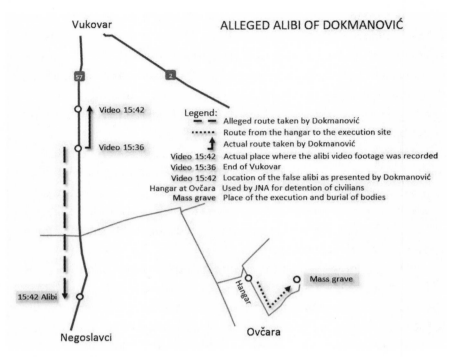

74. Sketch depicting the circumstances surrounding the alibi of Slavko Dokmanović. (Vladimír Dzuro)

cific location in Vukovar. For better orientation I sketched it all on a map. Clint then resumed his questioning:

Williamson: "After you returned from your first trip to Vukovar to verify the D-2 videocassette, did you have the opportunity to go back to Vukovar again?"

Dzuro: "Yes."

Williamson: "What reason did you have for it?"

Dzuro: "The D-2 video shows many different trees in certain places, but because I'm no expert on trees, I asked one, Professor Tabbush, to come with me to Vukovar to help me identify them."

Williamson: "Did Professor Tabbush have the opportunity to visit all of Vukovar and the villages of Negoslavci and Orolik?"

Dzuro: "Yes, he did. I took him to all the places in Vukovar he asked to see, and we drove together on the road from Vukovar to the villages of Negoslavci, Šidski Banovci, and Orolik."

Williamson: "Did Professor Tabbush recognize any of the trees captured in the D-2 video?"

Dzuro: "Yes, he did."

Williamson: "Were you present with Professor Tabbush when he looked at the trees and examined them in detail?"

Dzuro: "Yes, I was."

Williamson: "Did Professor Tabbush use for his investigation certain photos from the D-2 evidence and certain photos that you yourself took?"

Dzuro: "Yes, he did, and for a good reason. Professor Tabbush and I were in Vukovar in May, when the trees were full of leaves, unlike in winter. So Professor Tabbush used the photos that I took during my first visit, when the trees were bare. The professor himself chose the material he used to apply his methods of research."

When it was his turn, Fila smiled at me in a friendly manner and said he believed me of course, but he needed to clarify a few things. He then launched into a detailed cross-examination, which took up two full days, but for all his efforts he was unable to find any holes in my testimony. Next, since the defense had banked everything on the authenticity of the video, Clint called Agent Herold as his next witness.

Williamson: "Is it true that in June of this year you met Mr. Vladimír Dzuro, an investigator with the prosecutor's office, at the FBI laboratories in Quantico?"

Herold: "Yes, Mr. Dzuro had a videotape with him that he asked me to examine to see if it was authentic."

Williamson: "Is the cassette brought to you by Mr. Dzuro the evidence presented by the defense known as D-2?"

Herold: "Yes, it is."

Williamson: "Did you have the time and opportunity to go over the material?"

Herold: "Yes, I did."

Williamson: "And did you determine whether the copy of the video recording is identical to the original?"

Herold: "Part of the video recording is a copy of the first generation and part the second generation. What I mean is part of it is a copy of a copy. The part of the video that shows the date 20.11 is a copy of the first generation. It was taken from the original."

Williamson: "Was it possible to determine whether the second-generation copy is identical to the original recording?"

Herold: "No, it wasn't possible."

Williamson: "If a copy of a recording is made, can the sequence of segments be tampered with?"

Herold: "Yes, it's possible."

Williamson: "Can information like the date and time be added to the video?"

Herold: "Yes, it's entirely feasible."

Williamson: "Is there a way to determine whether the date and time on the second generation copy are from the original or were added there later on?"

Herold: "There's no way to prove it one way or the other."

Williamson: "Would it be possible to erase certain sequences from a videocassette that were originally made with the original recording?"

Herold: "Yes, it would be possible to erase certain sequences, but because this is a copy here, there's no way to prove whether something from the original has been erased or not."

Fila told the court that he was unable to provide the original recording and offered nothing of substance in his cross-examination of Agent Herold. It wouldn't have mattered. We had established that the value of the video recording as evidence was in doubt.

Our last witness was the dendrologist, Paul Tabbush. Clint started off by telling the court how Tabbush came to be contacted by the prosecutor's office, how he had conducted his expert analysis and come to the conclusion he was about to present to the court. The main questioning focused on the village of Negoslavci.

Photo Taken by Dzuro in 1998

Alibi video D-2
15:42
20.11.1991

75. Simplified version of the analysis prepared for the tribunal by Paul Tabbush. (Vladimír Dzuro)

Williamson: "When you visited the village of Negoslavci, did you notice certain characteristics that were different from the ones that appear on the videocassette at time 15:42?"

Tabbush: "Yes, the distances between the houses and the road in Negoslavci are much greater. And very often there are two rows of trees between the houses and road. It's very typical for Negoslavci."

After explaining to the court that the video at time 15:42 is not from Negoslavci, Tabbush began to explain just exactly where the location was and how he was able to prove it. He had captured a photo of the scene, scanned it into the computer, and then drawn a straight line across all the major branches of the walnut tree that appear in it. He then extended this line to the edge of the roof of the adjacent house, which hadn't changed in either height or shape between 1991 and 1998. Next he drew angles between the edge of the roof and all the straight lines of the major branches. When he finished, he had applied the same method of measurement to the photo I had taken in 1998. He explained to the court that if they were a complete match, the resulting number of the measurement should be close to the figure 1.00. The measurement he came up with was 0.99, not enough to say it is the exact same spot where I took the picture, but considering a difference of seven years, pretty darn close.

Based on this measurement, Tabbush said he was absolutely sure where the video at time 15:42 was recorded in 1991. It was actually north of the footage shot at 15:36, namely, in Vukovar and not in Negoslavci.

Williamson: "Professor Tabbush, do trees have certain unique characteristics that distinguish them from other trees?"

Tabbush: "Yes, the arrangement of the main branches of every tree is the result of a combination of genetic factors and the effects of the environment, so no two trees can be exactly the same."

Williamson: "So trees are basically like humans?"

Tabbush: "Yes, basically, yes."

Williamson: "If two genetically identical trees were planted next to each other, would they look the same?"

Tabbush: "That would be highly unlikely. Even if the environmental conditions were the same, it's quite impossible for genetically identical trees to have the same appearance."

Williamson: "Do you have any doubt that the walnut tree you had the opportunity to study in Vukovar is the same one captured on video D-2 at the time 15:42?"

Tabbush: "No, I have no doubt about it. It is the same tree."

Williamson: "Thank you, I have no further questions."

It was time for the cross-examination, something none of us working on the case wanted to miss. Fila may have known enough about Scotch to presume he could trip up an Englishman, but we were positive he didn't have a clue about the science of trees. Indeed, the questions he asked Tabbush showed he didn't even understand the basics of his testimony. The professor had explained that only the tips of branches grow longer, so the point where a branch splits in two remains at the same height above the ground. Branches naturally grow thicker over time, but the angle between them basically stays the same. Fila just couldn't get it, and so he found himself hopelessly entangled in the questioning.

Fila: "So a tree grows like a person? For example, a person has a big nose and it grows and grows but it's still the same height from the ground."

Tabbush: "No, as I have been trying to explain this whole time, it's not like that for trees. For example, these two branches in the photo from time 15:42. At the time they were formed, they were in the same place as they were when filmed in 1991 and also in 1998, when Mr. Dzuro photographed them. They look only bigger, because as I said, trees only grow from their tips."

Fila: "So back to the same photo. For example, this particular point just above the passing bus—has the position to the edge of the roof changed between 1991 and 1998?"

Tabbush: "I can't say in which year the branches were formed . . ."

Fila: "Exactly my point."

Tabbush: "But if you will let me finish—I do not know exactly when the branches were formed; all I can tell you is that whenever it happened, that's it. The branches stay in the same position because trees only grow from the tips of the branches. I have already explained that to the court."

Fila: "I apologize to the court, but I really feel like either a fool or a teacher trying to explain something to a child, but I will try to make my questions more precise. Sir, during the seven or eight years that have passed since the video was filmed and Mr. Dzuro took this photo, has the relationship between the house and the tree changed in regards to the height of the tree? Not the angle or anything else, just the height of the tree."

Tabbush: "The tree has grown, of course, from the tips, but that has had no effect on my analysis, because the branching I studied already existed in 1991 as it did in 1998. That has not changed at all."

Fila: "Thank you, I have no further questions."

No one following the trial had any doubts that we had proved the actual location of the individual sites in the D-2 video. The witnesses for the defense had clearly perjured themselves. My quest in Vukovar had been absolutely crucial for our case. But that wasn't the end of it. Fila still had plenty of tenaciousness in him. He summoned several witnesses who testified that Slavko Dokmanović was an exemplary man, a devoted husband, and a doting father. All of it was testimony to his character, with no connection at all to the case. It was probably already clear to Fila that he could no longer defend his client against the charges; he just wanted to show the court that Dokmanović was at heart a decent man and in that way gain him some leniency.

While we were discussing whether and how to respond to these new facts, Swiss lawyer Stefan Waespi, who had recently been added to our team, came up with an idea. In a book about the war in the former Yugoslavia, he read about a Syrian doctor who had lived for many years in Vukovar and who had met Dokmanović in a POW camp after the city was occupied. We could try to find this doctor and see what he had to say. So I flew to Zagreb to meet Colonel Grujić and ask for his help in finding the doctor. Grujić gave me his address, and later that same day Vlatka and I rang at his door. The doctor was at home; he invited us into his apartment and told us everything he experienced in Vukovar in 1991. He even agreed to a formal interview, which Kevin conducted a few days later.

Clint and Stefan evaluated his statement and decided to summon him as a witness. He asked the court if he might testify under a pseudonym, so he was identified as Witness R. Under questioning from prosecutor Grant Niemann, he was asked if he knew Slavko Dokmanović. Witness R said he knew him very well because they had worked together at the same football club, where the witness worked as a doctor. In addition they were close family friends, and before the war in 1991, the two families often visited each other. A week didn't go by without the two men seeing each other. Witness R and Dokmanović were together almost every day at work or at the football club.

Even before the fall of Vukovar, in early August 1991, Witness R was called to the village of Trpinja to treat a disabled child. He took his wife with him, and while he was in the village, he treated several other patients. As he was going back, he met Dokmanović by chance on the street. He had five or six armed men with him, and he was wearing the olive-green pants and shirt worn by Yugoslavian military reservists. Witness R said he had never seen Dokmanović dressed that way before, as he always wore a shirt, tie, and suit. At the meeting in Trpinja, they greeted each other and chatted about life in Vukovar, in Borovo Naselje, where Witness R lived, and also in Trpinja. They said their goodbyes, and Witness R returned home. After the occupation of Vukovar in November 1991, he was detained and, with other men, shipped off to a prison camp in Serbian Vojvodina near the town of Zrenjanin.

Niemann: "What was the situation like in the prison camp?"

Witness R: "There were Serbs who had been detained with us because they refused to leave their homes in Borovo Naselje during the military operations. When the soldiers and reservists started beating us, these Serbs protested that they were not Croats. Some of them managed to save themselves this way, so I thought I would try the same by saying I was a foreigner. I told them I was neither Croat nor Serb, but it didn't help. The guards accused me of being a foreign mercenary and dragged me to a place where they started beating me viciously with anything they could get their hands on. After fifteen minutes, I was lying on the floor, I couldn't move, and some person in civilian clothes came up to me and said in a friendly voice, 'Doctor, they're beating you too?' And he took me to another room, where he promised me that he would make sure no one hurt me, and because I was a doctor, I could help take care of the wounded. So I did that. The conditions were appalling. We were locked up in sheds where pigs had been raised not long before. The dirt and stench were nauseating. There were about 1,500 people and they brought in another 200. The JNA operated this detention camp, and it was the military police that began interrogating us. They wanted to know what we were doing during the war in Vukovar."

Niemann: "Did you meet anyone you knew during your imprisonment in the camp?"

Witness R: "About the fourth or fifth day after my interrogation ended, I met Slavko Dokmanović in the corridor."

Niemann: "How was Mr. Dokmanović dressed?"

Witness R: "He was wearing the soldier's olive-green uniform."

Niemann: "Was Mr. Dokmanović alone?"

Witness R: "No, there were several other men with him, all dressed in camouflage uniforms and armed with automatic rifles."

Niemann: "In your opinion, what was Dokmanović's position among the men who were with him?"

Witness R: "He was their superior. He was their boss."

Niemann: "Can you describe the circumstances under which you met Mr. Dokmanović?"

Witness R: "Yes, the corridor was about one and a half meters wide, and I was walking toward him. When he saw me, he didn't look at me and passed by without a word."

Niemann: "Are you sure he saw you?"

Witness R: "Absolutely sure! He was walking straight toward me. The corridor was narrow. There was no way we could avoid each other."

Niemann: "Did you try to speak to Mr. Dokmanović?"

Witness R: "No, it was impossible. I was under detention. I was not allowed to speak to anybody."

Niemann: "What was your feeling about seeing him?"

Witness R: "I was disappointed, deeply disappointed."

Niemann: "Why were you disappointed?"

Witness R: "Because my close friend, Slavko, knew very well that I am a foreigner and a doctor and that I stayed behind in Vukovar so that I could help the wounded. He could have helped me."

Niemann: "Why do you say he could have helped you?"

Witness R: "He had authority and power as the mayor of Vukovar, no doubt about it."

Niemann: "Before the conflict broke out, did you have the opportunity to hear Mr. Dokmanović make any nationalist speeches and sing Serbian nationalist songs?"

Witness R: "Yes, on the anniversary of our football club."

Niemann: "In your opinion were the views of Mr. Dokmanović moderate or radical?"

Witness R "His views were radical."

Niemann: "Finally, could you please look around the courtroom and tell us if you see Slavko Dokmanović here?"

Witness R: "Yes, I see him here."

Niemann: "Can you show us where you see him?"

Witness R: "He's sitting there in the back, wearing the gray suit and white shirt."

Niemann: "Your Honor, it's clear beyond a doubt that Witness R has identified Mr. Dokmanović. I have no further questions."

When Witness R pointed out his former friend in the courtroom, Dokmanović seemed to shrivel up; he stared at the floor and looked like a completely broken man. Fila still had fight in him, however, and he attacked Witness R with the intention of discrediting his testimony.

Fila: "My question is simple. Did Mr. Dokmanović say anything bad about anyone else in your presence?"

Witness R: "Yes, in 1990. I was invited to the anniversary of the football club, where I got an award for my work. They were singing these offensive songs about Croats."

Fila: "We understand, but did Mr. Dokmanović himself say anything bad?"

Witness R: "He was the one who started it, who let them sing those songs, so he had to have the same mentality as them. He was the organizer."

Fila: "So someone at the celebration was singing nationalist songs?"

Witness R: "Not someone, but all of them."

Fila: "When you met Mr. Dokmanović in the camp, how did you know he was in command of those around him?"

Witness R "Slavko went first, was leading the group. The distance between him and them was so small that they had to be together."

Fila: "So that was your personal observation?"

Witness R: "It was no promenade where everyone could go where they wanted, it was a prison camp. Nobody could just come and go there as they pleased."

Judge Cassese to the prosecutor Niemann: "Would you like to reexamine your witness?"

Niemann: "No, your Honor".

Judge Cassese to Fila: "Mr. Fila?"

Fila: "I am tired, your Honor. I would like to apologize for my mistakes."

End of the Trial

In any trial the closing arguments are crucial because they allow the prosecutor and the defense attorney to clarify the evidence that had been presented.

Most of the witnesses summoned by the defense had nothing to do with Dokmanović's alibi. Only five were involved in that bit of chicanery, and their reasons for doing so were many. It's possible that some, even all of them, went with Dokmanović to Ovčara on that fateful day. Who wouldn't want to go to see the recently captured Croatian terrorists they thought were behind all the crimes and destruction? Who wouldn't want to see those bastards finally in Serbian hands? Ovčara was not far from the road they were traveling, so why not turn off to go have a look? If they had really gone there, then it was only natural that they would want to hide the truth. Maybe they lied to protect their friend, or perhaps it was some half-baked attempt to defend Serbian honor. What their real motive was, we don't know.

The irony of the situation is that the position shown at time 15:42 is of no importance in itself. As far as we know, no crime had been committed at that spot. Dokmanović and his friends had only stopped there and filmed some buses that came out of nowhere and left ahead of the person making the video. But they saw it as an opportunity to extricate Dokmanović from the sorry position he now found himself in. If they claimed it was in Negoslavci and backed it up with their sworn testimony, that meant they were south of the turn to Ovčara. Testifying that the voice of Dokmanović could be heard at that factual point aimed to prove the alibi he needed for the time when he left Vukovar and headed in the direction of Ovčara. It didn't entirely prove his innocence, but it might have strengthened his version of the events. But because the purpose of an alibi is to show that the accused was somewhere other than a crime scene, the credibility of witnesses is crucial in the absence of direct evidence. Dokmanović was able to provide five of them, a definite show of strength, but forensics and detective work were their undoing. In the end the only thing these five proved was that they had lied under oath.

But to return to the credibility of witnesses, why would Dragutin Berghofer and Emil Čakalić lie about having seen Dokmanović at Ovčara? They had barely escaped the ghastly massacre that claimed the others. They themselves had been brutally beaten. There was no point in accusing someone who wasn't there when there were plenty of other perpetrators. Berghofer and Čakalić came from Vukovar and certainly knew the Serb extremists at Ovčara. According to their own testimony, neither had ever had a quarrel or dispute with Dokmanović. Equally important they had singled out Dokmanović on their own initiative, before the prosecutor's office had ever heard of him.

In his emotional statement, Emil said, "I would be happier today if I had never seen Dokmanović there, because I'm still racking my brains about how it's possible that such an intelligent individual, a person whom I talked with many times in his office, who knew those people at Ovčara. . . . I keep asking myself, how could he allow himself to participate in it!?"

The defense tried to change history and show Dokmanović as something other than what he really was. According to the defense, he was neither mayor nor minister, and was certainly never an extremist out to get the Croats. He was a moderate and peaceful citizen, an ordinary civilian who never visited the prison camps in uniform. But the bodies pulled out of the mass grave at Ovčara and the loved ones they left behind tell a different story. There were the facts that counted at this trial, the facts that would some day ensure that the world knew the truth.

But in the end, it was neither his victims nor the judges who passed the ultimate sentence on Slavko Dokmanović.

The Sentence That the Tribunal Would Have Never Issued

It was with the old Roman expression "Bis dat qui cito dat" (paying quickly is worth twice as much) that Judge Casesse wrapped up the case of the *Prosecutor versus Slavko Dokmanović* on June 26, 1998, at 3:52 p.m. The verdict was expected within two weeks.

Throughout the trial none of us had taken any time off, let alone a vacation, so practically all of us took off at the end of it. I took my family on a long-promised trip to Sicily. We had just driven through Zell-am-See in Austria when my cell phone rang. Since we were just then rounding curves, I had to wait until we came to a rest stop before digging out the phone. Clint had called. My first thought was that Casesse had arrived with the verdict. I eagerly called Clint back, and the first thing I said when he answered the phone was, "So how many years did he get?"

The answer out of The Hague was completely different from what I had expected. It floored me, in fact. Sometime during the night of June 28 and 29, Slavko Dokmanović had slipped a tie around the top hinge of his closet and hanged himself. He had chosen a penalty not even the judges at the International Tribunal were at liberty to sentence him to. He had shown signs of depression during the trial and was under medical care. We told ourselves his demons had finally caught up with him. On June 23, even before the end of the trial, he was put under closer supervision. During recess the guards were supposed to check him every thirty minutes. It was the second strictest mode of supervision allowed at the prison in Scheveningen, but apparently not strict enough. An examination of his body found that he had tried to kill himself already twice before then. Somehow these attempts went unnoticed by the guards. The third time around he was successful.

On June 29, immediately following the announcement that Dokmanović had committed suicide, Judge McDonald ordered an internal investigation into his death. On July 15 Casesse officially halted the case on account of the death of the defendant. Six days later, on July 21, Judge Almiro Simões Rodrigues published the final report on the cause of death: "The investigation did not uncover any signs of violence in the cell or on the body of the accused that would lead to the suspicion that a crime had been committed."

Justice Halfway

The suicide of Slavko Dokmanović accomplished nothing good at all. It gave no satisfaction to all those whose loved ones were murdered at Ovčara, and for us it meant we had to start all over again. Had the court been able to hand down a verdict on Dokmanović, it would have made convicting the others responsible for this massacre much easier, including General Mile Mrkšić, Colonel Veselin Šljivančanin, and Captain Miroslav Radić, followed by RSK president Goran Hadžić, Željko Ražnatović (Arkan), and President Slobodan Milošević.

The international community applied political and economic pressure on the authorities of the Federal Republic of Yugoslavia to hand the Vukovar Three over to the tribunal, but nothing could or would happen as long as Slobodan Milošević was still in power. In 1999 Chief Prosecutor Louise Arbour left the tribunal after the Canadian prime minister appointed her to the supreme court of that country. The Security Council then appointed a new chief prosecutor, Swiss lawyer Carla Del Ponte, whose primary task was to bring the remaining accused before the tribunal.

4

How a Police Officer, a Dentist, and a Warehouseman Became the Presidents of the Republic of Serbian Krajina

The Republic of Serbian Krajina

Less than three weeks after my arrival at the tribunal, we were given another case that Chief Prosecutor Richard Goldstone asked us to investigate urgently. It concerned the rocket attacks on the Croatian cities of Zagreb, Sisak, and Karlovac on May 2 and 3, 1995. We had just opened the case at Ovčara, but now had to put it on hold because it was, after all, already four years old, and these attacks were happening in real time.

We immediately set about analyzing all the available information, of which there was plenty thanks to the coverage by European and world news agencies. But first we had to become familiar with the situation in Krajina. With the exception of Clint, none of us knew much about the Republic of Serbian Krajina. Therefore, we looked into the history of this part of the Balkans to better understand the correlation of events between 1990 and 1995.

The History of Knin and Krajina

The name of this area comes from the name of an earlier province, Vojna Krajina (pronounced "Voyna krayeena"), which literally means military border. It was formed by the Austrian Empire from parts of Croatia and Slavonia between 1553 and 1578 as part of the empire's defense against the expanding Ottoman Empire. At that time many Serbs, Croats, and Vlachs left the territory occupied by the Ottomans and settled in this inhospitable part of the western Balkans.

The castle complex of Knin was built in the tenth century on the Spas hilltop near the Krka River to protect the trade route between Zagreb and Split. In modern times Knin fell under the administrative control of Šibenik-Knin County. In 1991 Serbs made up more than 50 percent of the population of Krajina, Croats 35 percent, and various ethnic minorities the rest. The first free elections held in the Socialist Republic of Croatia were won by the Croatian Democratic Union (Hrvatska Demokratska Zajednica, HDZ) led by Franjo Tuđman. Croatian Serbs did not recognize the new government, and relations between the Croatian majority and Serbian minority deteriorated rapidly.

In mid-July 1990 the Serbs held a popular assembly in Knin and in the presence of the Orthodox Church and local politicians declared the establishment of the Serbian Autonomous Region (*oblast* in the Serbian language) of Krajina, or SAO Krajina, and resolved to hold a referendum on July 31. In December of that year, the Croatian parliament adopted a new constitution, which formally identified the Serbs and other ethnic groups living in Croatia as national minorities. In March 1991 another referendum called for the unification of SAO Krajina with Serbia and therefore continued existence within Yugoslavia. The Croatian government declared the referendum illegal and ordered all police units in areas inhabited by Croatian Serbs to surrender their weapons.

Serb officials responded to this move by blocking roads with logs. Since the Croatian word for log is *balvan*, it became known as Balvan revolucija—the Log Revolution. On May 19, 1991, the Croatian government declared a referendum on independence from Yugoslavia. It was boycotted by the majority of Serbs. The Croatians overwhelmingly voted for independence, but under pressure from the European Community, they postponed the official declaration until October 8. Seven months later, on December 19, 1991, the Serbs living within SAO Krajina formally declared the Republic of Serbian Krajina, RSK, and by

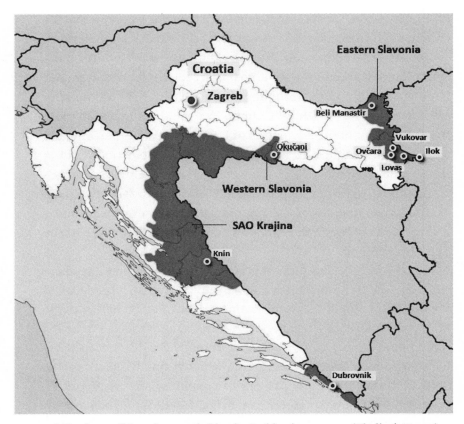

76. Territory of Croatia occupied by the Serbian insurgents. (Vladimír Dzuro)

February 26 had added SAO Western Slavonia, SAO Eastern Slavonia, Baranja, and Western Srijem to the RSK.

In October 1992 the name of the regional Territorial Defense Force was changed to the Serbian Army of RSK. It numbered forty thousand men under Lieutenant General Mile Novaković. In 1994 he was replaced by Lieutenant General Milan Čeleketić; after the loss of Western Slavonia, his replacement was Lieutenant General Mile Mrkšić, who was well known from the battle of Vukovar. The first president of the RSK was a dentist from Knin named Milan Babić, who held the post between December 1991 and February 1992. He was succeeded by a warehouseman named Goran Hadžić, who turned over the office in January 1994 to the police inspector Milan Martić.

At the beginning of 1995, a plan called z-4 was worked out in cooperation with the UN to give a greater degree of autonomy to Krajina and to a somewhat lesser extent to Western Slavonia, Eastern Slavonia, Baranja, and Western Srijem. Martić refused to accept not only the plan but also any further negotiations. On August 2 Babić, now head of the RSK government, accepted z-4 and so became a traitor in the eyes of many Serbs. RSK was never internationally recognized and ceased to exist after the Croatian army launched Operation Storm between August 4 and 7, 1995, and retook control of the region.

Rocket Attack on Zagreb

A few months before the demise of the RSK, between May 1 and 3, 1995, the Croatian army launched Operation Lightning against SAO Western Slavonia and reassumed control of this territory for Croatia. The RSK decided to strike Zagreb in retaliation. On May 2, at about half-past ten in the morning, its army based in Petrova Gora fired ORKAN rockets tipped with antipersonnel cluster warheads into the center of the capital and into the Pleso district, where Zagreb International Airport is located. They struck Juraj Strossmayer Square and the streets of Stara Vlaška and Križanićeva, killing five civilians and wounding forty-six.

A day later at about noon, the RSK army fired more ORKAN rockets. This time they hit the Croatian National Theater and Klaićeva, Medulićeva, and Ilica Streets. Two civilians were killed and forty-eight wounded. The number of wounded eventually climbed to more than two hundred. Peter Galbraith, the U.S. ambassador to Croatia, informed us that he had had a meeting with Martić in October 1994, and already then Martić was threatening to shell Zagreb in the face of Croatian army attacks against the RSK. In March 1995 the RSK army commander Milan Čeleketić was quoted in a newspaper article published in Serbia: "Croatian aggression is almost certainly daring us to hit them where it hurts the most. We know their weaknesses, we know the squares of their cities and who goes there, the civilians."

Police Officer Milan Martić

Shortly after the rocket attacks in May 1995, RSK president Milan Martić appeared on Serbian television and said that he had ordered them in retaliation for Croatian army attacks against SAO Western Slavonia. This public admission earned him a spot on our list of war criminals. Kevin, who had joined the tribunal on May 1, flew to Zagreb on May 17 to talk with the Croatian police and obtain their complete documentation of the rocket attacks. Time was short, and the chief prosecutor wanted action on this war crime as quickly as possible.

Kevin met the local bomb squad, who showed him the places where the cluster munitions landed. He asked if he could seize one of the unexploded bombs that had been made safe, to present as evidence in court. The disposal unit removed the explosive material from inside the casing and after getting their confirmation that it was safe, Kevin put it in his bag together with other evidence. He then went directly to the airport for a flight back to The Hague and placed his bag on the conveyor belt to be x-rayed. Before he knew it, airport police with weapons drawn rushed in and arrested him for attempting to take a bomb aboard a plane. He was taken to an interrogation room, thoroughly searched, and because the police didn't speak any English and his Croatian at the time was limited to *dobar dan*, *hvala*, and *pivo* ("hello," "thank you," and "beer"), the situation hung in limbo.

Finally, Kevin remembered the documents in his bag and gestured to them. They included a copy of the passport of the chief of pyrotechnics and his telephone number. The subsequent call to this man changed the mood inside the room entirely to the point where even the Croatian policemen were smiling. The situation was completely resolved after an interpreter arrived. Kevin got an apology and was escorted to the plane with his bomb. Everybody was all smiles as the door to the plane was shut and they took off, but he then realized the same thing might easily occur at the airports in Frankfurt and Amsterdam. He somehow managed to get through them with no problem, and the

77. Sample of a casket bomb. (Vladimír Dzuro)

next morning when he went through the security check at the tribunal, nobody even noticed the bomb in his bag.

The chaos unleashed by Kevin with this particular piece of evidence was not yet over. While giving testimony in the courtroom, the prosecutor asked whether he had secured any material evidence in Zagreb. He calmly pulled out the bomb and raised it above his head so the court could take a good look. The guards immediately panicked because no one had told them there was going to be a bomb in the courtroom.

In its coverage of the event, the BBC showed a British police officer testifying about the bombing of Zagreb. Kevin's brother dropped a cup of coffee on the floor when he saw Kevin sitting there in the broadcast with the bomb over his head.

In two months' time, we had gathered enough evidence for Richard Goldstone to sign an indictment against Martić on July 25 for the attacks on civilians in Zagreb. The investigation showed that the rocket attack on Zagreb was not the first war crime committed by Martić, merely the culmination of his activities in the RSK. The further we dug into

Martić's political career, the more charges were added to the indictment against him, and it gave us reason to focus equal attention on Milan Babić and Goran Hadžić.

Martić graduated from the Croatian police academy, and until 1990, he had worked as a senior inspector for the Croatian Ministry of the Interior in Knin. In early 1990 he started his own police force in Knin made up entirely of Serbs. They called themselves Martić's Militia, and Martić was the head of it throughout its existence. In May the following year, he was appointed the minister of defense of SAO Krajina, and Martić's Militia fell under the authority of the militia of Krajina.

In August 1991 Martić was appointed deputy commander of the SAO Territorial Defense and later the RSK Territorial Defense, and his direct control of the police and defense forces strengthened his position further. By January 1994 he was the minister of the interior of the RSK, and all police forces, still including his personal militia, were under his command.

In 1999, with Dokmanović's trial and death behind us, Dennis Milner took over Team 4, and with his promotion to commander, I was put in charge. Clint and I elaborated a plan to further investigate the rocket attacks against Zagreb and also to expand the indictment against Martić for other crimes in Croatia. We obtained a list of the wounded survivors from the bombardment of May 2 and 3, 1995. Interviewing them would help us present these events before the court.

In the preparatory phase for the expansion of the indictment against Martić for crimes against Croats and the other non-Serbian inhabitants of the RSK, we drew up a list of towns and cities where such crimes, according to the reports available to us, were alleged to have occurred. The second phase involved asking the Croatian authorities for information about the victims and potential witnesses. We once again received help from Colonel Grujić, whose team had conducted the exhumation of mass graves found in this part of Croatia. In the third and final phase, we compiled a detailed plan of investigation in the villages of Škabrnja and Nadin and subsequently in Bruška, Dubica, Cerovljani, Baćin, Saborsko, Poljanak, and Lipovača.

Team 4 was reinforced with new investigators, lawyers, and analysts, and in early 2000 we launched investigations in the villages of Škabrnja and Nadin. The cases were initially assigned to Brent Pfundheller and William (Bill) Hardin. I first met Brent, a police officer and detective from Washington State, while on assignment in Kosovo in 1999. Bill, who used to work as a police officer in California and had spent a considerable part of his career working in antinarcotic operations, joined our team shortly after Brent. Due to the scale of the investigations, the team was later reinforced by Deon van Royen and Rajandiren (Rajie) Murugan from South Africa and Azim Arshad from Pakistan.

I recall that I guided Brent and Bill around for their first mission in Croatia, introducing them to local police officials and arranging their accommodation and offices. They went right to work conducting interviews and securing the evidence that Clint and I had outlined. Brent, Bill, Deon, Rajie, and Azim managed, in a relatively short period of time, to put together cases not only on Škabrnja and Nadin, but also on Bruška, Dubica, Cerovljani, Baćin, Saborsko, Poljanak, and Lipovača.

Meanwhile, my success rate in getting people to become informants led the chief of investigations, Patrick Lopez-Terrez, to name me in mid-2001 as the coordinator of a secret project called Insider. My task was to find, contact, and enlist people working for the Milošević regime to cooperate with the prosecutor openly or in secret, whether they came from the ranks of the police and the army or were political and governmental officials. The ultimate goal was to persuade those individuals to testify before the tribunal.

John Cencich, an American investigator, took over Team 4 and successfully finalized the amendment to Martić's indictment, which was signed by Chief Prosecutor Carla Del Ponte on December 18, 2002. Martić had already surrendered to Serbian authorities on May 15 of that year and was shipped off the same day to the tribunal to face trial for the shelling of Zagreb. Our amended indictment significantly broadened the charges against him.

Martić pleaded not guilty to all the charges, but on June 12, 2007, the judges of the Trial Chamber found him guilty of nineteen of the twenty

78. Accused Milan Martić before the tribunal. (ICTY)

counts against him. They included war crimes, crimes against humanity, and violations of the laws and customs of war, such as murder, persecution, imprisonment, torture, inhumane treatment, deportation, the
destruction and devastation of villages, the destruction of institutions
dedicated to education and religion, and attacks on civilians. Martić
was sentenced to a total of thirty-five years in prison. In October 2008
the Appeals Chamber upheld the verdict of the Trial Chamber.

Dentist Milan Babić

In September 2001 Chief Prosecutor Carla Del Ponte submitted an
indictment against Slobodan Milošević for crimes committed in Croatia. Milan Babić was named as one of his accomplices in the indictment. A dentist by profession, Babić became one of the directors of
the medical center in Knin in 1989. He left the League of Communists
of Croatia and joined the newly founded Serbian Democratic Party,
SDP, a far-right nationalist party. In February 1990 he was elected
president of the Knin Council.

In November 1991 the international community attempted to negotiate a peaceful solution to the conflict and sent special envoy Cyrus Vance to assist. According to the plan submitted, Krajina was to be disarmed and put under the protection of UN troops. The RSK was formed in response to this initiative, which Babić, now the president, vigorously opposed. He personally tried to get the RSK parliament to reject the peace plan, but it was approved on February 16, 1992. Babić was then replaced as president by Goran Hadžić. In July 1995 Babić was named premier and served in this capacity until the fall of the RSK a month later.

Less than a month after the indictment against Milošević was published, Babić contacted the tribunal on his own to ask for a meeting with representatives of the Office of the Prosecutor. Since I was working on the Insider project, Patrick Lopez-Terrez tasked me with the assignment. I met Babić for the first time in October 2001 at the Hyatt Hotel in Belgrade. I intentionally chose the hotel restaurant because of its good security, which I assumed would refuse admittance to any armed individuals Babić might bring to the meeting.

Brent Pfundheller joined me because he was working on crimes in the RSK and knew important details about them. He was also an experienced police officer, so I could depend on him in any unforeseen situation. We spent a few minutes at the door to the restaurant studying the situation inside the lobby and the restaurant itself. We did not want to take chances rushing into a trap.

Babić was sitting alone at a table sipping his black coffee. While he fidgeted in his seat, his eyes kept darting around the room. We walked up to him, introduced ourselves, and shook hands. His was warm and sweaty. He was no longer President Babić, the self-assured, passionate, and radical Serbian politician we knew from his television appearances in the early nineties. The man before us was now a broken, ex-dentist named Milan. His forehead glistened with sweat, and he was clearly scared to death.

We were there because we wanted him to cooperate in the case against Milošević and Martić, but we first had to determine what he knew and under what conditions he would testify. I asked him about people from the RSK and government agencies in Belgrade, while Brent wanted to know about specific war crimes in Krajina. What he told us could be verified and deemed credible, but because we didn't have an official mandate to negotiate cooperation between Babić and the tribunal, at the end of our conversation we could only say that we would be in touch. We lingered a bit in the hotel, however, to see if someone might join him, but Babić paid and left alone.

Our initial meeting at the Hyatt opened up a well of information about the RSK and the influence of Milošević in areas controlled by Serbs outside Serbia. We were certain that Babić would be the star cooperating defendant whom the tribunal needed in its case against Milošević and Martić. Lopez-Terrez asked me to set up a formal interview with him. I tried several times to call him, but no one picked up. I was beginning to worry that he had changed his mind or possibly been killed when I finally got him on the phone and arranged a meeting. The interview with Babić lasted several days; it was conducted by Bill Hardin and assisted by a prosecutor, Hildegard Uertz-Retzlaff. It eventually resulted in a plea bargain between him and representatives of the Office of the Prosecutor.

On November 17, 2003, that same office indicted Milan Babić for crimes committed between August 1991 and February 1992, specifically crimes against humanity, persecution on racial and religious grounds, and violations of the laws and customs of war, such as murder, inhumane treatment, the destruction of villages not justified by military necessity, and the destruction of institutions dedicated to education and religion. Nine days later Babić surrendered to authorities in Serbia and was handed over to the tribunal. He exercised his right not to enter a plea against the charges. Under his agreement with the prosecution, he appeared before the judges on January 27, 2004, and pleaded guilty to the charge of committing acts of persecution on racial and religious grounds.

In his statement of guilt, Babić said: "I come before this tribunal with a deep sense of shame and remorse. I have allowed myself to take

79. Accused Milan Babić before the tribunal. (ICTY)

part in the worst kind of persecution of people simply because they were Croats and not Serbs. Innocent people were persecuted, innocent people were evicted forcibly from their houses, and innocent people were killed. Even after I learned what had happened, I kept silent. Even worse I continued in my office and I became personally responsible for the inhumane treatment of innocent people. The regret that I feel is the pain I have to live with for the rest of my life. These crimes and my participation in them can never be justified. I am speechless when I have to express the depths of my remorse for what I have done and for the effect that my sins have had on others. I can only hope that my expression of the truth and admitting to my guilt and expressing remorse can serve as an example to those who still mistakenly believe that such inhumane acts can ever be justified."

Babić admitted that between August 1991 and February 1992 he was part of the persecution of Croats and other non-Serbs. He formulated policy, then instigated and took part in the forcible and permanent expulsion of the majority of Croats and other non-Serbs from an area accounting for approximately one-third of Croatia. He took part in the reorganization and movement of members of the Territorial Defense of SAO Krajina; cooperated with the commander of Martić's police forces involved in war crimes; participated in providing financial, material, logistical, and political support for the military takeover of the territory of SAO Krajina; and made speeches that encouraged the collection and distribution of arms among Serbs for the purpose of persecuting the non-Serbian population.

He testified before the tribunal that the RSK authorities had participated in the murders of non-Serbian inhabitants in the villages of Dubica, Cerovljani, Baćin, Saborsko, Poljanak, and Lipovača; in the long-term imprisonment of hundreds of civilians under inhumane conditions on the premises of the old hospital and barracks of the Yugoslav army in Knin; and in other war crimes. The judges rejected the recommendation of the prosecutor for a sentence of fewer than eleven years because they reasoned that such punishment did not reflect the purpose of justice. On June 29, 2004, they sentenced him to thirteen years in prison. The Appeals Chamber confirmed the sentence on July 18, 2005. On March 5, 2006, Babić returned to court as a witness in the trial of Milan Martić, but he killed himself in his prison cell during the course of it.

Warehouseman Goran Hadžić

It was in connection with the cases of Milošević and Dokmanović that we first came across the name of Goran Hadžić. In mid-November 1999 I asked the Office of the Prosecutor for an indictment against Hadžić for crimes committed in Croatia. The case was given the code name Matrix. In August 2000 Chief Prosecutor Carla Del Ponte signed the order that tasked Clint and me with opening and conducting the formal investigation. We first had to collect all the information available about Hadžić that dated to the period before the outbreak of armed conflict in Croatia.

In June 1991 Goran Hadžić, the warehouseman, became leader of the Serbian National Council and the Serbian Democratic Forum, which included the regions of Eastern Slavonia, Baranja, and Western Sriem. It was widely known that Hadžić was supported by Slobodan Milošević, who was working to reinforce his position within the Serbian community in Croatia. Our sources said that between June 1991 and December 1993, Hadžić took part in war crimes and crimes against humanity as a member of a criminal organization, whose main objective was to forcibly expel thousands of Croats and non-Serbian inhabitants from Croatian territory controlled by Serbs. He publicly advocated the creation of an ethnically pure Serbian state in Croatia and urged no mercy in the fight against Croats. With the evidence in hand, we concluded that he was part of a joint criminal enterprise composed of, among others, Slobodan Milošević, Jovica Stanišić, Franko Simatović, Željko Ražnatović (Arkan), Milan Babić, and Milan Martić.

Under Hadžić's leadership the Serbs occupied Croatian territory that they considered belonging to the Serbian people, namely, Serbian Krajina, Eastern and Western Slavonia, Baranja, and Western Sriem. They used mainly military force to drive at least ninety thousand non-Serbian residents from their homes. Those who remained were subjected to inhumane treatment that included sexual assault and murder. Hadžić provided Željko Ražnatović (Arkan) and his paramilitaries with a training ground in the village of Erdut, arranging both financing and impunity for their operations. Our evidence clearly showed that Hadžić was responsible for the deaths of many non-Serbian civilians in and around the villages of Dalj, Erdut, and Lovas and directly within Vukovar.

Reaction to the news of Hadžić's impending indictment was not long in coming. In late February 2002, Slobodan Vukčević, a lawyer from Belgrade, contacted Hildegard Uertz-Retzlaff of the Office of the Prosecutor on behalf of Hadžić to discuss his questioning by investigators of the tribunal. Events were set in motion immediately, and in March 2002, I flew to Serbia with my colleague William Fulton to question Hadžić.

Hadžić stipulated that our meeting be held in the Hotel Park in Novi Sad, which was owned by his friend Ratko Butorović, a controversial businessman also known as Bata Kan Kan. As soon as we arrived at the hotel, I noticed about fifteen bodyguards mulling around him and in the lobby. They looked like street thugs from a Balkan thriller. Hadžić had an attorney with him, Miroslav Vasić, who was from the Belgrade law office of Toma Fila.

We set up our recording equipment in the room and drank the obligatory black coffee as we prepared for the questioning. Hadžić suddenly burst into the room and greeted us. He then, in an aggressive gesture, pushed aside the front part of his jacket and, much to our amazement, revealed a handgun in a belt holster. No doubt the bodyguards also had their own weapons, suggesting that Fulton and I were the only unarmed people in the hotel. Fulton looked at me with an expression of concern that was not alleviated by the Serbian interpreter cowering in his seat. We weren't sure whether the menacing atmosphere was meant to be provocation or payback for arresting Dokmanović. It didn't matter. We couldn't call the local police, and our office in Belgrade was in no position to help. We waited with an uneasy feeling as Hadžić readied himself to speak. When he did, it was to stress that he would not allow the tribunal to arrest him under any circumstances and warned us that bullets would start firing if we attempted it. He concluded by declaring that he would never be taken alive.

My feeling was that we were in deep. I knew the kind of person before me and what kind of people he surrounded himself with: the same hoods who had murdered innocent civilians and tossed their bodies into water wells, if not into the Danube. But his welcome speech also had an air of desperation about it, the tough guy who knows his time is up.

Only very slowly the tension in the room relaxed, and we were able to get on with the questioning. It continued on and off for six days, and after our return to Belgrade, I wrote up an official report about the gun and bodyguards and sent it to our office in The Hague.

I later heard Hadžić claim during his trial that he came armed to our interview only so he could protect us: "Dzuro was an urbane gentleman and a guest in my town, you see, and I was worried about his safety. It would have been worse if he had been attacked than if I had been killed, and therefore I was ready to step between him and any danger." I laughed like hell when I read that. The gun and bodyguards were meant to intimidate us, to give us a taste of what would happen if we tried to haul him in. And yet, truth be told, even the accused always has the inalienable right to defend himself.

In the spring of 2002, I started spending more time in Belgrade on the Insider project than at The Hague. I developed and maintained a network of informants from among high-ranking officers of the Yugoslav army and the Serbian State Security.

It was from my informant codenamed Ikea, from the Serbian State Security, that I learned of Hadžić's whereabouts. It seems that on the night of July 2, 1997, just a few days after the arrest of Dokmanović, Hadžić, fearing that he would meet the same fate, had secretly crossed the Danube from Croatia to Serbia in a little boat. Ikea gave me his home address in Novi Sad, where he was working for the local NIS petroleum company. He gave me his home phone number, work number, a description of the cars that he drove, and their license plates.

The secret indictment against Hadžić was confirmed by a judge on June 4, 2004. Count 1 of the charges accused him of persecuting Croats and other non-Serbs; counts 2 to 4 of murder and the extermination of inhabitants; counts 5 to 9 of imprisonment, torture, inhumane acts, and cruel treatment; counts 10 and 11 of deportation, the forcible transfer of up to ninety thousand Croats and non-Serbs from different parts of Croatia; and finally counts 12 to 14 of the wanton destruction and plunder of public and private property, including homes and religious and cultural buildings.

Even before the indictment was confirmed, Chief Prosecutor Del Ponte decided to use the indictment against Hadžić to prove that although the Serbian authorities claimed to be cooperating with the tribunal, in fact this was only a pretense, and in many cases they were actively working to sabotage its success. Ikea was key to her plan because we needed a reliable source of information about the movement of Hadžić without the local authorities learning about it. I had already spent a considerable amount of time and energy working with Ikea, and it cost me even more effort to verify his information. In early July 2004, Patrick Lopez-Terrez briefed me on the chief prosecutor's plan. We agreed that I would oversee the surveillance in Novi Sad with the help of investigator Roel Versonnen and an interpreter from our office in Belgrade.

The date for serving the arrest warrant was July 13, 2004. We had been able to use the services of a friendly country to install hidden surveillance cameras around Hadžić's home to capture his possible flight. Early in the morning of the appointed day, we left in two official cars from Belgrade to Novi Sad and got there around nine. Our black Toyotas had diplomatic license plates, making them easy to spot, so no one could later accuse us of carrying out a covert operation on the territory of Serbia. We did a drive-by of his home and then went to a nearby café to await instructions from Lopez-Terrez.

Patrick called around half past nine and told us the indictment against Hadžić had just been handed over to Serb officials. Carla Del Ponte expected someone to warn the accused about the arrest warrant so that he could flee. We immediately went back to his house, and I parked in front of the driveway. Versonnen and the interpreter took up positions behind his house to make sure we covered all avenues of escape. Our goal was not to arrest Hadžić, only to be witnesses to his making a run for it.

Before long an unknown woman emerged and drove away in a Fiat Punto with the license plate number NS-13004. At 12:38 the gate opened, and the Ford Mondeo sedan driven by Hadžić left. He was alone, and as he passed me, I quietly took his picture. Then someone closed the gate from the inside. Hadžić drove toward Cara Dušan Street and turned right onto Cara Lazarusa Boulevard. After forty-five minutes he returned home and spent the rest of the afternoon there.

At 4:30 p.m. he came back out of the house carrying a large bag, which he put in his car and drove away again. This was the last time we saw Goran Hadžić. Just before seven in the evening, a man brought his car back and parked in front of the house. We kept our positions. After seven o'clock a Honda with the license plate number NS-212847 pulled up at the house. A young woman got out and went inside. A moment later the driver of the car got out and headed toward me. He stopped about two meters away to check out my license plate and looked at me in a manner that suggested he was a career heavy. He went inside the house, presumably to discuss the situation with the woman, then came out, and walked up to my car again. He took out his phone to make a call, which even through the closed windows I could hear was about this stranger hanging around the house. He then got into his car, circled around the block, and stopped when he saw Roel, who informed me about it over the walkie-talkie. There he repeated the same scenario of checking out Roel and the interpreter and then calling someone.

We agreed that hanging around there any longer would be too risky, and Patrick concurred after a phone call. As soon as our two cars pulled away, the man in the Honda began tailing us. I could see him through the rearview mirror talking to somebody on his cell phone. I radioed Roel to say that we should try to lose him. We did a few loops, drove repeatedly through red lights, and eventually lost him. We returned to Belgrade and made a full report.

On July 19, 2004, Del Ponte called a press conference to announce that on July 13, a secret indictment against Hadžić was handed over to representatives of the Ministry of Foreign Affairs in Belgrade, adding that an international arrest warrant was also provided together with Hadžić's home address. The chief prosecutor also declared that on July 14 the president of Belgrade District Court had appointed an investigating judge and transferred the warrant over to the Serbian police. The next day the police reported that they couldn't find Hadžić at his address, and on that same day someone leaked the text of the secret indictment to the Belgrade daily *Internacional*. The following day, on July 16, a judge in Belgrade sent a message to the tribunal that it was not within the authority of Serbian officials to track down and arrest Hadžić.

80. Goran Hadžić in the yard of his house in Novi Sad (*top*); Goran Hadžić fleeing (*bottom*). (ICTY)

81. Accused Goran Hadžić before the tribunal. (ICTY)

The reporters at the press conference were interested in the information that Hadžić had fled his home on July 13 at 4:29 p.m. The chief prosecutor was delighted to confirm that her office would indeed publish photos proving this to be the case. Carla Del Ponte said, "This typical failure of the Serbian authorities to cooperate with the criminal tribunal simply amazes me, because not even ten days ago President Boris Tadić declared in his opening presidential address that cooperation with the tribunal would be the priority of his foreign and domestic policy, to prove their responsibility and commitment to European values and the strengthening of Euro-Atlantic integration."

She ended the press conference with these words: "Belgrade must now decide. Either keep their word and promptly arrest Goran Hadžić, or I will be forced to ask the president of the International Tribunal to inform the UN Security Council that Serbia and Montenegro have failed to fulfill their obligations under Article 29 of the Statute of the Tribunal."

Goran Hadžić was not apprehended until July 20, 2011, the last of the 161 indicted war criminals. His trial started a year later but was suspended in 2014, when doctors discovered he had a malignant brain tumor. The tribunal stopped the proceedings for good on March 6, 2016, and on July 12, 2016, at the age of fifty-seven, Hadžić died. Only the existence of a higher authority would ensure that he faced the justice he escaped on earth.

5

The Case of Dubrovnik

The City That Should Have Been under UNESCO Protection

Dubrovnik, originally called Ragusa, well deserves to be called the pearl of the Adriatic coast and was included on the UNESCO World Heritage List in 1979. To make the list, the Yugoslavian authorities had to completely disarm Dubrovnik, and this meant closing down all military installations and moving the munitions stores for the Territorial Defense Force to the city of Grab in neighboring Herzegovina. In 1991 Dubrovnik was home to more than seventy-one thousand inhabitants, of which 84 percent were Croats and 7 percent Serbs. Ethnic minorities made up the remaining 9 percent.

In August 1991 the Croatian government ordered its units to blockade the JNA barracks and cut off their electricity, water, and telephone lines. The Croats had acquired a certain amount of weapons from operations against the JNA elsewhere. In the regions of Prevlaka and Konavle, they repeatedly attacked JNA convoys moving arsenals between Boka Kotorska in Montenegro and Trebinje in Bosnia. In late August and early September 1991, the JNA began moving troops from Pula, Split, and Šibenik southward toward Dubrovnik.

In mid-September 1991 the JNA formed the Second Operational Group, numbering seven thousand men under the command of Lieutenant General Jevrem Cokić. After a month he was replaced by General Pavle Strugar. The Second Operational Group included the Ninth Boka Kotorska Military-Maritime Sector deployed in

82. Old Town of Dubrovnik. (Vladimír Dzuro)

Kumbor, where Admiral Miodrag Jokić was named commander on October 7 following the mysterious death of Krsto Đurović two days earlier. The chief of staff for Jokić was Vice Admiral Milan Zec. Major General Nojko Marinović was in command of the 472nd Motorized Brigade, which was likewise under the Second Operational Group, but in mid-September he resigned his post and joined the defenders of Dubrovnik. On October 25 the command of the Third Battalion of the 472nd Motorized Brigade fell to Captain Vladimir Kovačević, who was also known as Rambo.

We received information from the former Montenegrin minister of foreign affairs Nikola Samardžić that at a government-level meeting on October 1, General Strugar deliberately misled the president of Montenegro, Momir Bulatović, with a report that thirty thousand Croatian soldiers were moving toward the border between Croatia and Montenegro to invade Boka Kotorska. The Yugoslavian Ministry of the Interior therefore gave the green light to Territorial Defense units and the special police force of Montenegro to engage in operations on the border. In fact the Croatian troops and police in and around Dubrovnik were poorly armed and, according to our information, numbered fewer than a thousand men. They had to protect a coastline of seventy-five kilometers.

On September 30, 1991, the General Staff of the Yugoslav People's Army ordered General Cokić of the Second Operational Group to blockade Dubrovnik. Early the next day, JNA infantry units from Bosnia and Herzegovina and Montenegro began an assault on the city with help from naval and air force units. They succeeded in cutting off all access. There were no Croatian forces in the area of Konavle south of Dubrovnik capable of stopping the JNA advance, and the defense forces in the north were very weak. The Yugoslav Air Force knocked out utility facilities around the city, disrupting telecommunications and the supply of electricity and water. Dubrovnik had to bring in all its drinking water by sea until December of that same year.

As soon as the news spread that the Yugoslav People's Army had attacked Dubrovnik, the European Monitoring Mission contacted their leaders to persuade them to negotiate with representatives of Dubrovnik. In November the JNA submitted to international pressure and prohibited shelling of the historic part of the city. Despite this order forces under Strugar, Jokić, and Kovačević intensified their attacks on the Old Town.

The Republic of Dubrovnik

The Republic of Dubrovnik arose in southern Dalmatia in the fourteenth century and fell on January 31, 1808, after it was occupied by French troops. On October 15, 1991, after JNA troops occupied the town of Cavtat, situated south of Dubrovnik, the city prosecutor, Aleksandar Apolonio, proclaimed a new Republic of Dubrovnik. It covered roughly the same area as the old republic, from the town of Neum on the Adriatic coast to Prevlaka on the border of Croatia and Montenegro.

The declaration of the Republic of Dubrovnik took place at the Hotel Croatia, attended by about two hundred citizens who elected a symbolic Small Council, a gesture evoking one of the governing bodies in the days of the historic republic. Apolonio declared himself the interim president. Although opposed to the plans for a Greater Serbia, he understood it provided an opportunity to restore the Republic of Dubrovnik. He felt it was therefore in the interests of the Republic of Dubrovnik to remain in the former Yugoslavia. The political elite in Belgrade and the Bosnian Serbs intended to annex the republic to the projected Greater Serbia, this way giving Bosnian Serbs access to the Adriatic Sea. The self-declared but unrecognized state disappeared when Dubrovnik was liberated by the Croatian army in May 1992.

Investigating the Case—Code Name Frost

At the start of 1998, the case of the shelling of Dubrovnik was assigned to our team, which had grown to include several researchers tasked with analyzing publicly available information. In July and August 1998, Clint Williamson and I visited Dubrovnik and subsequently evaluated bits and pieces of information we had managed to gather from the local authorities. Then in April 2000, I returned with Clint and analyst Ivo Lupis. We planned to collect all the documentation, including photographs and video records, gathered by the Croatian police in 1991 so that we could launch an investigation. Carla Del Ponte met representatives of the Croatian government and reassured them that it was her intention to arrest and punish those responsible for war crimes in Dubrovnik. They in turn provided us with access to their police files.

Naturally our arrival in the city did not escape the attention of the local media. We had Del Ponte's agreement to meet with local reporters in the belief that positive coverage of our investigation would help gain the trust of witnesses for the expected indictment. The chief prosecutor opened the formal investigation on August 8, 2000, with her instructions labeled OTP-INV-04-2000.

She assigned Clint and me the case of the alleged imprisonment and killing of civilians and the bombing and shelling of Dubrovnik between September 1991 and October 1992. I formed the initial team of investigators—Rajandiren Murugan, Azim Arshad, Michael Stefanovic, and Dirk Hooijkaas—and we focused our inquiries on General Strugar, Admiral Jokić, Vice Admiral Zec, and Captain Kovačević. The case was given the code name Frost. The team was later reinforced, and John Cencich, as a team leader, supervised completion of the indictment.

Unlike at Ovčara this time we relied much more on photographic documentation, video records, and various expert reports, as well as on the testimony of both local and foreign experts who were working in the area during the time of the conflict, and on the negotiators who came into direct contact with the JNA command. Our tables also began piling up with interviews from those who were injured during the bombardment of the city, eyewitnesses to the shelling of the historic center, prisoners from POW camps, and doctors and medical staff who had treated the wounded in 1991.

In addition to copies of the autopsy reports of civilians killed and records pertaining to the damage inflicted on cultural sites, we obtained direct evidence that units of the JNA under Strugar, Jokić, Zec, and Kovačević launched their attack in order to separate the Republic of Dubrovnik from Croatia and annex it to Serbia and Montenegro. Their offensive ended in October 1992, when a peace agreement was signed, and the JNA had to withdraw its units from the area. Furthermore, we provided evidence that nine people had been killed during the attack on the suburb of Mokošica on October 7, another ten civilians during the shelling of the historic center between November 9 and 12, and fourteen across the Dubrovnik area on December 6.

The suffering of civilians and the destruction of cultural monuments at the time of the blockade and shelling of Dubrovnik by the JNA were briefly captured by a young chronicler of the war, Croatian photographer Pavo Urban. On the morning of December 6, 1991, Urban was out and about as usual. He was preparing to take pictures of Stradun, the main street in the Old Town center of Dubrovnik, when a shell exploded next to him. The local press reported that the slain twenty-two-year-old photographer left behind several rolls of film and black-and-white photographs. We were able to track down and interview several witnesses who saw what had happened. One of them later testified under the pseudonym Witness A.

Question: "Did you see Pavo Urban on December 6, 1991?"

Witness A: "Yes, around two o'clock in the afternoon I heard some male voices through the window. They were standing on the street corner west of my home. In panic, everyone was screaming, 'Pavo got hit!' I ran to the window and looked out. I saw Miro Kerner and Mr. Djukić. Then I looked to the right under the city bell tower and saw a motionless body lying there."

Question: "Was it Mr. Urban's body?"

Witness A: "That's what I heard them saying, but I couldn't recognize his face from that distance."

Question: "In what position was the body lying?"

Witness A: "He was lying on his left side, facing west, motionless, but almost like he was crawling."

Question: "I would like to show you a photograph, but before that could you tell the court what this person lying on the street was wearing?"

Witness A: "He was wearing the vest that Pavo Urban normally wore. It had lots of pockets where he kept the film and other things he needed for taking pictures. It was a civilian vest, not a military one."

Question: "What kind of pants was he wearing?"

Witness A: "I think they were jeans."

Question: "Now I would like to ask you to look at the photograph the bailiff will show you. Can you identify the person in the photograph?"

Witness A: "Up close, yes."

Question: "Who is it?"

Witness A: "Pavo Urban."

According to our investigation, forty-three people were killed because of military operations in the city and surrounding areas. Of the 824 buildings in the Old Town section, 563 were hit by various projectiles. A study conducted by UNESCO and the Institute for the Rehabilitation of Dubrovnik estimated the total damage caused by the bombardment of the city to be valued at nearly US$10 million.

On February 22, 2001, Del Ponte signed an indictment based on our recommendation to prosecute Strugar, Jokić, Zec, and Kovačević. They were accused of grave breaches of the Geneva Conventions, violations

83. Pavo Urban killed in Dubrovnik on December 6, 1991. (ICTY)

of the laws and customs of war, and crimes against humanity related to murder, cruel treatment of and attacks on civilians, unjustified devastation, unlawful attacks on civilian objects, and the destruction of and deliberate damage to historic monuments and institutions dedicated to religious purposes. The indictment also covered the widespread destruction and looting of private property. Five days later Judge Patricia M. Wald confirmed the indictment and at the request of the chief prosecutor ordered that it be issued under seal.

The Questioning of President Stjepan Mesić

To allow us to navigate the complex political control over the JNA in 1991, we approached Stjepan Mesić, the former president of the Presidium of the Federal Republic of Yugoslavia. The initial preparation for the interview began in 1997, but the actual interview did not take place until June 5–6, 2000. Mesić told Clint that, in enforcing the rights and duties of the federation, the presidium was supposed to harmonize the common interests of the different republics and autonomous provinces and protect constitutional order. The Croatian parliament named Mesić as its delegate to the presidium on August 24, 1990. At that time the presidium had eight members, each representing one of the six republics and two autonomous provinces that formed Yugoslavia. Borisav Jović represented Serbia; Janez Drnovšek, Slovenia; Branko Kostić, Montenegro; Jugoslav Kostić, Vojvodina; Sejdo Bajramović, Kosovo; Bogić Bogićević, Bosnia and Herzegovina; Vasil Tupurkovski, Macedonia; and Mesić, Croatia. Already by the end of 1990, it appeared that Slobodan Milošević, the president of Serbia, was doing everything to gain control over the Presidium of Yugoslavia, and according to Mesić, he had succeeded by April 1991. Jugoslav Kostić, the delegate for Vojvodina, declared himself a Serb and publicly supported Milošević, as did Borisav Jović of Serbia and Branko Kostić of Montenegro.

On May 15 this troika tried to prevent Mesić from assuming the presidium at any cost, but on July 1, after six weeks of their obstruction, which created international protests, Mesić became the last official president of the Presidium of Yugoslavia. However, the actions of Slobodan Milošević meanwhile marginalized the office of the Socialist Federal Republic of Yugoslavia (SFRY) president, which left Mesić powerless. Two months later threats to his personal safety forced him to move his office from Belgrade to Zagreb, where he held the post until December 1991, when the constitutional institutions of Yugoslavia disintegrated.

About the situation in Dubrovnik, Mesić said: "At the end of 1991, after Dubrovnik was surrounded by the JNA together with various Serbian and Montenegrin paramilitaries, I decided to visit the city in my capacity as the president of the presidium, which made me the supreme commander of the JNA. So that it wasn't an empty gesture, we dispatched a humanitarian convoy of forty ships. I tried to get permission to enter the port through the minister of defense, General Veljko Kadijević, and JNA chief of staff, General Blagoje Adžić, but all my efforts were in vain.

"I then communicated with the deputy defense minister, Admiral Stanislav Brovet, and requested permission from him. Although the JNA command virtually refused to recognize my authority, I was allowed entry on October 31 under condition that I issue no orders to JNA soldiers. That's when I realized that the JNA was taking orders from elsewhere, ignoring the presidium in violation of its duty. I got the suspicion that the JNA was acting under the authority of Slobodan Milošević through General Kadijević."

On March 20, 1998, while still engaged with the case of Dokmanović, we summoned Stjepan Mesić as a witness. Clint asked him about Dubrovnik because for us it was important to clarify the situation over who had actual control of the JNA.

Williamson: "Did you try to break the naval blockade of Dubrovnik at the end of October 1991?"

Mesić: "Yes, we put together a convoy of about forty ships, and I was in the largest of them, the *Slavija*. We had announced our humanitarian mission well in advance because we wanted to give hope to the inhabitants of Dubrovnik, to let them know they had not been abandoned, and we were making every effort to bring them food and medicine. But our convoy was stopped, and Admiral Brovet asked us to sail to Montenegro, where our ships would be searched because the JNA said we were smuggling weapons. The negotiations took three days before we were allowed to anchor in the harbor."

Williamson: "In your position as the president of the Presidium of Yugoslavia, specifically in 1991, did the JNA obey any of your orders?"

Mesić: "Unfortunately, I have to say that not a single officer or member of the JNA followed any of my commands."

In 2000 Mesić was elected president of Croatia and held that office until 2010. The prosecutor decided not to summon Mesić as a witness in the trials of Strugar and Jokić, but instead prioritize his testimony for Milošević. Mesić appeared before the tribunal on October 1 and 3, 2002, and his testimony also covered the crimes committed in Dubrovnik.

The Questioning of Prime Minister Milo Đukanović

The case of Dubrovnik continued even after the indictments, and at the beginning of February 2003, while I was working in Belgrade on the Insiders project, Geoffrey Nice assigned me the task of interviewing the former president of Montenegro, Milo Đukanović, who was then serving as prime minister. Interviewing presidents, prime ministers, and other senior politicians is always legally complicated, and Đukanović was well aware of this, but the mandate given to the tribunal conferred considerable powers on us. Carla Del Ponte talked with Đukanović about it beforehand, and he agreed to the interview.

The team dispatched to Podgorica, the capital of Montenegro, was led by Geoffrey Nice. I was to be assisted in the interview by analyst Nevenka Trump and an interpreter from the Belgrade office, while a security officer, Žaneta Dufková, kept close at hand. A VIP convoy was waiting for us at the airport when we landed on February 9, 2003, and took us to a government mansion on the Adriatic coast for our meeting with Đukanović. We were welcomed by his political adviser Milan Roćen, who told us that dinner and our accommodations were ready, but that the prime minister would see us in the morning in Podgorica. It was unpleasant news because going to the coast and back just for dinner was a waste of time, but as the guests of the government of Montenegro, it would not have been undiplomatic to snarl at these arrangements.

In the morning the same VIP convoy took us back to Podgorica. Đukanović received us in a beautiful government mansion reminiscent of the era of Yugoslavian president Josip Broz Tito. After going through the initial formalities, we commenced the interview.

Đukanović: "Novak Kilibarda was the leader of the National Party, which was a very radical pro-Serbian group in Montenegro in 1991, was heavily influenced by Slobodan Milošević and other politicians from Belgrade. At that time Kilibarda supported Radovan Karadžić and the Bosnian Serb leadership. I heard about the formation of the Republic of Dubrovnik from representatives of the National Party. I was under the impression it was not so much Milošević but rather the Bosnian Serbs who had an enormous interest in the area around Dubrovnik. It would give them access to the Adriatic.

"As for the actual work of political parties in Dubrovnik, you have to remember that it was a turbulent time and the mood of the population was full of passion for preserving Yugoslavia. The declaration of independence by Croatia and Slovenia was seen as something ready to completely cripple Yugoslavia. A strong propaganda campaign was launched in Belgrade in connection with the situation in Prevlaka. The media at that time was full of rumors about Croatian forces moving to the border of Montenegro with the intention of attacking Prevlaka, which was a gate to the Kotor Bay, where the SFRY Navy had its main strategic base. The media was intent on arousing nationalist passions in Montenegro, which didn't have any of its own troops around Dubrovnik. It was the JNA that recruited Montenegrin citizens and sent them to the front under their command. I know there were Montenegrin police units operating around Dubrovnik, but I did not make the personal decision to involve them. They were also deployed by the command of the JNA, which acted together with federal authorities to launch military operations in Dubrovnik. They mobilized men in Montenegro and Serbia to reinforce their units deployed around Dubrovnik. If I remember correctly, roughly five thousand soldiers and officers from Montenegro were incorporated into JNA troops in the vicinity of Dubrovnik. The government of Montenegro was not consulted about the military operations. I recall the words of Momir Bulatović, the president of Montenegro, who said he tried to get Slobodan Milošević to order the commanders of the JNA not to shell the Old Town of Dubrovnik. The answer he got was that the attacks on the Old Town would be minimized and that any rockets that had landed there were fired in response to Croatian provocation. But we can only guess whether this information is true and, then, how much of it.

"These JNA operations caused many of ill-feeling in Croats against Montenegrins, who were suspected of committing war crimes in Dubrovnik and around Konavle. The JNA later investigated a few of these cases, but the dire conditions gradually made future positive relations between Croatia and Montenegro impossible. In 1999 I met Croatian president Mesić and apologized to the Croats for the war crimes committed against them by Montenegrins wearing the uniforms of the JNA. It was a political gesture that really helped to greatly improve relations between us."

I met Đukanović once more, this time accompanied only by my interpreter and Roćen. I asked him a number of additional questions, and the interview ended with his signature on his statement.

From Podgorica I returned to Belgrade, where I concluded several interviews before leaving for The Hague a week later. At the airport I boarded, as so often before, an older Boeing 737 of the local airline company. I sat down in my seat, strapped myself in, and as usual began to doze. I faintly remember hearing the passenger safety instructions. I woke up to the sound of the engines revving up and our plane rumbling down the runway, but I didn't look out the window until we started lifting off from the runway. The ground receded from view when I suddenly felt a stabbing pain in my lungs and an unpleasant pressure in my eyes and ears. A moment later I could barely breathe. As panic began to overcome me, I looked around and could see the other passengers weren't doing any better. Several of them began screaming hysterically, and the lips of the elderly woman next to me were blue, her face white, and she started gasping. The plane banked sharply to the side and abruptly began to fall.

At that moment an alarm sounded, and the oxygen masks above our heads dropped, just like in the safety film. My neighbor held her throat, still gasping, and I was worried that she was going to collapse. We all had it bad, with our lungs burning as we desperately tried to breathe. There was a rasping noise in the speaker before we heard the voice of the captain, completely calm in contrast to our panic, ordering us to immediately put on our oxygen masks because there was decompression in the cabin. My mask swung from side to side just above my head. I grabbed it and tried to put it on, but it wasn't as easy as I thought it would be, or at least as it seemed to be in the safety films. With my survival instincts fully kicked in, I yanked on the mask and managed to get it on my face. It was the sweetest breath I ever drew. I breathed deeply twice more before I realized that my neighbor was still struggling in vain to fully extend her mask. I clawed it from the air and pushed it up

84. Decompression in the cabin of the JAT airplane. (Vladimír Dzuro)

against her face. She too took a breath like there was no tomorrow, then another and one more, and then shrank back into her seat.

In the meantime there was still a problem in the cabin. Several passengers became nauseous as we continued in what felt like a freefall, and the fuselage shook terribly. With some deafening jolts of the engines, the pilots managed to level the plane off. The captain announced over the speaker that the plane had experienced difficulty pressurizing the cabin, but the crew had everything under control. Still, we were returning to Belgrade airport.

After safely touching down, we all breathed a sigh of relief. The flight attendant offered her apologies and told us that ground staff would be waiting at the gate ready to take care of us. Most passengers, however, flew past them and headed straight for the airport bar. We had a wait of a couple hours while the planes were switched, and then we took off again for Amsterdam.

I gave my interview with Đukanović to the lawyers and plunged further into the case of Dubrovnik. On September 7, 2003, the prosecutor issued a public statement expressing her deep disappointment that Đukanović had refused to testify before the International Criminal Tribunal.

We questioned other witnesses and discovered new evidence. Regardless of the outcome of the siege of Dubrovnik, it was increasingly apparent that the military operation and the shelling of the historic center of the city, had struck a raw nerve in the public consciousness. The reaction of the international media only strengthened the opinion that first arose at the time of the operations around Vukovar. The actions of the JNA and the Serbs were barbaric, with the goal of dominating Croatia, and if that meant destroying a priceless cultural heritage, then so be it. Nikola Samardžić, the former minister of foreign affairs of Montenegro, was asked if he knew of any time in the history of modern warfare when the historic part of Dubrovnik was damaged by shelling or bombardment on the scale of what happened in 1991 and 1992.

Samardžić put it like this: "Not even in the fourteenth century was Dubrovnik damaged in any way. Even the armies that came up to the city always drew a line at the fortifications. It was a rule respected by all. In 1944 the Allied armies occupied Italy, and the United States and Britain sent their air squadrons across the Adriatic Sea to bomb targets in Romania, which were still under the control of Nazi Germany. These squadrons used Dubrovnik as a navigation point because they didn't have radar at the time. A colonel in the Yugoslav Liberation Army forced General Petar Peko Dapčević to send a telegram to the commander of Allied forces in Italy, saying: 'Please don't fly across Dubrovnik because the bombers could accidentally drop a bomb on the city. Go south or north of the city, but never over it.'

"All armies in the past did their best and refused to wage war or to target and bomb the city of Dubrovnik. In the 1800s Dubrovnik was captured by Napoleon but without a fight. The Russian fleet of Admiral Senyavin came to attack Dubrovnik, but the ships lowered their guns and gave up on the attack. There was not a single shell or bullet fired at Dubrovnik. That's Dubrovnik's history, and that indicates the level of human civilization, the level of respect afforded to Dubrovnik. What we did in 1991 was the greatest possible shame that could have been done."

The actions of Captain Kovačević during the attack on Dubrovnik confirmed Samardžić's statement. It was proven that by October 25 the JNA had control over most of the strategic positions around the town. At this point negotiations with the Croatian side were in full swing. At a meeting of the Ninth Military-Maritime Sector held in the city of Kupari on December 5, it was decided that the 472nd Motorized Brigade would attack Mount Srđ the next day, which was the only strategic point around Dubrovnik still held by Croatian units. The operation was supposed to end at noon before the prenegotiated cease-fire went into effect.

The attack was launched at five o'clock on the morning of December 6, starting with an artillery assault. The infantry brigade divided into two groups and attacked from two directions. The Croatian forces hit them with artillery and rifle fire, and the JNA responded with more artillery fire. In his position as commander of the Third Regiment of the 472nd Motorized Brigade, Kovačević asked that the 130-millimeter howitzers be deployed south of Dubrovnik at the Čilipi airport to hit back at the Croatian artillery, but his request was denied. The Croatian defenses were stiffening, and the JNA was losing men. Around six o'clock that morning, Kovačević decided that a tactical assault on the city would force the defenders on Mount Srđ to surrender sooner. He gave the order for hundreds of shells and rockets to fall on the historic part of Dubrovnik. He even lent a hand and helped fire a dozen Malyutka rockets. JNA casualties forced Kovačević to withdraw, but the shelling continued until half past four that afternoon. The attack on the historic city partially or completely destroyed many residential and cultural heritage buildings, caused many injuries, and killed several civilians.

The Reckoning for Dubrovnik

In the years 2001–8, the tribunal charged and prosecuted several individuals in connection with military operations in Dubrovnik and its surroundings. General Pavle Strugar surrendered to the national authorities on October 4, 2001, and was extradited to the ICTY seventeen days later. He pleaded not guilty to committing war crimes and maintained his innocence throughout his trial. He was found guilty, and in January 2005 he was sentenced to eight years in prison for not preventing the attack on the civilian population and for the destruction of historical monuments in Dubrovnik, which were within his immediate authority. In July 2008 the Appeals Chamber reduced his sentence to seven and a half years on account of his worsening health.

Admiral Miodrag Jokić surrendered to the authorities of the Federal Republic of Yugoslavia on November 12, 2001, and was handed over to the tribunal on the same day. He pleaded not guilty but then had a change of heart and admitted to the indictment in full. His speech was laden with sincere remorse and regret. In March 2004 he was sentenced to seven years in prison, and the Appeals Chamber upheld the sentence.

Captain Vladimir Kovačević was arrested in Serbia on September 23, 2003, and extradited to the tribunal a month later. On July 2, 2004, the prosecutor asked for a temporary adjournment of his trial on account

85. (*top*) Accused Pavle Strugar before the tribunal. (ICTY)

86. (*bottom*) Accused Miodrag Jokić before the tribunal. (ICTY)

87. Accused Vladimír Kovačević before the tribunal. (ICTY)

of his mental state. On November 17, 2006, the judges ordered that Kovačević be handed over to the authorities in Belgrade for prosecution. The prosecutor in Serbia in charge of investigating war crimes, Vladimir Vukčević, charged Kovačević on July 26, 2007, with committing war crimes against civilians. The indictment provided a rather detailed look at the events surrounding Dubrovnik but also described the specific actions of Kovačević and the JNA units under his command. According to the indictment, Kovačević was totally sane at the time of the military operations. He started suffering from mental illness in 1995 but refused hospital treatment. In 1998 he was diagnosed with posttraumatic stress disorder. A year later he was found unfit for duty in the army, and in 2003 he was diagnosed with paranoid psychosis. He was hospitalized at the Military Medical Academy in Belgrade and remains under the care of doctors today.

Vice Admiral Milan Zec never appeared in The Hague. The indictment against him was dropped due to lack of evidence.

6

Everything Is Controlled from Belgrade

Jovica Stanišić and Franko Simatović

When in 1995 we undertook the investigation of war crimes in Croatia, Jovica Stanišić sat firmly in his chair as the head of Serbian State Security. In the former Yugoslavia, he was clearly number one when it came to intelligence, and for years as a close associate of Slobodan Milošević he was considered one of the untouchables. His deputy, Franko Simatović, known as Frenki, was an ethnic Croat who established the Special Operations Unit, the JSO, within Serbian State Security. He had some five thousand men under his command. The proceedings against Stanišić and Simatović are still ongoing, so I cannot comment on them, but I would like to share my personal experience with these men.

I met Stanišić at his mansion in Belgrade on November 8, 2001, and was amazed at how a government official in the Balkans could afford such luxuries. The floor was made of green marble, the furniture was all glossy, and his bar offered only the best drinks and cigars. It felt more like the home of an oligarch than a former chief of a national intelligence agency. We sat down at a table with my colleague Bernie O'Donnell and interpreter Marc Jeffery.

For six days I peppered Stanišić with questions about Croatia, while Bernie took up Bosnia. Stanišić wasn't giving anything away. He carefully calculated every word underneath a piercing gaze, as if moving figures on a chessboard. He showed no visible emotion, just the stony face of a poker player.

88. Accused Franko Simatović (*left*) and Jovica Stanišić (*right*). (ICTY)

On December 12, 2001, we had to break off the questioning after Stanišić fell ill. Before leaving I asked if he would call Franko Simatović and give him my cell number so that he could phone me. Stanišić replied: "We will see." We left with his promise that the questioning would resume as soon as he was able.

I met Stanišić next on May 20, 2002, when I organized a meeting between him and Geoffrey Nice. It was about the possibility of Stanišić testifying in the Milošević trial. The negotiations were very intense and strategic and concluded with a stalemate. It was my last personal encounter with him. We looked into each other's eyes and firmly shook hands. He left our office, got into a waiting car, and drove off.

A few days after our questioning of Stanišić, my cell phone rang. The urbane male voice asked for my name. He said he was somebody I supposedly wanted to talk to. I asked who he was, but the caller only told me to call him Petar. After a while I got the sense from our conversation that it was Franko Simatović himself on the line.

I told the caller that I would like to meet, but he avoided giving me a direct answer. I wasn't going to take no for an answer because we

89. Hotel Metropol in Belgrade. (Wikimedia Commons)

really didn't know much about Simatović up to that point. It had been a superhuman effort just getting his photo. Finally, this person agreed to call me at the beginning of January 2002, perhaps to set something up.

When the phone rang on January 16, I had more or less written him off. To my surprise the caller said, "Good day, Vladimír, Petar is calling." We agreed to get right to it and set up a meeting on Saturday, January 19. As for where, Petar said he would call on Saturday at 10:00 a.m.

I was in the office staring at my phone from 9:30 onward, but it continued to remain quiet until ten minutes past ten. Finally, it rang, and Petar told me to meet him at the Hotel Metropol in Belgrade.

I called my interpreter, Marc Jeffery, and explained to him what was up. This English teacher by profession, who had lived in the former Yugoslavia for over a decade, was hardly excited by the news. Marc liked to prepare for big meetings, which this one could definitely be, but here I was telling him to get over here quickly. There was also the covert nature of it to consider, so while driving to the hotel I did a couple of extra rights and lefts to lose anyone who might be following us. We parked and went inside the restaurant. We ordered coffee, which tasted revolting. After waiting more than half an hour, I decided Simatović was going to be a no-show. We paid and left to go back to the office.

We got in our car and slowly exited the parking lot onto the main street. A moment later I noticed a green Audi A4 with Belgrade license plates pull away from the curb as we passed. There was no way one could not notice it. It was a shiny, clean car among dozens of dirty, banged-up Volkswagens, Skodas, and the like. Looking in the rearview mirror, I told Marc, "Looks like we got a tail. Probably somebody from State Security." I grabbed the walkie-talkie and contacted our Belgrade office.

"Sierra Bravo Base, this is India Bravo One, over."

"Go ahead, India Bravo One."

"We're on an official ops and have picked up a tail."

"Location and description, India Bravo One."

"Audi A4, green metallic, license plate BG 212063, repeat Bravo Golf two-one-two-zero-six-three."

"Roger."

"Sierra Bravo Base, location Hotel Metropol."

"Should we contact the local authorities?"

"Negative, Sierra Bravo Base, operation not for disclosure. Inform the prosecutor's office and prepare a vehicle with security detail. Will inform you to dispatch, if necessary."

"Roger, India Bravo One, over and out."

The traffic light in front of me was red, but I drove straight through it. I jerked hard on the wheel for a sliding turn across the median so that we were going in the opposite direction. I turned right at the intersection and quickly parked. As expected the Audi pulled the same stunt, and as soon as the occupants saw us, they parked nearby. We were off again a second later, heading toward the roundabout at the Slavija Square, where I started going around and around in an endless circle. A few laps into it, and the Audi joined us. When its occupants realized that I saw them, they turned off, and now I was following them. They stopped at the traffic light, and I pulled up next to them. I rolled down the window and yelled at the driver, "Tell Mr. Simatović this isn't what we agreed on." I then continued on, through my second red light that day. That did it. They left us alone.

A couple of minutes later the phone rang. It was Simatović calling to ask why we missed our appointment. I calmly told him that I had no use for his little spy games around Belgrade. I knew perfectly well who was behind the Petar facade, and if he truly wanted to meet, to let me know. No, no, he said, come back to the hotel; he was waiting for us. I hung up and told Marc to hang on, that we were going back to the Metropol. In the meantime I needed to let our office know.

"Sierra Bravo Base, this is India Bravo One, over."

"India Bravo One, go ahead."

"Sierra Bravo Base, returning to the Hotel Metropol; we got rid of our tail. Send a security detail by the hotel. They should case the place and report anything that happens."

"India Bravo One, dispatching vehicle, on location in ten minutes. Their call sign is Sierra Bravo Mobile."

"Sierra Bravo Base, roger, let the boss know, out."

I drove around for a couple of minutes before entering the hotel parking lot for the second time. Next to the door to the restaurant sat two men, both with a cup of coffee and a bottle of mineral water in front of them. One had a bulldog face; the other one looked sharp in an expensive suit. They x-rayed us with their eyes, then let us in without a word. The place was empty, so it wasn't hard to spot Simatović. He didn't flinch a muscle as we walked up and introduced ourselves.

The first thing Simatović asked was where Marc was from, and when he heard that he was an Englishman who worked for us as a translator and not a Serb, he simply acknowledged his presence. The conversation commenced with no pleasantries or formalities. I asked him right off what was the meaning of sending those goons to follow us. Simatović didn't feign surprise and said that he had to take precautions about his safety. He said he wasn't going to let the police or the tribunal arrest him. He gave me a piercing look and said: "Mr. Vladimír, I know who you are. I have my information; you have yours. Before we reach an agreement, we should clear up one important thing. Neither of us is an amateur: you do your work, I do mine, we know what will work with the other. So let's cut to the chase and tell me why you are here."

We stuck to the point of it all, namely, the conditions under which he would give us an interview. I described the procedure to him, and he said he would have to talk to his lawyer first. He refused to give me any contact information, saying he would contact me himself through my cell phone because he understood that all the phones in our office were bugged. If the interview were to happen, it would be later that January and again the interpreter must not be a local Serb.

He called me right at the end of January 2002, and we agreed to meet on February 2, but he still insisted on doing all the contacting. We put together a team; I made the proper security arrangements and waited by the phone when the day arrived. Within twenty minutes of his call, we were pulling up in front of a little house on an obscure street. The familiar green Audi was parked nearby. I rang the bell. A scruffy man with a lot of hair appeared and invited us in. I asked him about Simatović's whereabouts. Just then his phone rang. The entire conversation from his end was "yes," "no," "yes," "no," "okay." He hung up and handed me a slip of paper with an address written on it.

After my previous experience, I wanted assurances that Simatović would really be there, but this fellow merely shrugged his shoulders and mumbled that he was only doing what he was told. More than that he had no clue. We got in the car and headed to the address provided. The green Audi had already beaten us there. Again we parked on the curb, and I again rang the bell and somebody let us in. We had a big crate with us for our recording gear and were lucky that we had managed to get into an elevator with it. We arrived at the door indicated, and this time Simatović himself greeted us. His eyes still had that steely coldness of concentration and alertness. He stepped aside and allowed us inside his sumptuous duplex apartment. We assembled our equipment and commenced the interview with his lawyer present.

Naturally we took some breaks, and in that time he would tell us that he was writing a cookbook and talked about sailing on the Adriatic Sea and his other hobbies. If I didn't know any better, I would think we were doing an interview for a home and garden magazine. But this was clearly Simatović compartmentalizing his thoughts so that he could remain fully focused and precise where it counted most. Like Stanišić, and probably like most every feared head of a secret police organization, his mind worked like a chessboard where the principal strategy was to survive when the chips were down.

The suspect interview of Simatović lasted a number of days. Several colleagues from various investigation teams in the Office of the Prosecutor participated in questioning, since Simatović's men had allegedly been involved in war crimes not only in Croatia but also in various places in Bosnia and Herzegovina and Kosovo.

On March 13, 2003, Stanišić and Simatović were both arrested during a special operation designed to capture the killer of Serbian prime minister Zoran Đinđić. The indictment signed by Del Ponte on May 1 accused Stanišić and Simatović of involvement in the formation, training, and financing of special units of the Serbian State Security, as well as supplying them with weapons and logistical support. Both men issued orders to their agents that resulted in the murder, persecution, inhumane treatment, and forcible deportation of the non-Serbian populations of towns and villages within the SAOs of Krajina, Western Slavonia, Eastern Slavonia, Baranja, and Western Srijem, and then in the districts of Bijeljina, Bosanski Šamac, Doboj, Mrkonjić Grad, Sanski Most, and Zvornik of Bosnia and Herzegovina.

According to our evidence, the units directed by Stanišić and Simatović included the following Serbian paramilitary units: the Red Berets, the Scorpions, the Arkan's Tigers, the JATD counterterrorism operational unit, the JSO special operations unit, and Martić's Militia. New evidence allowed us to refine the indictment so that it included only those crimes for which we were sure we could get a conviction. The trial should have started on February 27, 2008, but was adjourned by the judges at the request of Stanišić, who claimed ill health. It began on June 9, 2009, and

90. Dragan Samardžić, a prosecution witness in the case *Prosecutor v. Slobodan Milošević*. (Vladimír Dzuro)

lasted nearly four years, until May 30, 2013. To the dismay of both our team and the victims, both men were acquitted of all charges. But upon appeal by the prosecution, the Appeals Chamber ordered the full retrial.

On December 18, 2016, Stanišić and Simatović were recharged and again pleaded not guilty. As of this writing, the retrial is under way before the MICT (the legal successor of the ICTY).

The Extraordinary Story of an Ordinary Young Man from Bosnia

Many times our investigations brought us into contact with ordinary people whose lives had been completely turned upside down by the war, who found themselves in places where they had no wish to be. They included Dragan Samardžić, a Serb who was born and had lived his entire life in Mostar, Bosnia, and Herzegovina before the war broke out.

When Dragan was six months old, his parents divorced and neither wanted him, so his grandparents raised him. He was a street kid who had a passion for football and liked getting into the thick of things. He went to vocational school to learn how to become a mechanic but was drafted by the JNA. On March 19, 1991, he was assigned to the Sixty-Third Paratroop Brigade in Niš, Serbia. In May his unit was transferred to Slovenia, which is where he found himself when the war broke out. Dragan was interested in many things, but war wasn't one of them. He took the first opportunity to desert and secretly returned to Mostar, where he planned to hide out in his mother's home. The minute he told her about his desertion, however, she called the military police, and they hauled Dragan away to jail—the first of many times.

I first saw Dragan in July 2000 at a refugee camp in Debrecen, Hungary. He was no longer the carefree boy kicking a ball around in Mostar, dreaming of becoming the Maradona of Yugoslavia. He was nervous and frightened, almost like a dog you might see in the pound that had only been beaten and kicked its whole life. He had no papers, no money, and his entire belongings consisted of sweatpants, sneakers and a pack of cigarettes in a backpack. We were introduced by a Serbian journalist, Dejan Anastasijević, who had been writing an article about the refugee camp where he met Dragan. After hearing his story, Anastasijević called me to say that he might have a valuable witness for us at the tribunal. I discussed it with Clint, and together we caught a plane for Budapest.

Dejan met us at the airport and took us to a prearranged location in Debrecen. Dragan showed up in scruffy blue sweatpants; he was unshaven, had a cheap haircut, and held a cigarette in his hand. I could already tell that he posed some serious challenges. We suggested he come with us to a hotel in Budapest for a couple of days while we interviewed him. Dragan was naturally all for the chance to escape the dreary refugee camp. While I drove, Clint asked questions, and Dejan translated. It looked as if we had hit the jackpot because Dragan seemed to have been in all the places we were interested in. The problems started when we reached the reception desk at the Hotel Gelert. The three of us, respectably dressed, were in the company of an unshaven, unkempt young man with wild black hair, wearing dirty sweatpants and smoking one cigarette after another. He could have been a bandit for all the hotel staff knew. Only when we offered a credit card as a guarantee for our stay and expenses did the receptionist hand us keys to four singles. We encountered the same nasty looks when we tried to get Dragan into the restaurant. His table manners were those of a rustic, and this did not go unnoticed in the five-star Hotel Gelert.

We didn't care. What he had been through and all he had seen put him at the top of our witnesses to cultivate. After all he had moved around with the Red Berets, one of the most notorious of the special units set up by Serbian State Security as Yugoslavia disintegrated into its bloody nightmare. After our first, preliminary interviews, we drove Dragan back to Debrecen and went to work on verifying his testimony. First, we had to ask the authorities in Croatia and Bosnia whether they had any outstanding warrants against him, but the checks came back negative. William McGreeghan arranged a passport for him at the Bosnian embassy in Budapest, while our analysts evaluated the data he gave us. Clearly, here was another witness for our protection program.

I picked up our tickets in The Hague and headed for Budapest. I called Dragan to tell him to pack his personal belongings, such as they were. He didn't tell anyone in the refugee camp; he simply caught the next train to Budapest. There he met me as if I were an old friend. We picked up his passport, got him a visa for the Netherlands on the spot, and the next day we went to board our plane. While waiting at the gate, Dragan told me flat out, "Either they let me smoke on the plane or I ain't going nowhere." I was able to coax the flight attendant into allowing him to smoke a cigarette on the steps of the ramp.

God, was that a sight! The plane was full of jet fuel, and Dragan was standing there lighting one cigarette after another and flicking the butts on the tarmac. I was standing at the doorway, sweating buckets not just from the heat but also from the thought that they were going to throw us out of the airport and I'd have to stay in Hungary with this guy. I finally managed to get him into the plane, the attendant slammed the door shut, and we departed. Fortunately, Dragan fell straight to sleep, and so did I. We made it to Amsterdam with no in-flight problems.

The Dutch police and employees from the witness protection division were waiting for us at the exit from the plane. They loaded us into a car for the drive to The Hague. On the way Dragan demanded a stop for a cigarette and smoked three just to make sure he could make it the rest of the way. I left him at the tribunal building with a reminder that we would begin a detailed interview the next day. My head was throbbing after the trip, and I immediately grabbed Kevin for a beer at the Hotel Dorint, which was across the street. I definitely deserved that first gulp, but even with all the headaches still to come with this "dragon" on my hands, I never regretted going to the refugee camp in Debrecen. He was an almost inexhaustible source of information about war crimes committed in Bosnia and the activities of Serbian agents there and in Croatia. On a more personal level, his testimony was also the confession of a life that had suffered much during the armed conflict, and because I never lied to him or abandoned him, despite the headaches, I eventually became a sort of personal guru for him.

We picked up his story in Mostar, a historic city whose famed stone bridge built in the Ottoman era had been destroyed by besieging Croatian forces in 1993. Right after Dragan's mother turned him in to the authorities, he was sent to a cell in the local garrison. During the night he managed to send a message to his girlfriend, who arrived the next day with a thousand German marks. Dragan used the money as a bribe to escape, but he couldn't leave Mostar because the place was crawling with soldiers and police. He hid out at his girlfriend's place, waiting to see what would happen. Less than a week later, two soldiers from the Croatian army knocked on the door and told them that all Serbs had to leave Mostar. Dragan told them to piss off, so they beat him, handcuffed him, and threw him in prison, one operated by the Croats.

After two days behind bars, he was exchanged for a Croat who had been arrested by the Serbian police. The good news soon soured when, instead of getting his freedom, he was sent to another prison, this one run by Serbs in the town of Trebinje. He was interrogated and then shipped to an area called Buna, where there was a camp run by the White Eagles, a group of Serbian radicals. It wasn't a prison, but Dragan suspected that most of the Serbian combatants that went through the training camp had really long rap sheets. When given the choice between fighting or sitting in prison, he chose to join the White Eagles. He was given a gun, put inside a truck with a heavy machine gun mounted on top, and sent off to fight the Croats. It didn't take long to come across a Croatian squad. In a matter of seconds, he found himself in the middle of crossfire.

"We saw these Croatian soldiers running out of some houses along the side of the road," he recalled. "As soon as they saw us, they started firing, and we returned it. I jumped off the back of the truck and hid in the bushes. I prayed I wouldn't get hit because several Serbian soldiers with me on the truck were already lying on the ground, all bloody and looking like they were dead. It was the first time I had ever seen someone die. I was so afraid that I began crawling to one of the buildings so I could hide inside it. I made it and crouched up against a wall and waited. The shooting wouldn't stop. I told myself I'm no damn hero, and this certainly ain't my war. Finally, the shots died down, and I figured it was my best chance to get to safety. I slowly crawled to the corner of the building, got up on my feet, and peered around the corner. I saw this Croatian soldier doing the same thing I was doing, almost like I was looking at my reflection in the mirror. We stood there face-to-face for several seconds, but it felt like hours. With our eyes still locked on each other, we both pulled the triggers simultaneously, but because our guns were pointed toward the ground, the bullets started ricocheting everywhere. The noise was deafening, the rocks and dirt were flying everywhere, but neither of us was hit. I was completely paralyzed with fear, but just then my survival instincts kicked in. I bolted for the nearby woods and dived into the first bushes I found. I was shaking from head to toe; that first encounter with death completely unnerved me. I got into many other similar situations later on, but this first fire fight I will never forget. I had this terribly unpleasant taste in my mouth. I couldn't get rid of for the longest time."

Dragan was then taken to the training camp at Boračko Lake. It was run by the Red Berets under the command of Franko Simatović, whom he personally met during one of his visits. He and the other newcomers were given CZ-99 pistols straight from Simatović's hands. After some time Dragan was sent into battle again, and it only reaffirmed that war was not for him. As soon as the opportunity arose, he fled with an official car to the city of Nikšić in Montenegro. There, he sold the car and his guns to a local gangster and continued his flight further into Montenegro, where he hid out until January 1994. It was then that the Montenegrin police arrested him as a deserter and deported him to Sarajevo, where he again found himself in prison.

After a few days behind bars, he was again given a choice, prison or war, this time fighting for the White Wolves, which was a unit recruited from prisoners and mercenaries from Romania, Russia, Bulgaria, and Cyprus. The choice was simple because Dragan wasn't planning to stay with the White Wolves for long. He deserted and went back to Montenegro, but because it was no longer safe for him there, he made his way up to Eastern Slavonia, which at this time was run by Goran Hadžić and Željko Ražnatović (Arkan). When the Croatian authorities took control of Eastern Slavonia, Dragan didn't wait to see what they had in store for him and made his way to the Hungarian refugee camp in Debrecen.

The continuous smoking was an indication he was suffering from posttraumatic stress disorder. He had violent mood swings, ranging from boundless joy and enthusiasm to the deepest, darkest despair and depression. He began to deal with this while at The Hague, and little by little recovery set in. He learned English well enough that he no longer needed an interpreter. We agreed to meet two times a week, once for questioning and the other just for coffee. Dragan clung to me as someone to whom he could confide anything. After several months the authorities managing his protection succeeded in bringing Nataša, the love of his life, to the Netherlands. However, even she found it difficult to cope with the traumas of childhood and war etched into his soul. Dragan had a superb memory and natural intellect, but also a quick temper and frequent changes of mood—not easy traits to live with.

We prepared Dragan intensely for what would be the performance of his life, testifying at the trial of Slobodan Milošević. At the beginning of June 2003, he entered the courtroom and stood face-to-face with the suave, crafty former president of Serbia. None of us was sure whether Dragan was up to it. But he held his own, enduring three days of testimony without any serious problems. Milošević himself conducted the sharp cross-examination but realized that he had met his match in this scarred former street urchin of Mostar. Dragan looked haggard as hell when it was finally over, but he was rightly proud of himself and didn't need to hear it from me.

A few months later, Dragan was given a new identity and asylum in a country in Central Europe. We talked on the phone and wrote emails from time to time. Sometimes even his fiancée called me, during the periods when his demons were getting the better of their life together.

On February 3, 2008, I received a brief email from Nataša. "Vladimír, I am sorry to tell you the very sad news that Dragan died suddenly yesterday, from a broken heart. You were one of his few friends, and I thank you very much for it."

I was staggered by the news. I immediately wrote back to learn more details because Dragan was so young. Nataša replied and then we talked on the phone. Dragan was at work when he suddenly collapsed and died. The autopsy said the cause of death was heart failure due to an untreated disease. He was only thirty years old. Even then fate was ready to deal him a cruel hand. The local authorities wanted to have his body transported back to Mostar. Nataša was hysterical because Dragan had left Bosnia in search of a better life, and now, in death, they wanted to send him back there. In the end she was successful, and Dragan was buried in the country where he died.

The Story of Some Really Evil People

In early August 2000, Carla Del Ponte received a letter from Guido Papalia, the public prosecutor in Verona, Italy. The letter concerned a certain Njegoslav Njego Kušić, a Serbian criminal who was arrested in Italy on an international arrest warrant issued by the Serbian authorities.

Del Ponte sent the letter to the analytical department, and it learned that our witness Dragan Samardžić could write a whole novel about Kušić. According to him Kušić was a ruthless killer active in units of the Red Berets in Bosnia. He eagerly joined the war in the former Yugoslavia in 1990 and was among the first fifty-seven members of the Red Berets trained by Captain Dragan Vasiljković in the fortress of Knin in Croatia. The recruits underwent special training and were then deployed in various operations in Bosnia and Croatia. Important for us was that Kušić had been in direct contact with Simatović and, through him, Stanišić.

Dragan Samardžić described Njegoslav Kušić this way: "Instructor for the Red Berets, easily agitated, very aggressive, approximately 170 cm tall, burly figure, with wavy, dark blond hair. I heard from Pero Divljak that after the war in Bosnia, Kušić was directly involved in the slaughter of Bosnian civilians in Čačak. He was supposed to have killed five people and then fled to Italy. Divljak also told me that Kušić took part in the massacre of Doboj at the outset of the war. The Red Berets moved around by helicopter. They would surround a marketplace, and Divljak would order all the local Bosniaks to show him their identification cards. If Divljak threw somebody's identification card on the ground, it was a sign for Kušić to execute that person on the spot with an ax. Once they got tired of the killing, they would loot all the stalls and fly back to their base."

We evaluated the information about Kušić to see whether it might be worth interviewing him specifically in connection with the cases of Milošević, Stanišić, and Simatović. We went to Del Ponte to find out what she had learned from Guido Papalia, if she had the details of his arrest, and whether we should visit him in jail in Verona. We then received an arrest report based on an application to extradite Kušić to the Federal Republic of Yugoslavia for an alleged armed robbery. While he was being questioned by the Italian authorities, Kušić had intimated that the extradition request was just a cover. According to him the Serbian authorities wanted to get their hands on him so they could do away with him. He knew too much about the top brass in the police and the state security organizations. The Italian prosecutor said Kušić was in genuine fear for his life and wanted to avoid extradition at any cost. He was willing to work not only with the Italian authorities but also with the tribunal. The two prosecutors therefore arranged to have us visit Kušić.

In mid-August 2000 I left with Clint and an interpreter, Maja Draženović-Carrieri, for Verona. The local police picked us up at the airport and drove us to the office of the prosecutor, Guido Papalia. Clint wasted no time and dived right into negotiating the terms for meeting and questioning the prisoner, but the Italian prosecutor was in no hurry. The earliest time we could see Kušić, he said, was the following day, early in the afternoon. We got back into the police car, and the police drove us to the hotel.

Since none of our party had ever been to Verona before, we decided to use the unplanned free time as tourists. In the hotel lobby we had noticed a poster advertising the opera *Aida* playing that very evening in the local amphitheater. The idea of seeing an opera under the open sky was enchanting, and we had the concierge scour up three tickets for us.

The next day the police came to escort us to the detention center, where Papalia was already waiting. We went through the security check and sat in the waiting room. Nothing happened for the longest time, and we were beginning to suspect that talking with Kušić wasn't going to be so easy. Finally, Papalia arrived and led us to the interrogation room. Kušić was not at all happy to see us. He sat behind the table like an arrogant thug and glared at us. We tried to talk to him through Maja, but he just sat there contemptuously. When Clint assured him that we were genuinely interested in him testifying at the trial of Milošević, he just scoffed and said he would talk to us only after he was granted asylum in Italy. He wasn't going to testify against Milošević in any case. So he continued to sit there and ignore us.

That's when Papalia interjected, and a very noisy and aggressive exchange in Italian between him and Kušić followed; Maja tried to translate but soon gave up. I felt as if I were watching an Italian film with no dubbing or subtitles. As the screaming and rather vigorous gestures continued, we left the interrogation room, figuring we would leave it up to the prosecutor to get him to talk. An hour later Papalia came to us and said that he had had no luck either. We weren't prepared to give up, however, and asked him if we might try again with Kušić in the morning. We needed to get Kušić to confess to something as part of a plea bargain that would get him a reasonable sentence in return for testifying against Milošević and possibly other defendants. Papalia agreed but called before noon to say that Kušić had refused to bend. We left him to his fate and returned to The Hague.

In the end all we got from our trip to Verona was an experience in complete contrasts. On the one hand, a snarling, repugnant individual who represented the worst of humanity and, on the other, the atmosphere of a two-thousand-year-old amphitheater with scenes of Egyptian pyramids and heavenly arias on a fragrant summer night.

Arkan—the Scarlet King of the Serbian Underworld

Željko Ražnatović (Arkan) is a name that famously made Interpol's ten-most-wanted list in Europe during the 1970s and 1980s. He also went under the aliases Roberto Betega, Paul Betega, Marsel de Kok, Stefan Kartni, Bob Elis, Gojko and Damian Peno, Rodoljub Kaličanin, Marko Marković, Miroslav Petrović, Đorđe Rolović, Milko Sarvić, Mario Valentini, Pol Karsenti, Marko Markotić, and Mario Valentino. His share, or direct involvement, in robberies, bank heists, and murders was remarkable. It was widely known that Arkan had been either convicted or was wanted in Belgium, the Netherlands, Sweden, Germany, Austria, Switzerland, and Italy. He had been imprisoned several times, and his escapes in Western Europe were legendary. It was said that during one of his trials an accomplice tossed him a pistol, and together they fled the courtroom. His successful escapes were attributed to his cooperation with the Yugoslavian secret police known as UDBA, which used his services to eliminate people whom Yugoslavia's leadership considered political enemies.

In 1991 he re-immigrated to Yugoslavia and appeared on the scene just after the elections in Croatia in 1990. As a leading representative of Delije (Red Star Belgrade football hooligans), Arkan participated in a huge fight in Zagreb with supporters of the Croatian team Dinamo Zagreb. This bloody battle between more than 1,500 fans is considered the beginning of the violent conflict between Serbs and Croats in Croatia.

In October 1990, acting on instructions from State Security, Arkan took a group of hardcore Delije hooligans and formed a squad of irregulars known as the Serb Volunteer Guard, later called Arkan's Tigers, and he became its commander.

The Arkan's Tigers' activities in the years 1991–95 were ostensibly to protect Serbian interests, making him a national hero in the eyes of many of his countrymen, but in fact he and his crew were bullies and brigands. They targeted only places where the plunder and pickings were easy. Forever the gangster he amassed a huge fortune, and with it naturally came political power. During his heyday he could strut about Serbia and do whatever he pleased.

One notable example is when he opened a coffee shop with an entrance on the street in front of his mansion in the exclusive Dedinje quarter of Belgrade. Several diplomats living nearby complained that he made the street impassable, but no one from the Ministry of Foreign Affairs dared asked this protégé of Milošević and Stanišić to be a nice guy and move his coffee shop elsewhere. Out of curiosity I went to visit it and found that it was more like a military camp, with hulking security guards everywhere and a clientele that did not exactly inspire trust. Halfway through the door I decided that any other coffee would taste better than in this place and went in search of it.

It was Goran Hadžić who provided Arkan and his Tigers with training ground in the small village of Erdut, which he used as a base for the war crimes he was suspected of committing in Eastern Slavonia and Bosnia. According to our initial information, they struck the Bosnian cities of Bijeljina, Zvornik, and Sanski Most, but it was their rampage in Croatia, between Erdut and the village of Borovo

91. Željko Ražnatović (Arkan). (REUTERS / Alamy Stock Photo)

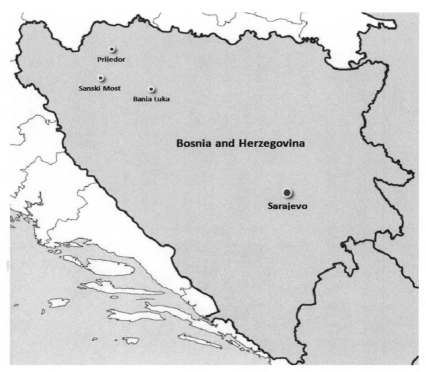

92. Map of Bosnia and Herzegovina depicting Sanski Most. (Vladimír Dzuro)

Selo, that allowed our Team 4 to launch an extensive investigation codenamed Scarlet King.

The first part of the eventual indictment actually involved Sanski Most in northwestern Bosnia. Before the breakup of the federation, the sixty thousand inhabitants consisted of 47 percent Bosniaks, 42 percent Serbs, and 7 percent Croatians. In the three years following the spring of 1992, most of the Bosniaks and Croats fled the city or else were expelled by the Serbs. In September 1995 the Serbian population began to panic as the Bosnian army approached. At the invitation of local Serb leaders, Arkan and his men arrived in the middle of that month to repel the attack and prevent the city from being occupied. He set up a command post in the Hotel Sanus and dispatched patrols throughout the city. Within a week they had apprehended eighty Bos-

93. Hotel Sanus in Sanski Most. (Vladimír Dzuro)

niaks and Croats and taken them to the hotel, where they interrogated, beat, and tortured them. The prisoners were left in totally inhumane conditions, without food or water, in the boiler room of the hotel.

We received reports that sixty-five of them were forcibly dragged onto a bus, driven to the village of Sasina, and shot there. Two survived their wounds. Another twelve from Sanski Most were taken to the village of Trnova and shot. One survived this massacre. While the men were being hauled away, one of the Bosnian women was raped by the soldiers in the hotel. Two years after these events took place, we found ourselves accommodated in this very hotel, not because it was directly linked to the crimes, but because it was the only functioning hotel within miles. The wartime front had gone back and forth across Sanski Most, destroying most of the accommodations in the process.

There was no heating, and running water was a luxury of the distant past. At times it was easy to forget that these inconveniences were nothing compared to what the locals had had to live through. Stefan Waespi, a lawyer who had only been with the tribunal for a few months, came from Switzerland, a place where everything always worked. He refused to pay the full price for his stay because there was no running

94. NATO-SFOR helicopters helping ICTY investigators in Bosnia and Herzegovina, a necessity due to unlocated minefields. (Vladimír Dzuro)

water in his room. The receptionist could speak neither German nor English, so he asked me to apologize for him to my colleague, since he couldn't give a discount. It was a state hotel, and the water and heating weren't working because of the miserable war. I explained the difficulties to Stefan, who instantly apologized.

To survey the terrain, we often had to travel by helicopter because the area around Sanski Most was still heavily mined. The air forces of the NATO countries operating in Bosnia and Herzegovina as part of SFOR troops provided this transportation. The Bosnian government representative delegated to work with the tribunal in Sanski Most was Zijad Ibrić. I was not able to establish the same trusting relationship with him that I had with Colonel Grujić in Croatia, but whenever we needed to find a witness or a location or get a telephone number, it was enough to call Zijad. He helped us find the three survivors of the Sanski Most executions and the Bosnian woman raped by Arkan's men. Their testimony and the evidence obtained from exhumations and subsequent autopsies were submitted as evidence for prosecuting Arkan.

One of the men who had survived a mass execution in Sasina recounted: "I don't remember how long before the bus turned off onto a dirt road. Arkan's soldiers were playing the radio, it was turned on loud, full of Serbian nationalist songs, and we couldn't hear what was going on around us. The bus stopped, and the soldiers took us out in pairs. Even over the loud music, I could hear the sound of screams and gunfire. When it came my turn, the soldier grabbed me by my arm and dragged me out of the bus. As I stood there, somebody kicked me from behind and ordered me to go to the left. There was this machine-gun fire behind me, and I was hit in the left side of my body. I immediately fell to the ground, my face and hands were smeared in blood, but I didn't feel any pain. I lay there absolutely still; there were more shots and the sound of falling bodies. From all around me I could hear the shouting and swearing of Arkan's soldiers. Then the shooting died down. There was this silence, with only the groans of the dying and steps by one of the soldiers going around the bodies and shooting anyone who moved. He shouted: 'You Muslim scum, I'll give you one in the mouth to make sure you're dead.' Finally the footsteps faded, and the bus drove off. It took me a long time to get the courage to move because I was afraid they had left somebody there to make sure there were no survivors. I slowly got up and quietly called out the names of several of the people I knew. But nobody answered, so I figured they were all dead.

"I decided to go back to the road that brought us there. It started to rain, and in the distance I saw some lights that started to get closer. I hunkered down in the ditch and waited. A truck and some cars passed me. Then I heard over and over again the shouting, machine-gun fire, and the same convoy returning to the same road. I stayed lying in the ditch, paralyzed with fear for what would come next. It was a bulldozer that came to bury the dead. Only when it left did I crawl out of hiding and walk toward Sanski Most.

"I went to the hospital because I needed treatment. I told the doctor that I was wounded at the front, and he didn't ask any questions. He treated me, x-rayed my wound, and wrote up a report for me. But I was worn out and didn't have the strength to make it home, so I sat on a bench at the entrance to the hospital. Suddenly, a blue Mercedes stopped in front, and two of Arkan's men got out and started heading in my direction. I just sat there resigned to whatever would happen. They could tell from my name that I was a Bosniak, so they bundled me into the trunk of the car and drove off. When the car stopped, they opened the trunk, and I discovered to my horror that I was back at the Hotel Sanus, where they had dragged me away from the day before for execution. But I was lucky because none of Arkan's men recognized me. They took my medical records and locked me up again in the boiler room."

We created a mosaic of the barbaric conditions in the boiler room from the witnesses we found. They included a certain Numin, a married father of four children, whose statement I took in Sanski Most in 1997. In 1991 he was a little over thirty-five years old.

"Arkan's men tortured us and forced us to do unthinkable things," Numin recalled. "They beat this one young man from the village of Kijevo so hard that he crapped in his pants. One of the soldiers then made him lick it all up until his underwear was clean. He was also forced to yell how good it was. Sometimes the soldiers scattered broken glass on the floor and made us get on our knees and pick up the pieces with our hands. If we weren't quick enough, they beat us with an iron pipe. They hit me in the back. My wound got infected, and I was all but paralyzed. When they found out I couldn't walk, they left me in the boiler room, but it wasn't much better. It was terribly hot and the air unbreathable. I found a rusty nail on the floor and used it to carve a little hole between the bricks so we could get a little fresh air in there.

"Their methods of torture were incredibly sick. There was a small window above the door to the boiler room, and they forced us to go through it into the room. One fellow with us was a little fat, and he got stuck halfway. The soldiers kept beating him from behind until he finally fell through. By then he was almost dead.

"They gave us no food and water only sometimes. Usually they just opened the door and pushed a bucket of water inside. Out of desperation, we took this old can we found down there and started drinking our own urine out of it. It was absolutely degrading, but after going days without a drop of water we prayed that one of us was still able to urinate in the can so we could at least wet our lips with it. At that point your life is nothing more than desperation.

"Two men died in the boiler room as a result of the beatings and dehydration. Their bodies stayed down there with us for several days because the soldiers wouldn't let us take them outside. Not until the stench of the decaying corpses reached the courtyard outside would they let us remove them. There was a garbage truck parked at the gate, and we threw the bodies inside it. They then forced us back into the boiler room.

"One evening they decided to humiliate us even more. They ordered us to gather in the courtyard. Again, we had to get on our knees, and one of Arkan's men put a bucket of water in front of us. We were told we could drink from it, but as soon as one of us lowered our head into the bucket, we were ordered to pass it to the next person. So none of us got to drink from it."

The rapid progress of the Bosnian Army Fifth Corps and their numerical superiority forced Arkan's Tigers to pull back from Sanski Most. Only a few of the prisoners in the boiler room survived. Our search for them led us to interview one Muharem, who had also survived a massacre in the village of Trnova.

Muharem offered the following account: "I climbed out of the truck with the man I was tied to. One of Arkan's soldiers walked in front of us and one behind us who had a very strong flashlight. They kept screaming at us to move faster. We passed one house and then came to another one that was partly built but had a garage. One of the soldiers ordered us to put our bound hands up over our heads. I realized then what they were going to do to us. I half turned and asked what they wanted to let us go. One of them said 5,000 dollars in German marks. The man who was tied to me said he had only 200. The soldier shouted, 'That ain't shit!' and took off the handcuffs. He then aimed the flashlight toward the walls to light up the garage, and there in the darkness we saw a pile of bodies with blood everywhere. They ordered us to go inside. We took just a few steps when we heard the deafening gunfire. A bullet hit me in the back close to my shoulder blade, and I fell to the ground. I fell on my back, and the other man fell on top of me. I lay there totally limp. A second later they brought in two more prisoners and repeated the whole process. The shots, falling bodies, cries of pain, and then the next two. I heard how one of them got on his knees and begged the soldiers not to kill him. I could tell from his voice that he was the same man I saw at the Hotel Sanus speaking with Arkan. The soldier shouted curses at him, and then I heard the sound of a knife being taken out of its sheath. There was this horrible shrieking and gurgling as they cut the throats of the two men. The one who had been kneeling fell on top of me, and I felt his warm blood dripping on me. My face was completely covered in his blood, but that probably saved my life.

"When they finished, there was only the moaning of a few prisoners, which Arkan's soldiers heard. One of them was ordered to put a bullet in each of our heads just to make sure. My bullet narrowly missed me, just tearing away the skin on my chin. Blood squirted from it, the pain in my face was horrible, but I was alive. Someone said we were all dead, the footsteps began to fade, and soon there was the rumble of the truck leaving.

"I couldn't stand it any longer. I tried to get up to see if anyone else was still alive. I heard some grunting and crawled over to a man who had a hole in his head and was bleeding heavily. He had no chance. I crawled out of the garage and just managed to get to my feet. I slowly staggered toward the road. I saw this half-destroyed house and went inside. I crouched by the wall waiting for the shock of it all to pass. Everything started hurting, and I was terribly thirsty. Luckily, I found water, drank as much as I could, and walked out. I didn't know where to go but stumbled on this factory hall, where they helped me."

The testimony given by Safet and Muharem was valuable from two perspectives. First, they helped us locate and exhume the mass graves in the villages of Sasina and Trnova. Second, there was also a psychological element. You would think that a person who had survived his own intended execution would be burning with hatred for those who were responsible. The emotions of these two survivors naturally came out in their description of the horrors they went through, yet neither said anything about wanting to take revenge on the Serbs.

The Bosnian woman raped by Arkan's soldiers at Hotel Sanus refused to give any testimony for reasons of trauma and stigma. My interpreter, Vlatka Leko, managed to establish a friendly and trusting relationship with her, and in the end she agreed that the men who did this to her needed to face the authorities.

Later in 1999, when I was in charge of running our office in Priština, Kosovo, I came into contact with various humanitarian organizations helping Kosovar refugees return home. One of them was a Swiss organization that also helped women who had suffered abuse or rape during the war. I thought about our witness in Sanski Most. She had been gravely injured in the attack but lacked the money for an operation. I gave her name and phone number to them, and two months later, when I was again working in Croatia, Vlatka's phone rang. After the call was over, she looked at me and said in a soft voice, "If you have

95. Esad Agičić (*first from left*) in Sanski Most. (ICTY)

any sins, God will surely absolve you of at least one of them." It was our witness on the phone, overcome by tears of gratitude and thanks. The promised financial assistance for her operation had arrived.

Our investigations in Sanski Most confirmed the veracity of the information that we had received from the Bosnian government. The massacre in the village of Trnova occurred on September 20, 1995, and the executions in Sasina a day later. Two years later, on September 23, 1997, a secret indictment was confirmed against Željko Ražnatović (Arkan), accusing him of war crimes, crimes against humanity, and violations of the laws and customs of war such as murder, persecution, imprisonment, torture, inhumane treatment, and deportation. Our team continued the investigation into his other crimes in the cities of Zvornik and Bijeljina, as well as in Croatia, especially at Ovčara and in Erdut.

Vlatka Leko and I spent much of 1997 occupied with witnesses against Arkan. They included Esad Agičić, a former prisoner in Banja Luka who described the conditions under which he and many other Bosnian soldiers and civilians were held:

"One evening Arkan's men brought in four men from the 727th Brigade of the Seventh Corps of the Bosnian Army. The one they called Mujo told us that they stabbed him twice in the buttocks after they captured him. He pulled down his pants and showed us the wounds. Another was called Tragalović, and the other two I don't remember. All four were handcuffed and looked like they had been beaten severely like me and the others."

By itself, this testimony wasn't special, because the beating and torture of prisoners was routine in Arkan's camps. We were intrigued when Agičić mentioned that after the war he saw an article in a Serbian newspaper in Banja Luka that showed a photo of other detainees along with several of Arkan's soldiers. I asked him if he could get a copy of the article and send it to The Hague. It would not only bolster his testimony but could also provide useful information about the perpetrators of these war crimes. Esad promised to try, and we wrapped up the interview and left Sanski Most after a few days. I heard nothing more about the article and moved on to other cases once the indictment against Arkan was filed.

Four years later, in June 2001, I met a fellow investigator in Belgrade who had just returned from Banja Luka, where he was working with Vlatka. He told me in a doorway that he had something for me. He reached inside his briefcase and pulled out a crumpled envelope containing a letter and a newspaper article written in Cyrillic.

Banja Luka, June 9, 2001

Hi,
Today I had the most incredible coincidence. I met the witness we interviewed together in Sanski Most some years ago. His name is Esad Agičić, and he was one of the three Bosnian army

soldiers who were captured by Arkan. He remembered that he promised to find the article from the newspaper *Glas Srpski* in Banja Luka. The article was written by a Serbian journalist who came to visit the prisoners in jail. Esad got the copy just a few days earlier and had it on him all this time. He asked me to send it to you, and he also sends his warmest regards. He is back in Banja Luka, but he says the situation there is not exactly rosy. The newspaper article is not all there, but it should be no problem to trace it, as it was published on October 14 or 15 in 1992 or 1993.

I hope that when you get this letter, you will be as surprised as I was to hear that I met Esad today near Sanski Most purely by chance. We needed to ask someone for directions, so we pulled up next to someone walking by. I rolled down the window and completely didn't recognize who it was, but he asked me if I was the Vlatka who works with Mr. Vladimír from The Hague. And my mouth fell open. We talked for a bit, and I of course promised him that I would send this article to you. So I am fulfilling my promise.

My best,
Vlatka

I read the letter again, completely amazed that after four years, Vlatka speaks to somebody on the street in Bosnia and not only does it turn out to be the person who promised to send me an article, but it also turned out that he had that very article in his pocket.

I handed over the article as evidence, but kept Vlatka's letter as a reminder that Bosnia is this beautiful part of southeastern Europe where literally anything can happen.

A Professional Snitch from Borovo

In our hunt for witnesses around Erdut, I stopped in a café in the village of Dalj. I fell into conversation with the owner, Boško Orlović, whose real name, Boro Perković, reflected his hometown of Borovo. He was slightly taken aback when I told him that I worked for the tribunal, but he then began to recall the war years in Eastern Slavonia in vivid detail. His knowledge was so extraordinary that I asked one of my contacts in the Croatian police about him. To my surprise I learned that Boško was a total scoundrel. He had been an informer for the Yugoslav State Security, then for the Serbian State Security, and the Croatian State Security, and he supposedly collaborated with the BKA, the German federal police, in Frankfurt. What's more, he was the prime suspect in the murder of Vlasta Petrović, an officer in the Yugoslav State Security and a friend of Arkan, for whom he worked in Sweden and Germany.

I started going to the café now and then, hoping to clarify his information. Boško was wary. He was always armed and wore a bulletproof vest under his shirt. His VW Golf was semi-armored and had bulletproof windows. In one conversation he hinted that I shouldn't be surprised to walk into the café one day and find him not there or else learn that he was dead. He was still moving in dangerous circles, which was good for me because his information was exceptional and really helpful. There was, for example, someone Boško referred to only by nickname, but after a while I managed to get the real name out of him. He was a local Serb who in 1991, although barely twenty years of age, took part in the massacres of Croats and Hungarians living in nearby Erdut. Boško also told me the country where this man was currently living, even the town. I called my contacts in the police to see if it was indeed true, and the next day my cell phone rang with the man's telephone number and address, as if served up on a silver platter.

I called and established contact with him. Because he was living with his family in a relatively safe place outside the former Yugoslavia, he was not included in the witness protection program, but I arranged for him to get the code name T4-20. When I went back to the café with additional questions about T4-20, I found Boško in a nervous and surly mood. He asked me to leave immediately and never come back. Apparently, something had happened, and he had to go underground. I went back to the café once more, but it was as if Boško Orlović had never existed. He had disappeared without a trace, and rumors spread around the village that he had been shot dead. I never did learn what became of him.

Witness T4-20

As expected my first encounter with T4-20 was very cold and tense. He was scared, worried about himself and his family. He felt his own responsibility for what had come to be known as ethnic cleansing. Despite his fears of being prosecuted, we eventually got past the mistrust, and he gave me a statement. He confirmed what Boško had said about him, that he became a member of the SNB, a Serbian National Security group providing protection for members of the Hadžić government and their official guests. This group was directly involved in the killing of Croats and Hungarians who had lived for generations around Erdut. He managed to flee prior to the Croatian authorities retaking control of Eastern Slavonia and the border crossings. He ended up in the country where I found him and was granted asylum there.

He added greatly to the list of insiders whom I eventually persuaded to cooperate with us. It was a nerve-racking game of cat and mouse because here I was going unarmed around people who, to put it politely, were no angels. Indeed, as the actual perpetrators, the ones who did the torturing and killing, they had a lot to be nervous about. But it was the big fish we were after, the ones who planned, ordered, and directed the criminal operations, and for that we needed evidence from the underlings, the ones who were "only following orders." I certainly wasn't in it for the fun of detective work. The endless stories of their utter depravity and cruelty always sickened me, but it's also what spurred me on, to seek justice for their victims.

One advantage I had over my colleagues was that I came from a fellow Slavic nation. I was able to empathize with the people and culture of the former Yugoslavia. I had visited it before all the death and destruction, had spent my honeymoon on the Adriatic coast. After a time I became fluent in Serbo-Croatian, which shares common root words and grammar with other Slavic languages like Czech. Even the most stubborn among these hoodlums was apt to talk when given the opportunity of doing it face-to-face.

It was in this atmosphere of familiarity that T4-20, as a member of the SNB, told me of his direct contact with Arkan, Hadžić, and employees of the Serbian State Security forces then operating in Eastern Slavonia: "After the fall of Vukovar in 1991, the Arkan Tigers established a regular presence in Eastern Slavonia, while members of the Vukovar Territorial Defense conducted exercises at a training center in Erdut. At that time the SNB was still carrying out its original assignment of protecting members of the government. The head of our group was Stevo Bogić, who was called Jajo. He kept in close contact with Arkan and his followers, in particular with Mile Ulemek and Milorad 'Puki' Stričević. Bogić met with them almost every day.

"One day Ulemek burst into our office and excitedly shouted that the Tigers had arrested some Croats and were bringing them to the training center. All of us in the office got up and followed him there. We entered a room on the first floor, which Stričević was using for interrogations, and there I saw Arkan and a man known as Šuco, who was holding a baseball bat. They brought in the Croatian prisoners one by one. First, they asked them questions and then Šuco beat them with the bat. When they brought in a villager who spoke with a Hungarian accent, Arkan kicked him in the genitals. A soldier nicknamed Cope put a revolver in his mouth and asked out loud whether he should shoot him or not. Arkan said maybe they might need him, so he decided against it.

"There were about fifteen to twenty villagers in the prison, mostly ethnic Hungarians. After a few days, the prison was empty, so I asked Stričević what became of them. 'They swam against the tide' is how he always described those who had been liquidated. About a week later, the wife of one of the prisoners came into our office to find out about her husband. We insisted we didn't know anything, and she left, at which point a drunk Ulemek again burst in, this time screaming that the old woman was talking to someone from the UN or perhaps ECMM, that there was going to be trouble, and we were a bunch of pussies for not taking care of her on the spot. In the morning Bogić returned from

Arkan, who was complaining that none of us had yet to kill anyone. All of us would have to go through a baptism of killing, otherwise they couldn't consider us dependable.

"The next day they brought the woman, who was about fifty, in for questioning at the Erdut police station. There they told her not to talk about her husband anymore. But she refused and kept asking around. Bogić felt she was provoking him, so ordered me and some other people in our office, Siniša Galić, who we called Gaja, and Milenko Dafinić, called Dafo, to arrest her and anyone with her. We were also told to search her house and take any money or valuables we found. So we did. The woman gave us a tin box, which contained about 15,000 German marks. We arrested her along with her son and daughter-in-law and bundled them into the car.

"They asked us where we were taking them, and Galić told them to a camp where other members of their family were being held. When we reached a place called Savulja, we turned off and continued on a road that leads to an abandoned house called Lovački dom (Hunting Lodge). Galić stopped there, and we got out and walked a little way to the side. Dafinić told us that Bogić had ordered him to shoot these people and throw them into the old well out back.

"I was supposed to be the first to go through this baptism. We took the old woman and led her to the house. I went in first, she was behind me, and behind her was Galić. Suddenly there were two shots, and the bullets whizzed by my head. I quickly turned around and saw that Galić had shot her in the neck. I stared wide-eyed as blood sprayed from the woman in all directions, and she collapsed toward me. I lost my balance, she fell on top of me, gasping, her blood pouring over me, and I couldn't move for fear. I screamed at Galić, what the hell was he doing, and I struggled to get out from under her. I was only twenty at the time, had never seen a dead body before. Galić yelled at me not to be a pussy and ordered the other ones to be brought in. I begged him not to make me do it. He just smirked and spat at me, saying I was a coward and that he would have to do the other two himself. He also killed them with a shot to the neck.

96. Exhumation from a water well at Lovački dom. (Vladimír Dzuro)

"I was still sitting on the floor next to the woman's body, too shocked to move, when Galić came up to me and promised me he wouldn't tell anyone that I had failed and didn't kill anyone. He then ordered me to at least help them drag the three bodies to the well and throw them down there. We dumped the woman first, then the girl, and finally the man. Dafinić collected the shells and threw two or three grenades into the well to cover up the bodies as much as possible. We then threw some bricks and trash down there, made some makeshift brooms out of grass, and used them to dust up traces of blood."

T4-20 drew a detailed map for me of where to find the well. That same day Vlatka and I left for Croatia, and on our way she contacted Colonel Grujić to inform him of our destination. He was waiting for us when we arrived the next day in Vinkovci. We drove together to Borovo, and with the help of some local residents, we were able to find the abandoned Lovački dom and the partially filled-in well. The colonel's team went right to work. They built a makeshift pulley above the well and lowered one of the specialists into the depths. They were able to expose the first remains before dusk. Grujić called in the local police to guard the well until morning. The full examination was carried out the next day in the presence of a judge, a police investigator, and a crime scene specialist from Vukovar.

Three skeletons, two females and one male, were recovered. They were identified as Juliana Pap, age fifty, her son Franjo Pap, thirty-one, and her other son's fiancée, Natalija Rakin, twenty. They had been kidnapped, murdered, and tossed down a well, all seemingly for a rite of passage, and T4-20 had told us the truth about where to find them.

Networking in Croatia—a Gentlemen's Agreement in Practice

Our work was far from over. There were other bodies to find, more abducted local residents who had fallen victim to these marauding thugs, whether Arkan's Tigers, the Territorial Defense, or SNB. I questioned Serbs from Vukovar who had left Slavonia after the war. I even tried to pinpoint the locations from former members of the JNA, including several of the Tigers who had been active in Vukovar. The colonel's team studied old maps from the archives to get a fix on various abandoned homes and wells and then scoured the area in search of them. Well after well had to be checked. Sometimes it was enough to drain water and then send somebody down to search the bottom of it. Most of them, however, had to be cleared of dirt and garbage before the bottom could be reached.

I was able to persuade some of the Serbian witnesses to talk about mass-grave sites in Croatia. However, I needed to get them into the country to show me the exact locations, an improbable prospect without first informing the Croatian officials. And not only that—once I got them in, I had to make sure they got out safely again. This meant absolute trust and secrecy, and I knew just the man to go to for it, Colonel Grujić. When we started our work in Croatia, it was clear that he was going to be one of our key contacts, but there was naturally some suspicion in the beginning. We quickly overcame it because our objectives were the same, and in no time our professional relationship became one of friendship.

I went to discuss the situation of a particular witness with Colonel Grujić. He agreed it was good for both sides to have him come to Croatia, but he would first have to make sure this person wasn't wanted by Croatian authorities. When the witness didn't appear on any lists, we discussed how to get him in and out and then agreed on it with a simple handshake.

On the appointed day at the appointed time, I arrived at the border in a UN vehicle. Grujić had already arranged for us to be waved through without any check. A column of police cars was waiting to take us to the alleged grave site. I was on the mobile telephone with Grujić giving him directions based on my witness's recollection. When we got there, the witness stayed seated, simply cracked open his window, and described the exact location to Grujić in mumbled tones. These were tense moments because extremely intense emotions were still pouring out of Eastern Slavonia with every new exhumation undertaken, whether we were dealing with three bodies or fifty. Although I knew the team with Grujić by sight, I didn't know any of them personally. I had no idea what they had done during the war or whether some of the missing we were looking for in these graves could be their family members. I couldn't be sure that any of the colonel's team members had scores to settle with any of the Serbs I was planning to bring into Croatia.

We weren't talking about reunions between former neighbors here. Every secret crossing would be unpredictable and full of hidden dangers, so to minimize what could be some very unpleasant encounters, only Grujić was privy to the identity of my witnesses. The moment we arrived, one could feel the air around us thicken. We never left the car because often the discussion through the window grew heated. Still, the witness had to know there was nothing anyone could do if someone suddenly whipped out a gun and aimed it at him. Had Grujić broken his word and the individual come to a bad end, I was going to have a hard time explaining what the hell I was thinking when I concocted a covert operation like this. Indeed, with only one exception, I did not inform my superiors about these covert border crossings because I suspected they would not have approved them. Everything absolutely depended on the goodwill of everybody involved and on Grujić keeping his word.

It wasn't only Serbs I was bringing into Croatia. There was a certain Zoran, a Bosnian Croat, who was captured in the war by Serbian irregulars belonging to Željko Ražnatović (Arkan) and who spent 1995–96 doing hard labor for them in Erdut, Croatia. Grujić knew about Zoran. After the war Zoran returned to his native town of Jajce in central Bosnia. The Croatian newspaper *Večernji list* published an interview with him, in which it wrote that Zoran had helped cover up a mass grave in Erdut. I got a copy of the article, plus a phone number for Štefica Krstić, the representative for the nongovernmental group Family Members of the Missing who had met Zoran in Jajce. Working from his memory, Krstić sketched out the probable location of the grave, but her attempt to find it with Grujić was unsuccessful. I called Krstić to arrange a meeting. She called Zoran on my behalf, but he was hesitant about getting further involved. To avoid a subpoena from the tribunal, he eventually agreed to help us find the grave, but he still wasn't willing to cross the border into Croatia. We had to try to work it out with Zoran over the telephone.

On a Saturday morning, I went to meet Grujić in Erdut. By arrangement we called Zoran at exactly ten o'clock and, listening to his instructions, set out to find the grave. We walked here and there, the cell phone to the colonel's ear, but before long it occurred to both of us that we would never find it this way. It was decided that I would head south for Bosnia in the morning with my interpreter, Dolores, to get a more detailed map. We set out before daybreak because the winding roads meant we needed a good four hours to reach our destination. We also had to pass through many NATO checkpoints, and even though our UN vehicle received priority of some sort, it still took time.

We rented a room at a local hotel for our interview with Zoran. Dolores drew a detailed map according to the description he gave of the site. It was late at night by the time we started our journey home. We were both very tired when we reached Croatia, but we felt good

97. (*top*) Exhumation from a water well in Erdut Žarkovac. (Vladimír Dzuro)

98. (*bottom*) Croatian police taking photographs and video footage of artifacts found in a mass grave in Erdut. (Vladimír Dzuro)

about the interview and were convinced that we would find the grave the next day. It was a Monday, and we met Grujić in Erdut around noon.

My head was still swirling with the story Zoran had given us: "Sometime in March 1996, Arkan decided to move his base of operations from Erdut to the village of Đeletovci, which was closer to Croatian oil fields that he had been illegally exploiting. One day my work detail got a special assignment. About nine of us were loaded into the back of a small truck, where there were shovels and pickaxes waiting for us. They took us to a part of Erdut called Žarkovac, where I could see a tractor parked with a trailer hitched behind it. The driver obviously knew the fields well and took us to a nearby orchard. There we dug and filled the trailer to the top with soil. Captain Vuković, the commander of our work detail, led us to some ruined houses and one of them had a deep well. The order he gave us was 'fill in the well and conceal the location.'

"It was while we were filling it in that we heard the soldiers talk about how they used the well for burying inconvenient corpses. I gathered from this that we were covering over a mass grave, but how many bodies were in there, I couldn't tell. The well was deep, and it took us some time before we topped it off with soil. Vuković then ordered us to create an embankment about a meter high and plant a young pine tree there. Using the tractor and our picks and shovels, we were able to dig up a tree in a nearby wood. To disguise the location, we scattered some leaves and branches about and then went back to the camp in Đeletovci."

And yet even with more details, we were unable to find the grave. We decided that it was absolutely necessary to bring Zoran to Erdut; otherwise the victims would never be found. Colonel Grujić promised him free passage across the Croatian border in both directions, but the problem was getting Zoran across the border on the Bosnian side. He didn't have any identification papers and would need a passport of some sort. For help with this problem, I called Kevin Curtis in Zagreb, which meant coming clean with the truth about my covert operation. He went to the head of our office in Zagreb and arranged for Zoran to receive a temporary ID card as a local employee of the United Nations. The next morning Kevin knocked on my door and with a mischievous grin handed me an envelope with the ID card. Dolores called Zoran and told him everything was ready. We picked him up, all of us showed our ID cards through a closed window on the Bosnian side of the border, and we drove on to meet Grujić and his convoy.

Zoran took us to the place where his work detail had dug up the soil and then to the front of a home lying in ruins, number 167 in Erdut-Žarkovac. He used it as the starting point to the spot where he was sure the well was located. The pine tree he had planted next to it, however, wasn't there, just an old stump. Looking around the terrain, we found another lone pine tree about fifty yards away. Zoran was sure we were in the correct place. Grujić decided to do a test dig at both sites. We did not see any reason for Zoran to stay any longer in Croatia. We got him back in the vehicle and drove him across the border to Bosnia without incident. Kevin and Dolores were certainly relieved. It was their first and probably last illegal crossing of an international border. We told Zoran we would be coming by again after the exhumation to interview him. If no well or bodies were found, his credibility would suffer. Otherwise, any further details he could give us would prove invaluable at a trial before the tribunal.

The first order of business in Žarkovac was to have Croatian army engineers check the area for mines. Two days later Grujić brought in an exhumation team with heavy machinery, and they went to work under our supervision. By the end of the second day, the well had been located where Zoran had said it was. This raised the suspicion that the killers had come back and chopped down the tree to remove any landmark that might reveal the well. We later learned that the owner of the house and his family had fled after the area was occupied by the JNA and Serbian irregulars. Oddly enough they found safety across the river in Serbia, through which they crossed back to Croatia and lived for years in the town of Osijek. When in 1997 the owner came back to Žarkovac, he found his home in complete ruins with tons of garbage all over the grounds. In the cleanup work, he noticed that the well had been covered up, and the pine tree next to it was half-dead, so he cut it down.

It took us two days to clear out the rubble and complete the exhumation. We brought up the remains of four people. Their hands had been bound with plastic handcuffs, and a preliminary examination by a coroner confirmed that they had met a violent death. Grujić had them transported to pathology in Zagreb, but to this day their identity remains a mystery. A German driver's license and passport were found in the grave, but we were unable to make a positive identification.

Clandestine crossings like these allowed us to discover several mass graves and exhume the bodies of dozens of murdered men and women. It was a cathartic experience for both sides. We had the victim's body and could determine the cause of the person's death, and the Croatian authorities were able to give the relatives the dignity of a farewell. On more than one occasion, the survivors sought me out personally to thank me. The risk had indeed been worth it.

Throwing bodies into wells had been the hallmark of Arkan's men. It was an easy way to dispose of corpses. Exhumation in wells is, moreover, very time consuming and dangerous, because the walls could collapse at any time and bury those working inside.

Between January 1999 and December 2000, we exhumed seven bodies from Dunavska Street in Erdut and the four previously mentioned in Žarkovac. The number of victims ranged from twenty-three found in the Daljski Atar well, three at Lovački dom, to just one in the Dalj planina well. DNA was used to identify the victims when possible, and the results were handed to us to be included in the indictments we put together, principally against Goran Hadžić, Slobodan Milošević, Jovica Stanišić, and Franko Simatović.

The Elusive Scarlet King

In the second half of 1995, after the Dayton Accords were signed, Arkan left the occupied territories of Croatia and went back to Belgrade. He turned his attention from slaughtering unarmed civilians to sports, business, and politics. During the war he had accumulated a vast fortune in Croatia and later in Bosnia and Herzegovina, from robbing his victims; smuggling cigarettes, alcohol, and diesel fuel; and chopping down whole forests in Eastern Slavonia. His close contacts in the Serbian State Security made him virtually untouchable in the criminal underworld.

As a politician he came to the forefront in 1992 as the candidate for an independent group of citizens and became a member of parliament. He struck out on his own the next year and hastily founded the far-right nationalist Party of Serbian Unity (Stranka Srpskog Jedinstva, SSJ). In 1994 he gave a speech in parliament calling for the creation of a United States of all the territories of the former Yugoslavia where Serbs live. He was rewarded with thunderous applause. His party ran an intense election campaign, supported by among others the popular singer Svetlana Veličković, known as Ceca. She would later become Arkan's wife. They didn't win a single seat, but his party remained active and moved from Belgrade to Jagodina. Not until 2000 did they win any seats, fourteen in fact, but it would be their only success.

An incurable thief and thug, Arkan didn't let the end of the war slow his illegal activities. With the help of contacts in the Serbian Customs Administration, he imported scarce goods and sold them for a huge profit. He had already set up shop in Kosovo when he opened a bakery there in 1993 and took over the sponsorship of a football club in Priština, which he took into the top division. In 1996 he bought the Belgrade football club FK Obilić and led it to the championship of the Yugoslav Football League in the 1997–98 season, qualifying the team for the UEFA European Football Cup. Given his checkered past, UEFA demanded that he step aside before his team would be allowed to take part in European matches. Arkan solved the problem by making his wife, Svetlana, the head of the club in his place. Since he had met their demands, UEFA couldn't prevent FK Obilić from taking on Bayern Munich on August 12, 1998, and getting drubbed 0–4.

Our informants confirmed our belief that football fanatic Arkan would not miss an opportunity to accompany his team to these prestigious matches. At our request the German police kept their eyes out for him in Munich but reported no sighting. The information was so credible that for the next international match of FK Obilić, against

Atletico Madrid, we decided to go to Madrid to work together with the Spanish police in the hope of nabbing him. We arrived four days beforehand on September 11. Clint and I proceeded to the Ministry of Foreign Affairs, where we were expected by the director-general for European and North American affairs, José Rodriguez-Spiteri Palazuelo, and his deputy, Enrique Mora Benavente. On behalf of the chief prosecutor, Clint Williamson had formally requested their assistance, and the director-general promptly arranged to have the authorities in the Ministry of the Interior and Civil Guard assist. Enrique Benavente then informed us that an operative session would convene at ten in the morning on September 14 with Colonel Pablo Martín Alonso of the Spanish State Security Service.

Just as New York has its Madison Square Garden and Rio de Janeiro Maracanã Stadium, Madrid has the Plaza de Toros de Las Ventas, called Las Ventas for short, and that's where we headed that evening for a bullfight. We got there at the last minute, so we did not have to waste time choosing good seats. We simply took what was left.

Since it was my first time, Clint explained that three matadors usually slaughtered six bulls in one "corrida." That evening we were lucky, because the matador was El Juli, who was already a megastar yet only sixteen years old. He certainly looked like a champion in the ring. It was fascinating watching this young man dispatching all the bulls himself.

Unlike the other five, the last bull did not roll over in its death throes; rather it flopped on the ground with a thud, its nose buried in the dirt. It was almost as if he was saying to El Juli and the twenty-five thousand roaring spectators, "I never had a chance against you and your lance, not to mention your sword. Yes, you killed me, but don't even think it was a fair fight!"

My adrenaline was worked up by the blood, death, and enthusiasm of thousands of people all around me. It was fascinating and morbid, and I knew right away that I would never go to another bullfight.

We arrived at the State Security Secretariat on September 14, a half hour before our meeting. We were introduced to the chief commissioner, Angel de Miguel Bartolome, the head of the organized crime investigation unit for the Spanish police. He would be coordinating the entire operation, which consisted of thirty police officers from special units trained in everything from racketeering to investigating the criminal activities of the Basque terrorist group ETA. After one look at them, Clint leaned toward me and jokingly said in a low voice, "I wouldn't want to meet any of these guys in a back alley at night." We then made our presentation, accompanied by photographs and videos, and wrapped it up by pointing to an enlarged photo of Željko Ražnatović (Arkan) and reiterating that this was the person we were after, so we could bring him before the justices of The Hague.

Later in the day, we went to Vicente Calderón, Atletico Madrid's home stadium, which can hold up to fifty-five thousand spectators. After looking the place over with the police units, we concluded our tour in the control room, where the police normally monitored the action from cameras situated all around the stadium and its surroundings. The police also had surveillance set up for the representatives of FK Obilić who came to Madrid. Everything was ready.

We got to the stadium on September 15 well in advance of the match. Our operatives and uniformed police officers were patrolling all the sectors, the cameras were scanning everybody row by row, and the match got under way. Clint and I were sitting in the VIP section one row behind the Belgrade team management. They included Arkan's wife and his spokesman, the well-known international conman and money launderer, Giovanni Di Stefano. We noticed him dialing a number on his cell phone, which the special units immediately traced to a local house. In no time their forces descended on the occupants, but none of them was Arkan. Later on we learned that Di Stefano had allegedly dialed a wrong number.

The match ended in another defeat for FK Obilić, this time 0–2, but the investigators of Team 4 didn't do so well either. After a lot of work, organization, and expense, we still didn't get our man. Other attempts to arrest him, made in conjunction with the police in Belgium, Germany, and Sweden also ended in failure.

On March 31, 1999, Chief Prosecutor Louise Arbour announced at a press conference that the tribunal had secretly indicted Željko Ražnatović (Arkan) for war crimes, but fearing for the safety of our witnesses, she declined to offer any specifics.

Then in June the American TV station MSNBC quoted a prosecutor in Belgium who said that Arkan had contacted the authorities there to float the idea of his voluntary surrender to the tribunal. On the fourteenth of that month, Deputy Chief Prosecutor Graham Blewitt said at a press conference that the tribunal knew about the report, but neither Arkan nor his legal representative had contacted them. He confirmed that the indictment went back to 1997, and several attempts had already been made to arrest Arkan. That, said Blewitt, should lay to rest the speculation that the tribunal wasn't taking any action against Arkan or wasn't ready to prosecute the case.

It was clear that Arkan's voluntary extradition would have repercussions for leading government officials in Serbia, whose lives he could make equally miserable. We decided to wait and see what the response from the Balkans would be, and it wasn't long in coming.

On the afternoon of January 15, 2000, Arkan was hanging out with his friends in the lobby of the Hotel Inter-Continental in Belgrade. At about five o'clock, a Serbian policeman by the name of Dobroslav Gavrić walked up from behind and shot him three times in the head. Arkan died on the way to the hospital. As a result of his death, the indictment against him for war crimes in the Bosnian towns of Zvornik and Bijeljina and Erdut in Croatia was quashed. At his funeral held four days later, more than ten thousand of his supporters came to say their farewell. They remembered him as a mythical tough guy, not the gutless hoodlum who brought shame and disgrace to their homeland.

Slobodan Milošević—Code Name Viper

The fish we wanted more than any was former president Slobodan Milošević, for crimes committed in Croatia, Kosovo, and Bosnia and Herzegovina. This investigation was given the code name Viper.

Milošević had been a typical Communist apparatchik in the good old days of Yugoslavia. As that world began to collapse, he saw his chance to achieve political power by playing the nationalist card. He was no true nationalist in the proper sense of the word, just a tactician and opportunist who would use any means to satisfy his ambition. Everything fell into place when he was elected chairman of the Presidium of the Socialist Republic of Serbia on May 8, 1989. The upcoming six hundredth anniversary of the Battle of Kosovo, a loss to the Ottoman Turks that Serbs nevertheless commemorate to this day, was just the platform he needed. He went to a place called Gazimestan in Kosovo to mark the occasion, and on June 28 delivered a nationalistic speech in which he played to very basic human instincts. He brought to life the old idea of a Greater Serbia that incorporated any region where Serbs lived. The people loved it, and when a new constitution was adopted by Serbia on September 28, 1990, he became the first president. After consolidating his power, he took complete control of the country's police, territorial defense, and intelligence services. He then moved to gain de facto control over the JNA.

Because Serbs made up the largest ethnic group in Yugoslavia, whose capital was located in Belgrade, the JNA command was largely dominated by Serbs, whether in Serbia or in Bosnia and Herzegovina. This gave the Serbs an undoubted advantage at the start of the war because the JNA commanders, although prohibited by Yugoslavian law from taking sides, lost their neutrality and came to the aid of the Serbian population in Croatia and later in Bosnia and Herzegovina.

At the start of 1991, the situation between the two largest ethnic groups, the Croats and the Serbs, grew ever tenser. The representatives of the six republics held meetings throughout the country but failed to find a peaceful way out of the Yugoslav crisis. Meanwhile Milošević had weathered demonstrations called by the opposition to protest his control of the media. Emboldened, Milošević gave a speech that outlined plans for the possibility of adding a large part of Croatia to the new Yugoslavia. The response was quick. A clash broke out between Serbs and Croats at the Plitvice Lakes in Krajina on March 31, 1991, the JNA was brought in, and the Croatian War of Independence was on.

The basic problem we faced in investigating Milošević was obtaining evidence of his direct control over institutions that should have been subject to the Yugoslavian Federation and not to the president of Serbia. Our findings showed that in August 1991, Milošević used his position as the president of Serbia and likewise as the leader of the SPS, the Socialist Party of Serbia, to become actively involved in committing war crimes and crimes against humanity as a leader of a joint criminal enterprise. He participated in the planning and directing of the policies of local Serbian governments outside the territory of Serbia and helped them create Serbian Autonomous Regions, which he then provided with material, financial, and logistical support. He issued orders to Serbian authorities to form armed paramilitary units and send them to Croatia and Bosnia and Herzegovina. He also used his control of the state media to spread misinformation and incite ethnic hatred between Serbs and Croats.

The team that dealt with Milošević was led by British lawyer and prosecutor Geoffrey Nice, who joined the tribunal in 1998.

Geoffrey recalls: "In 2000, I was appointed by Chief Prosecutor Carla Del Ponte to head the team investigating war crimes committed by Slobodan Milošević. You need a large team of professionals when preparing complex indictments for large cases, but going after the head of state for crimes in three wars calls for an exceptional team of experienced lawyers, investigators, and political and military analysts. The success of the case ultimately comes down to the credibility of the evidence that has been collected over the years by investigators. They are the first to come into contact with the witnesses. They have to take into consideration that the witnesses may be severely traumatized and in many cases politically opposed to those they are testifying against before the tribunal. These issues, among many others, we had to face during the investigation of Slobodan Milošević."

The indictment against Milošević ran to 140 pages and was divided into three parts: Kosovo, Croatia, and Bosnia and Herzegovina.

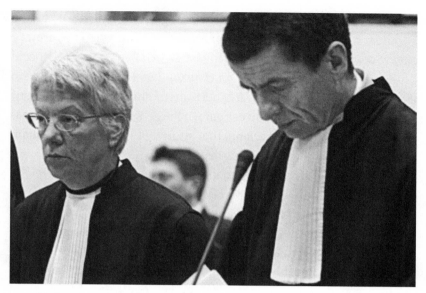

99. Chief Prosecutor Carla Del Ponte and a principal trial attorney, Geoffrey Nice, in the courtroom during the case against Slobodan Milošević. (ICTY)

Team 4, composed of investigators, lawyers, analysts, interpreters, and support staff who worked on the Croatian part of the indictment, included Alex Nereuta (Romania, analyst); Alex Whiting (United States, trial attorney); Andrea Božić (Croatia, interpreter); Ari Kerkkanen (Finland, investigator); Arne Kristiansen (investigator); Azim Arshad (Pakistan, investigator); Brent Pfundheller (United States, investigator); Carmel McGloin (team assistant); Clint Williamson (United States, trial attorney); Dayse de Oliveira (Brazil, team assistant); Dean Manning (Australia, investigator, team leader); Dennis Milner (United Kingdom, investigator, commander); Deon van Rooyen (South Africa, investigator); Dirk Hooijkaas (Canada, investigator); Hildegard Uertz-Retzlaff (Germany, trial attorney); Jan Wubben (the Netherlands, senior trial attorney); John Cencich (United States, investigator, team leader); Kevin Curtis (United Kingdom, investigator, team leader); Malena Rembe (Sweden, criminal analyst); Marie Tuma (Sweden, trial attorney); Mark McKeon (United States, trial attorney); Michael Stefanovic

(Australia, investigator); Monika Ora (Hungary, investigator); Morten Torkildsen (Norway, investigator); Nataša Milasinović (interpreter); Nigel Stewart (United Kingdom, investigator); Paolo Pastore Stocchi (Italy, investigator); Philippe Oberknezev (analyst); Rajie Murugan (South Africa, investigator); Renaud Theunens (Belgium, analyst); Sabine Scholz (Germany, investigator); Serge Krieger (Canada, analyst); Stefan Waespi (Switzerland, trial attorney); Tanja Kučan; William Hardin (United States, investigator), and me.

Team 5, led by Bernard O'Donnell, investigated Slobodan Milošević's crimes committed in Bosnia and Herzegovina, while Kosovo inquiries were initially handled by our team (Team 4) together with the crimes committed in Croatia. However, in 2000 the chief prosecutor established Team 11, which addressed Kosovo exclusively, and she made Kevin Curtis responsible for managing the team.

The first part, the Kosovo indictment, was confirmed by Carla Del Ponte on May 22, 1999. More than two years passed before the other two indictments (Croatia and Bosnia and Herzegovina) were confirmed, but by then Slobodan Milošević was sitting in a prison cell in Scheveningen, brought there safely by Kevin.

Arrest of Slobodan Milošević—Kevin Curtis's Firsthand Account

It was Monday, the twenty-fifth of June, 2001, and I had been sitting for several days in the Belgrade office of the tribunal. I was on a secret mission to arrest the recently ousted president of the Federal Republic of Yugoslavia, Slobodan Milošević, and safely transport him to The Hague. He was to appear before the justices to hear charges of his involvement and responsibility for war crimes and crimes against humanity committed in Kosovo. I knew all about the horrific acts inflicted on Kosovar Albanians by Serbians because in 1999 and 2000, I led the team that investigated these crimes and found mass graves containing more than four thousand bodies.

Only a few people knew I was there because no one wanted to provoke an uprising by Milošević's supporters. As I sat there in the office, waiting for the phone to ring, my thoughts had returned to the case of Slavko Dokmanović. I played a significant role in his arrest, which came about through some nifty and honest police work. This case was completely different. I was supposed to arrest one of the most powerful presidents, or rather dictators, in modern European history and had close to no control over the operation itself.

The way had been cleared by the previous arrest of Milošević by Serbian authorities in his villa in Belgrade. That part of the plan was undoubtedly motivated by the promise of the United States to pay $50 million as assistance to Serbia in the event the arrest occurred by March 31, 2001. This whole operation was to be an act of goodwill, a sign of cooperation between the Serbian authorities and the tribunal. The payment of the money was linked only to arresting Milošević, not to his extradition to The Hague. It was a political compromise that was meant to inform us that we couldn't have our cake and eat it too. But there were plenty of people in government circles who knew that as long as Milošević remained in Belgrade, it would be only a matter of time before he was released and returned to power. We can only speculate what would happen to those who had arranged his overthrow and subsequent arrest, but they might clearly want to make a run for it.

The police operation against Milošević was launched by Prime Minister Zoran Đinđić an hour and a half after midnight on March 31 and proved to be very dramatic. At the time Milošević's residence was guarded by twenty heavily armed loyal followers. They immediately put up a fight that turned into a thirty-six-hour standoff. The arsenal used to defend the large compound included two armored vehicles, a rocket launcher, thirty RPGs [rocket-propelled grenades], two boxes of grenades, three machine guns, thirty automatic rifles, twenty-three guns, and ten boxes of ammunition. After twenty-four hours, with the defenders flushed out of their positions, Milošević threatened to kill first his family, then himself.

The shooting stopped in the early morning hours of April 1. The government negotiator promised Milošević that his arrest did not mean that he would be extradited to the tribunal in The Hague. At half past four in the morning, Milošević finally surrendered to the police and was taken to jail in an armed convoy. His daughter Marija went with him. She had actively defended the compound and according to police sources was found to have three pistols on her during the arrest.

While still waiting for the phone to ring, I had time to think about what might happen as I stood before Milošević to arrest him on behalf of the tribunal. I had watched the dramatic footage of the March arrest on television and had to wonder if there wouldn't be similar opposition to his extradition to The Hague. How will the man himself react? Would there even be an attempt to assassinate him, since he knew things that could get a lot of other people into trouble? If we did succeed in getting him on the plane, I decided that the best course would be to establish a relationship with him during the flight that might facilitate interviewing him over the following weeks.

On June 28 at around three o'clock in the afternoon, there was a power outage in the district of Belgrade where our office was located. The computer screens dimmed, and the air conditioning faded to a stop. It was around forty degrees [Celsius, i.e., 104° F.] outside, and my corpulent figure began to cook. As the sweat ran down my back, and my organs began to drone, I decided to go back to the hotel to rest and cool off in air conditioning. I told my suffering colleagues in the office that I would see them in the morning.

My plan for that evening was to take a cold shower and then go down to the local bar for a beer. The first part was a complete success. I took the shower and stretched out on the bed to enjoy the air conditioning. And then the phone rang. It was Deyan Mihov, the head of our office in Belgrade. He told me to get ready immediately because somebody from the government was coming for me. I got dressed and went down to find a black limousine with tinted windows waiting for me. I got in, and after ten minutes I was walking inside the gigantic building of the State Security Department.

In style I would compare it to a castle or the mansion of an eminent statesman. I was led through a tangle of richly decorated corridors into the conference room where many meetings at the highest levels of state had been held and serious decisions made. It seemed appropriate that the decision that was now being made in this room concerned the fate of the former president of Yugoslavia, Slobodan Milošević.

The minister of the interior Dušan Mihajlović was sitting at the far end of a long table speaking to someone. He got up and came over to meet me. He looked tense. Dispensing with formalities he asked flat out how much time I would need to get Milošević airborne. I told him it all depended on where and how we managed it. He told me there was a helicopter at the back of the building waiting to fly us to Bosnia, where an escort would then take us to The Hague. I asked who was making the trip, and he replied curtly, "You, Milošević, and the pilot."

I insisted that before we set out, I needed an interpreter and member of our security detail. Irritably, he said there was no need, that Milošević spoke fluent English, and there was no danger to us. I nevertheless insisted on them. He became even more irritable, but within half an hour our interpreter and security guard were there. I took them to the side and explained what was going to happen. Mihajlović then led our little group to the rear of the building, and we magically found ourselves in the middle of a war zone. This part of the building had been completely destroyed, most likely when NATO carried out its bombing campaign against Belgrade. The contrast was absolutely incredible.

Standing on the manicured lawn outside were secret service agents responsible for our security. There were three helicopters nearby, one large and two slightly smaller ones. They were to start at the same time and fly away in different directions just in case the Yugoslav army decided to take action against the one transporting the former president, which of course would be the same one I was in.

As with the arrest of Dokmanović, I intended to record the reading of the rights of the accused and attached the equipment for it to the wall next to the entrance. We patiently waited for the arrival of the former president. It took only a few minutes before two black vans pulled up at the rear of the building. The first man to get out was wearing a black suit, white shirt, and tie. Then came Milošević, who stepped out of the back of the van. He also wore a black suit, black shoes, and a white shirt

100. Investigator Kevin Curtis in Belgrade arresting Slobodan Milošević.
(Vladimír Dzuro)

unbuttoned at the neck. I went to meet them and brought them to the place set up for the recording equipment. I asked Milošević whether he spoke English, and he said only one word: "No."

Since he wanted to play it this way, I introduced him to our interpreter, who translated everything I said regarding the rights of the accused. I officially introduced myself and informed him that in the name of the tribunal he was under arrest and would be transferred to The Hague.

That was the first time I saw some sign of emotion in his face. He was really surprised. When I informed him that he would be searched by our security officer, he testily snapped that he was coming straight from prison and therefore no search was necessary. I said equally sharply, "You are my prisoner, and you and your bag will be searched before boarding the helicopter." He was then searched and taken to the helicopter. He got inside with his little briefcase, followed by the security officer and the interpreter. I took the seat directly opposite him.

We flew in a military helicopter with camouflage paint. The pilot asked me in English if we were all safely strapped in. That seemed to goad Milošević. Speaking English with a slight Serbian accent, he sarcastically asked me, "Do you enjoy arresting innocent people? How long have you been doing it?" I assured him that I had been working as an investigator so long that I wasn't afraid of his type. "And yes, I like it when I can bring accused war criminals to justice. It will be up to the tribunal to decide whether you are guilty or not." He said nothing to that.

We took off and headed west toward Bosnia and Herzegovina. He silently looked at the landscape below. I can't say what was going through his head, probably the realization that he would never see Serbia again. Suddenly he roused himself and asked, "Do you smoke?" When I nodded, he politely asked whether I might not offer him a cigarette. I reached into my pocket but stopped short and said, "You can't smoke in here!" Milošević raised his eyebrows and pointed to the ashtray. "What do you think it's here for? Besides, it's my helicopter." I turned to the pilot, who just nodded, so we lit up together and pretty much chain-smoked the whole way from Belgrade to Bosnia.

Our helicopter landed at the U.S. military base Camp Eagle. A squad of special forces was waiting for us as we touched down at the end of the runway. I noticed that the names on their uniforms had been covered up. Milošević got out with an air of dignity, and the moment his foot touched the airfield he asked me in the tone of a statesman, "Where are we?" I told him Bosnia. Smirking as if he had just smelled some unpleasant odor, he quickly pulled a handkerchief out of his pocket, bent down, and wiped his shoes with it to demonstrate his disgust with coming into contact with Bosnian soil.

They took us to a nearby wooden shack that had only simple benches. As we entered, one of the soldiers began filming Milošević. He tried to strike up a conversation with the soldiers, but they all ignored him. That irritated him enough to prompt him to play a little game with them. He began pacing back and forth, and the soldier with the camera followed him around. Milošević turned to him and said, "You can film me from one position. All you have to do is use the zoom button." The soldier got it, and Milošević happily took a seat. After a while he again tried to talk to the soldiers, this time to ask for permission to smoke. One of the soldiers could no longer bear keeping quiet and told him that smoking was strictly prohibited. But this got the ball rolling. Another soldier left without a word and returned with a plastic mug containing water. We took this friendly gesture to mean silent assent, and we lit up after they brought us an ashtray.

After about an hour and a half of waiting, I heard the sound of an aircraft engine. One of the American soldiers went out and came back with another man, a member of the British SAS special forces. He had arrived in a small military aircraft with orders to deliver Milošević to The Hague. The former president was handcuffed and led inside the waiting plane. I followed with his suitcase. When we reached the plane, one of the SAS soldiers blocked my way and announced that I would not be flying with them. I told him in no uncertain terms that Milošević was my prisoner and that he didn't leave without me. Reluctantly, he gave way, and I boarded. I explained that I needed to record anything that Milošević said, and I was told that he would not be allowed to say anything. In fact, although it was a small plane, Milošević and I had been positioned at separate ends. The pilot then prepared for takeoff.

I could tell from the agitated conversation between the pilot and the soldiers that there was a certain suspicion about news of Milošević's extradition leaking to the press. It still wasn't clear where we were going to land in the Netherlands. Our final destination was supposed to be an airport with the fewest number of journalists or better yet with none at all. Eventually the airport at Eindhoven was chosen. As we began our approach, the atmosphere in the plane grew slightly ridiculous as the soldiers argued over which of them would be the one to bring Milošević out of the plane. It went on for some time before I informed them that I was doing it because he was still my prisoner. They smugly ignored me and continued jostling for the honor. We landed, the plane came to a stop, and we saw what appeared to be

101. Arrested Slobodan Milošević before the tribunal. (ICTY)

camera flashes outside the windows. The soldiers panicked because everything was supposed to be secret. They immediately began pulling the shades down over the windows and without a word of protest gave me the keys to the handcuffs.

And so with satisfaction, I brought Milošević out of the plane and handed him to the Dutch police, who escorted him by helicopter to the prison in Scheveningen.

When it was over, I learned to my great amusement that all the flashes that unnerved the SAS soldiers were not from members of the press but from a lone camera wielded by our colleague Dennis Milner on the tarmac.

The danger I had always suspected would arise with the arrest of Milošević occurred not quite two years later when, on March 12, 2003, Prime Minister Zoran Đinđić, who had authorized the extradition, was shot dead by a sniper on the orders of one of the former members of

Arkan's unit, Milorad Ulemek. The one who had done the actual killing was Zvjezdan Jovanović, a former operative of the Serbian special units.

I am firmly convinced that the arrest of Slobodan Milošević and his subsequent extradition to the tribunal was an important step toward the completion of the peace process in the Balkans, and I for one am proud that I was personally involved in it.

Of course, there was still the matter of putting Milošević on trial, and this created other complications.

As Geoffrey Nice explained: "Slobodan Milošević decided to defend himself. He conducted a thorough and often intimidating cross-examination of the witnesses we brought into the courtroom, which greatly extended the proceedings. To come face-to-face with someone who for many years was an authoritarian president, whom you saw only on television, was not easy for many. These were difficult times for our witnesses. We often saw tears in their eyes, and we came to empathize with their personal experiences. Often, I had to swiftly intervene with the judges during the cross-examination.

"I have personally visited the places where the most serious crimes were committed, including Vukovar, Srebrenica, and Ovčara. But we also had to be on our guard for unexpected surprises, because the investigation was still ongoing and ran concurrently with the trial. Our team of lawyers had to keep adapting our prosecution strategy as the evidence provided by the investigators kept coming in."

In 2001, while working on the Insider project in Belgrade, I was interviewing some high-ranking military, police, and government officials related to the trial of Slobodan Milošević. One of the most significant insiders I interviewed was Major General Aleksandar (Aco) Vasiljević, who was named as a co-perpetrator in the indictment against Slobodan Milošević for war crimes committed in Croatia. The interview was conducted in our offices in Belgrade over a period of almost three weeks. I was assisted by a political analyst, Philippe Oberknezev, and a military analyst, Renaud Theunens.

102. Major General Aleksandar (Aco) Vasiljević testifying as a witness before the tribunal. (ICTY)

General Vasiljević served as head of counterintelligence within the Security Administration of the SFRY Federal Ministry of Defense. On June 16, 1991, just before the most serious military confrontations in Croatia erupted, he was appointed head of the Security Administration. In May 1992, approximately a month after the war broke out in Bosnia and Herzegovina, General Vasiljević was prematurely pensioned off. However, seven years later, in April 1999 during the NATO bombing campaign against Yugoslavia, he offered his services and was appointed deputy head of the Yugoslav army's Security Service.

Interviewing the head of any military counter-intelligence service, a key position within military structures, always requires significant preparation. The head obtains critical, highly sensitive information and supplies it to the military command structures but also to the political elite of the country. Possession of information during military conflict makes the position of the head even more powerful.

None of us knew what General Vasiljević was prepared to talk about, but with the assistance of Philippe and Renaud, I did my best to prepare for the interview so that I could discuss the topics we believed were relevant to our investigations.

The volume and quality of information General Vasiljević shared with us during the interview was overwhelming. He gave a detailed explanation of how the JNA and the VJ military chains of command worked, showing the precise legal but also de facto authority of Slobodan Milošević and his co-perpetrators over military forces—the very forces that we alleged in the indictments had committed war crimes and crimes against humanity.

He also explained how the military's reporting channels worked, and he helped to prove that Slobodan Milošević had the means to know about the crimes that had been committed. General Vasiljević testified about Slobodan Milošević's control over appointments to key positions, including the Serbian Interior Ministry:

Question: "Did the accused exercise any influence over the appointment of people to the Serbian Ministry of the Interior? He obviously had the power to, but did he actually exercise that power?"

General Vasiljević: "The procedure for appointing ministers in the government is clear. They were nominated by the prime minister designate, and I think that there is no doubt that in relation to the key positions, one of which was always the post of minister of the interior, were certainly strongly influenced by the accused. The appointees were people he had special confidence in. However, the entire procedure, in formal terms, went through the assembly or the parliament, and there the Socialist Party of Serbia held the majority, and he [Slobodan Milošević] was the president of that party, so that it was very easy for votes to be in favor of what had already been planned."

Question: "To whom did it—to whom was it directly subordinate, the State Security of Serbia?"

General Vasiljević: "To all intents and purposes, it was subordinated to the president of Serbia at the time, that is to say Slobodan Milošević."

Question: "When he became president of the FRY, what was the position then about the [State Security Service] of Serbia? To whom was it then subordinate?"

General Vasiljević: "In a very short space of time, it was to be subordinated contrary to the provisions in force at the time. Once again, subordinated to President Milošević as the President of Yugoslavia."

General Vasiljević also explained the relationship between the Croatian Serb and the Bosnian Serb armies (the SVK and the VRS): "Objectively, there were two armies in two countries. And from a third country, the Federal Republic of Yugoslavia, they were treated as if they were both armies of the Federal Republic of Yugoslavia, because they were supplied with funds, personnel, matériel, and equipment."

However, General Vasiljević not only shared information with us related to relationships between Milošević and the military and police structures deployed on the territories controlled by Serbs in Croatia and Bosnia and Herzegovina, but he also had detailed information about the role that the Serbian Interior Ministry, its State Security Service, special units, and various volunteer and paramilitary groups played in the conflicts.

General Vasiljević confirmed that the real power within the Interior Ministry was in the hands of Jovica Stanišić, head of the Serbian State Security Service known as Državna bezbednost, who was directly linked to Milošević. General Vasiljević also explained that Jovica Stanišić stood behind most of the paramilitary units operating in Croatia as well as the territorial defense forces.

We also had a good opportunity to discuss war crimes committed in Croatia and specifically the massacre at Ovčara. We learned, for example, that since his retirement from army in 1992, General Vasiljević kept inquiring about the fate of the prisoners at Ovčara. He told us about an accidental meeting with Colonel Mile Mrkšić. They met sometime in spring 1998 at a street market in Belgrade.

General Vasiljević asked: "Mile, what happened at Ovčara?" Colonel Mrkšić responded: "I swear by my children, if I had known what they would do to them, we would have never handed them over." General

Vasiljević further questioned Mrkšić: "And when you found out what had happened, why didn't you report it?" Colonel Mrkšić: "When we found out what they had done, we swore to remain silent."

This short exchange proved that Colonel Mrkšić knew what happened with the prisoners and chose, together with his senior officers, to conceal the truth.

When the first part of the interview of General Vasiljević was completed, the analysts and lawyers from the prosecutor's office analyzed the information and supplied me with pages and pages of additional questions. Eventually Geoffrey Nice came to Belgrade and discussed the possibility of General Vasiljević testifying in the trial of Milošević in an open or closed session. General Vasiljević told us that if he ever testified before the tribunal, it would be only in an open session without any protective measures. We were surprised and concerned about his safety, since the security situation in Serbia at the time was still very volatile.

I recall General Vasiljević looking in our eyes and saying: "It was a great honor for me to be appointed as general, and I proudly served my country. My fellow officers and soldiers expect me to behave as general. I have nothing to hide; I want people to hear my testimony, so that they can judge my actions."

I worked with General Vasiljević on a number of occasions including when he was getting ready for his testimony during the trial of Slobodan Milošević. We developed a mutual respect, and whenever I traveled to Belgrade I would stop by at his home for a chat and coffee. General Vasiljević turned out to be a critical prosecution witness not only in the trial of Slobodan Milošević but also in the trials of a number of other accused.

Filming the Trial of Slobodan Milošević

One day in the summer of 2004, when I was spending more time in Belgrade than in The Hague working on the Insider project, the door to our office opened, and Geoffrey Nice walked in, followed by Dean Manning, an investigator for the Srebrenica case and behind him Michael Christoffersen and his film crew. Nice told me that a Danish

103. Map of Bosnia and Herzegovina showing Srebrenica and also the division between Republika Srpska and the Federation of Bosnia and Herzegovina. (Vladimír Dzuro)

television station had asked the tribunal for permission to make a documentary film about the trial of Milošević, and he wanted me to assist them with their filming in Croatia, particularly in Vukovar and Ovčara. Vukovar would be the first destination.

Like everything else in the former Yugoslavia, our cooperation began with a cup of coffee. We went to the banks of the Danube, where a restaurant with an outdoor garden had opened in a building still showing the scars of the JNA bombing in 1991. We discussed exactly what Christoffersen had in mind for the film and what scenes he wanted to shoot.

We first went to the bridge over the Vuka River, where Major Šljivanč-anin had blocked workers from the Red Cross and the ECMM from crossing. Then we visited Vukovar Hospital, the JNA barracks, and finally Ovčara.

The day ended with filming the memorial that stands over the mass grave, a permanent reminder of the suffering of the victims of the massacre. From Vukovar we moved 250 kilometers south to Srebrenica.

Before the war most of Srebrenica's inhabitants were Bosniaks, but the city and its surroundings had important implications for the Bosnian Serbs. Control of this region was necessary for the territorial integrity of Republika Srpska.

Shortly after the proclamation of this self-proclaimed republic, the Serbs unleashed ethnic cleansing around Srebrenica, but the local Bosniaks weren't about to give in easily. Under the leadership of Naser Orić, they raided neighboring villages, mercilessly slaughtering the Serb residents and looting their property. The Serbian side decided to choke off the Bosniak enclave and commenced a siege of the city. After three years the streets of the mining town, normally home to ten thousand people, were crammed with five times that number. The humanitarian debacle forced the UN to declare Srebrenica a safe zone and station the Dutch UNPROFOR contingent there to keep the peace.

Srebrenica was defended by soldiers of the Twenty-Eighth Division of the Bosnian army. On July 6, 1995, members of the Army of Republika Srpska, the VRS, with recruits from surrounding villages, began shelling the city in the early morning hours. Serbian artillery fire resumed two days later and hit the outpost of the lightly armed Dutch soldiers. The shelling intensified the following day, and thousands of civilians began fleeing the town. The Serbs took over another observation post of the UN without any fighting and took thirty Dutch soldiers hostage. The poorly armed Bosnian soldiers could no longer resist, and after losing about two thousand men, they retreated into the surrounding mountains. In panic thirty-five thousand Bosnians fled the city, and on July 11 Serbian troops moved in to occupy it.

In the afternoon Generals Ratko Mladić and Radislav Krstić, as well as other VRS officers triumphantly entered the city and began walking the empty streets in the presence of television crews. Mladić looked into the camera lens and boasted, "I present this city to the Serbian people. In remembrance of the uprising against the Turks, the time has come to pay back the Muslims."

Tens of thousands of refugees headed toward the UN compound in Potočari, about five kilometers north of Srebrenica. There they sought protection from the Dutch battalion. After five thousand people had squeezed into a makeshift camp close to the compound in just a few hours, the gates were ordered closed, and about twenty thousand civilians remained outside.

The next day the Serbs brought in dozens of buses and trucks to evacuate the women and children. The men, however, were marked for liquidation. Under Mladić's orders, they were driven to schools, factories, and the warehouses of nearby villages and systematically murdered. The mass slaughter of non-Serbs didn't stop until July 21. The tribunal later classified the massacre of civilians at Srebrenica as genocide.

Although the UNPROFOR units did not have either the mandate or the equipment to engage in heavy fighting, their operation around Srebrenica was seen as a failure, and the Dutch government resigned as a result. Starting in August 1995, mass graves with 8,373 bodies were uncovered, among which more than 6,000 of the murdered men have been identified.

Upon our arrival in Srebrenica, Dean Manning and I swapped roles. He became the guide and I the spectator. We went through the city, and Dean described to the filmmakers how the city was occupied by VRS units. We then visited the memorial site where the thousands of victims are buried. Just as Ovčara belongs to Vukovar, so does the village of Kravica to Srebrenica. The first of the victims were brought there on July 13, 1995. We looked through the warehouse of an agricultural cooperative, where in the late afternoon the Serbs dragged more than a thousand men captured around the village of Sandić. It

104. Reward of US$5 million for information on Radovan Karadžić and Ratko Mladić. (Vladimír Dzuro)

was right after one of the prisoners killed a Serbian policeman that the captors began executing the prisoners with automatic rifle fire, a bazooka, and by throwing grenades inside the warehouse. We found the walls peppered with holes from projectiles and the remnants of dried blood. It had been more than five years since the massacre and our arrival, but the sheer horror of what had happened in there was absolutely palpable. As in the case of the atrocities committed at the hangar in Ovčara, it was from the survivors, few as they were, that we got this information.

It's impossible to stand on the site of such a barbaric atrocity and not be affected. When it was time to go, the cameras were switched off, the microphones unplugged, and all the equipment put into the vehicles without a word. Silence prevailed during the whole drive back to Belgrade. Nobody from the television crew had any desire to talk because everything suddenly seemed trivial in the face of what had taken place in Kravica and other villages around Srebrenica in July 1995.

For the crimes committed at Srebrenica, the tribunal sentenced General Ratko Mladić, General Zdravko Tolimir, Colonel Ljubiša Beara, and Lieutenant Colonel Vujadin Popović to life in prison. The former president of the RS Radovan Karadžić was initially sentenced to forty years, but in March 2019 the appeal court changed the sentence to life in prison. Chief of staff Radislav Krstić and Lieutenant Drago Nikolić received thirty-five years, Momir Nikolić twenty-seven years, Vidoje Blagojević and Radivoj Miletić eighteen years, Lieutenant Colonel Dragan Obrenović and Ljubomir Borovčanin seventeen years, Lieutenant Colonel Vinko Pandurević thirteen years, Dragan Jokić nine years, and Dražen Erdemović and Milan Gvero five years each. Momčilo Perišić, the chief of staff of the Yugoslav army, was sentenced to twenty-seven years but was acquitted on appeal.

As for Slobodan Milošević, he did not receive justice in this life. At ten o'clock on the morning of March 11, 2006, he was found lifeless in his cell. The district prosecutor's office in The Hague ordered a thorough investigation into his death, conducted by the Dutch police and the coroner's office. A detailed autopsy was performed in the presence

Popović, Vujadin

Beara, Ljubiša

Nikolić, Drago

Miletić, Radivoje

Gvero, Milan

Pandurević, Vinko

Tolimir, Zdravko

Nikolić, Momir

Krstić, Radislav

Erdemović, Dražen

Karadžić, Radovan

Borovčanin, Ljubomir

Obrenović, Dragan

Blagojević, Vidoje

Jokić, Dragan

105. Individuals sentenced for war crimes in Srebrenica. (ICTY)

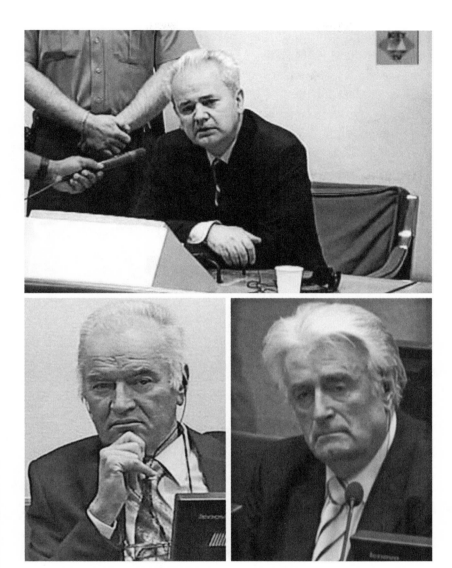

106. Accused Slobodan Milošević (*top*), sentenced Ratko Mladić (*lower left*), and Radovan Karadžić (*lower right*) before the tribunal. (ICTY)

of a pathologist from Serbia, and toxicological examinations were carried out by the Dutch Forensic Institute. The findings were submitted for assessment by specialists from several countries, including the Russian Federation, Serbia, Belgium, France, and Germany.

The results were conclusive. Despite the speculation in the media over the possibility that he had been murdered, investigators found no outward signs of violence, nor were there any traces of poisons or chemical substances in his body that could have caused his death. The investigation also ruled out the possibility that Milošević committed suicide. His death, which occurred between seven and nine o'clock that morning, was a natural one, caused by a heart attack.

7

Carla Del Ponte Visits Eastern Slavonia

One day in April 2002, I got a surprise call from Colonel Grujić, who asked for an urgent meeting. I said that I was at our Belgrade office at the moment but could drive to Vinkovci the next day for lunch at the Lady M. Since he didn't provide any details, I kept wondering what was so urgent and important as I headed west for Croatia in the morning.

The Lady M Hotel was almost like a second home for our team. The owners, Josip and Marija, welcomed me as usual with open arms and gave me a glass of wine as we caught up with each other. Suddenly I noticed the colonel standing in the doorway. He had arrived on time, and to judge by the serious look on his face, he had come to discuss something important. It turned out that Chief Prosecutor Carla Del Ponte had decided to visit the places in Eastern Slavonia that were related to the indictment of Slobodan Milošević.

The Croatian government had enormous interest in her visit and wanted to make sure it was to her complete satisfaction. It was on their behalf that the colonel wanted me to be personally involved in her visit, from planning to departure. Naturally I agreed, sure that our office would approve, and since fortune favors the prepared, as had certainly been our case a number of times, we embarked on the preliminary planning over a plate of delicious seafood.

We agreed that the chief prosecutor and Croatian government representatives, along with her entourage, would board a helicopter at the palace of former president Franjo Tuđman and fly to Erdut, where I would be waiting for them. Grujić told me that it wouldn't be just any helicopter, but Tuđman's. I understood what he was getting at. Tuđman had died in 1999, but many outside Croatia felt that he should have been brought before the tribunal for his part in the horrors of Bosnia. Anyway, the first briefing and meeting with survivors would take place in Erdut; then we would head south through the places where war crimes were committed around Vukovar. We would finish at a château in Ilok with a dinner party for Del Ponte. Her delegation would then fly back to Zagreb.

On May 6 I left Belgrade for Erdut accompanied by Žaneta Dufková, a sergeant from our security detail whom we nicknamed Action Janet.

We arrived to find Grujić there with local authorities and nongovernmental organizations, as well as a huge number of journalists from across the former Yugoslavia and foreign correspondents. The Croatian police were visibly on high alert. We looked up and trained our eyes on two black dots that were rapidly approaching. They circled overhead before one landed, and a squad of well-armed police officers in black coveralls jumped out and secured the perimeter for the second helicopter. After it landed, the chief prosecutor emerged along with Deputy Prime Minister Goran Granić, Justice Minister Ingrid Antičević-Marinović, and Patrick Lopez-Terrez.

The Croatian authorities made a determined effort to ensure not just the safety of the visit but to show who was really in charge in Eastern Slavonia. After a brief welcome, we left with a police escort for the former training center run by Arkan's irregulars and the seat of the Hadžić government. In the center itself, Del Ponte met survivors and the first group of nongovernmental organizations. She was often called the Iron Lady for the tough way she handled politicians and her own office, but here she was an ordinary woman, holding the hands of weeping mothers, oblivious to her crammed schedule. These too were ordinary people. They had come to share their tales of suffering with her, and that was the only thing that mattered at the moment. From Erdut our column of vehicles began Del Ponte's journey of discovery with

107. Sergeant Žaneta Dufková (*left*) and Vladimír Dzuro (*right*) at a shooting range in Belgrade. (Vladimír Dzuro)

108. Chief Prosecutor Carla Del Ponte in a helicopter flying to Eastern Slavonia. (Vladimír Dzuro)

helicopters watching overhead: Dalj, Borovo, Borovo Naselje, Vukovar, Ovčara, Lovas, Šarengrad, Ilok. My job was to inform her where we were going, what had happened there, and who was expecting us.

In Vukovar she held official talks with Deputy Prime Minister Granić. As soon as the door to the meeting room was closed, Del Ponte again became the Iron Lady. There was a press conference and another meeting with the families of the murdered or missing. From Vukovar we went to Ovčara, where she paid tribute at the memorial to the victims, and to Lovas, where in yet another dreadful incident villagers had been forced to walk through a minefield. Our delegation then went to the Catholic cemetery. Here Grujić showed us the place where his team had exhumed the remains of twenty-two murdered villagers.

We were two hours behind schedule by the time we arrived in Ilok. The Croatian government had organized a banquet in honor of Del Ponte at the local château. After it was over, she thanked me for the explanations, and I thanked her for coming to see what had to be seen. We shook hands, she got into a waiting BMW, waved to us, and the entire column sped off to an improvised heliport, where Tuđman's helicopter was waiting to take her back to Zagreb.

In spite of the tragedy that imbued almost my entire existence there in Eastern Slavonia, I couldn't help but feel elated by moments like these, to be in the center of such a major event. The entire security machinery of the Croatian government literally whirled around us; there was the personal security detail for the chief prosecutor, the bodyguards of the deputy prime minister, helicopters, special units, getting in and out of armored BMWs wherever we went, with hordes of journalists, television crews, and microphones at every stop. All this was quite normal for high government officials and for Del Ponte, who enjoyed this privilege as the chief prosecutor, but it was definitely not part of the normal life of a tribunal investigator, let alone a detective from Prague. On that day I basked in self-importance, and I have to say I rather liked it.

But fame is fleeting as they say and all but disappeared as the media circus moved on. I was standing in the dark with Žaneta, my bodyguard, at the intersection of some county roads in the middle of a

109. Chief Prosecutor Carla Del Ponte with the vice premier of Croatia, Goran Granić, at Ovčara (*top*) and at the minefield at Lovas (*bottom*). (Vladimír Dzuro)

field. Our solitude was a sobering reminder to get back to the work I was there to perform.

Because Žaneta had accompanied our convoy the entire day, she hadn't had the time or opportunity to fill up our Toyota service car. By our calculations we wouldn't make it back to Belgrade with what was left in the tank. We found a station in Ilok, but it was after ten o'clock in the evening and closed. We tried to find a local hotel for the night, but had no luck there either. Somehow I came up with the half-baked idea of calling our office in Belgrade to see if someone might not bring us a few canisters of fuel. They basically told me to get lost. So we crossed into Serbia in the hope of finding a gas station or hotel, but everywhere we went it was dark, and everything was closed.

We were absolutely desperate by the time we came to a little inn in Fruška Gora National Park. The bathroom had no running water, the bed linen spoke of one thousand and one nights, the shower reeked of mildew, and there was a mummified fly under my pillow. I took off my jacket, loosened my tie, and unbuttoned my shirt collar. I dared no more; I just carefully lay down on the bed and tried to sleep, but my head was still swimming with the day's events. Suddenly there was a soft knock on the door. It was Žaneta, still wearing her holster and Smith & Wesson gun. The door of her room had no lock, and there was no way she could fall asleep with her handgun under the pillow. The receptionist, not too convincingly, insisted there were no other available rooms, so my bodyguard took my bed while I went to crash on the sagging sofa against the wall. For a while we joked about the injustices of the world, lamenting how we were stuck in this fleapit while Carla Del Ponte was enjoying top-flight service and comfort in a suite at the Zagreb Sheraton.

In the morning we skipped breakfast and made our way to the nearest gas station. We were a pitiful sight when we checked in with our operating officer from UN Security. I went home, showered, and reflected on how I deserved that hovel in Fruška Gora for soaking up too much of the VIP scene. In the future I would do well to remember that the investigator's job isn't to walk on the red carpet; it's to look under it.

8

The International Tribunal in the Eyes of a Czech Prosecutor

For a long time, I was the only Czech national who employed at the Office of the Prosecutor. One day my colleague Brenda Hollis came to me and asked me to make a phone call to Prague. They were looking for lawyers to hire, and one of the prime candidates was a prosecutor they had made contact with but now couldn't reach. Soon I had Anna Richterová on the phone and was explaining the whole process of investigating war crimes to her. The call lasted for half an hour. Several months later my phone rang, and it was again her pleasant voice on the other end, but this time from the office of the tribunal. It was the start of many consultations on the cases before us, with Anna as the prosecutor and me the investigator.

Anna Richterová Recounts Her Experience with War Crime Prosecutions

In 1998, while I was working as a regional public prosecutor for Central Bohemia, I discovered a letter in our Prague office from the International Association of Prosecutors. It was written in English, and no one there gave it any thought. The chief told me to read it and do with it what I thought best. It said that the International Tribunal was looking for a new lawyer who was doing exactly what I was doing then in Prague. I jumped at the chance and sent my application to The Hague. Sometime in late September I got a call, and the male voice on the line informed me that they would like an interview with me, first over the phone. Two days later they called. I will never forget the question, what did I know about the conflict in the former Yugoslavia. My gut answer was, "Everything there is to know." They must have been impressed because they asked me to come in for a personal interview at the tribunal itself. Some three weeks later, I received a one-year contract from the UN.

I had two weeks to decide if I wanted to join the tribunal. Many people were telling me to forget it. My boss asked me, "What do you even know about war and all the legal aspects?" He was right: I knew practically nothing about the laws of war and crimes against humanity, but on the other hand, I had plenty of experience with investigating and gathering evidence and arguing cases in court. As I sat in my office and pondered whether to accept the offer, it suddenly occurred to me that another thirty years awaited me in this office if I let this chance go by. That same day I called to accept. Much later I learned that several hundred applicants from around the world had applied for that position. They chose seven lawyers, and I was one of them.

I was assigned to Team 1, which was led by British barrister Joanna Korner. We investigated crimes committed in Bosnia and Herzegovina by Bosnian Serbs of the Autonomous Region of Krajina (ARK). ARK was formed in September 1991 out of the original Association of Districts and Municipalities of Bosnian Krajina, which was dominated by Serbs and had its capital in Banja Luka. In January 1992 the Republic of the Serbian People of Bosnia and Herzegovina was declared a federal part of Yugoslavia, which also included the ARK. After Bosnia and Herzegovina was recognized as an independent country, the Bosnian Serbs declared themselves the Bosnian Serb Republic, later renamed Republika Srpska. They created their own army, the Army of Republika Srpska (VRS), which was essentially a former unit of the JNA.

Our investigations were focused on Radoslav Brđanin, the chairman of the Crisis Staff; Momir Talić, the commander of the First Army Corps of the Army of Republika Srpska; and Stojan Župljanin, the police chief of the ARK. All three had close links to the president of Republika

Srpska, Radovan Karadžić. They were indicted, and my first task was to modify the indictment to include newly acquired evidence. I was relieved because in Czech criminal procedure, once the indictment is issued, it means that all the material evidence has been gathered. It would be naive to presume the same here. When I asked where to find the evidence for a particular case, one of my colleagues led me to a corridor with a dozen giant metal cabinets. Each one was crammed full of various files. I was assured I would find it there.

A huge mountain of documents gradually rose on top of my desk, some of them naturally without reference numbers, so there was no point perusing them in the computer system. There were various reports and interrogation records; nothing was organized in the way I was used to in Prague. What was completely clear is that an indictment from the tribunal is different from the Czech system. It provides only a minimum of evidence justifying issuance of indictment against a particular person. It has to be approved by the court, and only then can an arrest warrant be issued. My despair was compounded by the fact that nobody explained anything properly to me. It was truly a case of learning how to swim, and time was of the essence.

Brđanin was accused of crimes committed in twelve of the sixteen districts of the ARK. The only possible approach was systematically collect and analyze the evidence for each district or municipality in chronological order. First, I created a time line of events in the individual districts, which not only facilitated taking statements from witnesses but also filled in gaps in the evidence as the investigation went along. At first glance it looked simple and, importantly, logical, but it had never been done by our team or by the others. My boss, Joanna, who had kind of ignored me because my English was far from the level of her Oxford training, suddenly began to take me seriously. My system for categorizing evidence according to place and time was greatly welcomed and adopted by the other teams in the Office of the Prosecutor. Also for the first time in my life, I could appreciate the Russian I had been forced to learn in school because it had taught me how to read the Cyrillic script, and my Czech gave me a fair understanding

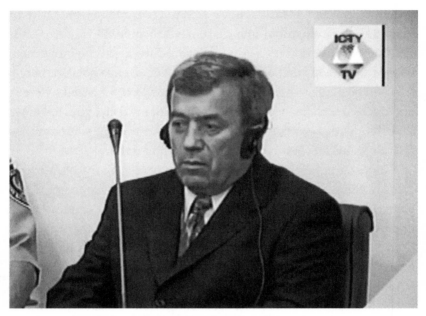

110. Accused Radoslav Brđanin before the tribunal. (ICTY)

of Serbo-Croatian, something the vast majority of my colleagues had no clue about.

In April 1992, after the occupation of Prijedor, the Bosnian Serbs were afraid of an armed uprising by the Croats and the Bosnians. To keep that from happening, they set up detention camps in Omarska, Keraterm, and Trnopolje the next month. These camps gradually filled with people suspected of organizing and taking part in an insurgency against the Serbian population. The condition inside them can be compared to the concentration camps run by the Nazis in World War II. They were originally supposed to operate for just a few days but were not closed until the autumn of 1992 and then only after pressure from the international community.

The statements of the witnesses were appalling. We simply couldn't believe these events could happen in Europe at the end of the twentieth century, just several hundred kilometers from Vienna, Budapest, and Prague—beatings, torture, rape, and murder. For their part in creating this atmosphere, Brđanin and Talić were put on trial by the tribunal. Brđanin was found guilty and sentenced to thirty years in prison, but Talić died of illness during the trial.

For me the most tragic moments came when survivors would describe the torture and murder of their children or parents. Every report I read could have filled an entire book. For the main trials involving Prijedor, we had the testimony of a number of survivors of these camps. Their testimonies were added to other indictments, including one for Karadžić.

One of the witnesses for the prosecution was Samir Polak. In 1992 Polak was just nineteen years old. After several weeks in the detention camp at Omarska, he learned that his father was also imprisoned there. After some time they managed to get the same cell. The Serbs often took his father away for interrogation, where he was brutally beaten. One day at five o'clock in the afternoon, they came for him, and he did not return until an hour before midnight. He was terrified and wouldn't say anything. An hour after midnight they came for him again. "I clearly remember how he stood up and went to the door," Samir recalled. "He turned around, looked at me, smiled, and walked out. I never saw him again." This was the everyday reality of everyone who ended up in these camps. One day they would come for your loved ones, and you would never see them again.

The district of Prijedor was the scene of many human tragedies. One day more than two hundred men from a place called Brdo were brought to the Keraterm camp and locked in one of the halls without any food or water. One of the witnesses who testified before the tribunal recalled how after several days some soldiers arrived and shot the lot of them. The witness described the events of the next morning: "The door to our hangar opened, and the guards herded in volunteers to haul away the dead. Outside we could see a pile of corpses with blood everywhere. A truck arrived, and the inmates were forced to load the dead bodies on top of it. It's a terrible sight, something that haunts me to this day. The thing I can't stop thinking about, which I suppose

111. (*top*) Map of the western part of the Republika Srpska showing the town of Prijedor and the concentration camps at Keraterm, Trnopolje, and Omarska. (Vladimír Dzuro)

112. (*bottom*) The Omarska concentration camp. (ICTY)

I will have to live with forever, was the sight of the truck leaving and all that blood dripping from it along the way."

A similarly cruel fate awaited another 190 men, also from the Prijedor area, who were detained at the Trnopolje camp. One day they were taken to a place called Koričanske stjene near the town of Dolnji Vakuf and shot. A witness who survived the ghastly ordeal told the tribunal: "Our bus stopped, and a man in a red beret ordered us to get out. We were lined up at the edge of the cliff and then told to take three steps back and drop to our knees. They started shooting, and the man in front of me slumped backward, causing me to fall on my back. The man behind me, who was missing part of his head, fell directly on top of me. When the shooting finally stopped, I could hear only the groans of the dying. After a while there was silence, and I realized that I was probably the only one to survive."

The mayor of Prijedor was Milomir Stakić, who incredibly was a doctor by profession. He was personally involved in establishing the detention camps of Omarska, Keraterm, and Trnopolje. In October 1992 Stakić also took part in the murder of two hundred people who were hastily taken away from the Keraterm and Omarska camps before they were closed. For these crimes, he was sentenced to forty years in prison. Also convicted for operating the camps were Zoran Žigić (twenty-five years), Mlađo Radić (twenty years), Duško Sikirica (fifteen years), Predrag Banović (8ight years), Miroslav Kvočka (seven years), Milojica Kos (six years), Dragoljub Prcać (five years), Damir Došen (five years), and Dragan Kolundžija (three years).

We investigated other crimes committed in Sanski Most. Most of the Bosniaks and Croats fled from the town in 1992 after a massacre of some inhabitants, one of which took place directly on the bridge across the River Sana. My work on this case brought me into contact with a survivor, Raif Begić. He managed to flee Bosnia and had been living elsewhere in Europe for several years. Like most of the people I met in the former Yugoslavia, he was very hospitable and agreed to testify before the tribunal.

Žigić, Zoran   Sikirica, Duško   Došen, Damir   Kolundžija, Dragan

Kvočka, Miroslav   Prcać, Dragoljub   Kos, Milojica   Radić, Mlađo

113. Sentenced before the tribunal for war crimes committed in the Omarska, Keraterm, and Trnopolje concentration camps. (ICTY)

In our interview with him, he described how Serbian soldiers rounded up the men from his village and brought them to the bridge: "One by one, we had to jump into the water so the soldiers could take shots at us there. When I jumped, the current luckily pulled me under the bridge. I quickly took off my white T-shirt and let it float downstream. The soldiers started shooting at it, and I swam underwater to the dense reeds on the side, where I hid."

After the main trials, Begić returned to Bosnia to put these events on film for me. He mapped out the village, the road leading up to the bridge, the river, and the place where he hid and later made his escape from. I still have this short film as a reminder of our encounter.

One of the witnesses I questioned in court in the case of Sanski Most was Grgo Stojić, a Croat who was the only survivor of an attack on the village of Škrljevita by Serbian gunmen under the command of Daniluško Kajtez. Stojić suffered serious injuries that left him an invalid. He often told us how he was permanently disabled, couldn't work, and only desired a life "with some decency." Because Stojić knew the perpetrators of this atrocity, he called them out by name during his testimony, which was broadcast in Bosnia, Croatia, and Serbia. A few months later, we received the news that he had died of gas poisoning. I found it hard to believe. He lived in a tiny house where there was next to no equipment, and the gas stop was outside on the front of the house. We asked the Bosnian authorities to investigate his death, but they still concluded it was an accident. I remain unconvinced.

Reading the interviews and listening to the stories of witnesses who survived these massacres or were forced to watch their loved ones murdered before their eyes sometimes brought tears to my eyes. But I was far from the only one who couldn't help becoming emotionally involved. I still think about the woman who was led away by Serbian soldiers along with her husband, two small children, and a large group of villagers. Along the way the soldiers took a group of men, including her husband, and shot them on the spot. The others were taken to an industrial building and locked up there without food or water. Maybe four days later, the soldiers dragged her away from her children and took her and several other women to an abandoned house. There they repeatedly raped them. She managed to escape and make it back to the village, where she believed her children had been taken, but they were nowhere to be found. She never stopped looking for them, and any time a mass grave is discovered, she goes there out of desperation.

Survivors know their family members are dead and that no miracle is going to bring them back. This particular woman also knew her children were gone, but she was still looking for them in the hope that she could at least give them a proper burial. She also perhaps harbored the secret yearning that miracles do happen and that one day her children might come home to her. When she was telling her story before the tribunal, everyone except the accused had tears in their eyes. As the prosecutor I had the duty to remain professional throughout, but I could not make it to the end without my emotions overcoming me as well.

The tribunal only goes after the people at the top and only in special instances after those who actually commit the murders, rapes, and nameless other atrocities. In one instance a woman whose husband and three sons were murdered by Serbian irregulars willingly offered her testimony, including the exact details of how it happened. Then she learned that the person to be charged for these heinous acts was a certain Radoslav Brđanin, the chairman of the Crisis Staff of Banja Luka. She was completely dumbfounded. I tried to explain to her that he had encouraged the hatred that gave rise to these crimes, but she did not understand our priorities or prosecution strategy. She said she didn't know this man and would not testify against him. She wanted the bastards who had slaughtered her husband and children, to look them in the eye and point them out for all the world to see what kind of scum they were.

Witnesses from all districts told us about the systematic beatings, torture, and murder. This persecution of the non-Serbian population reached such a fever pitch that most of them were happy to leave the ARK. We found the dead from the detention camps, from other camps, and those murdered directly in their villages in mass graves, not only in Prijedor but throughout Bosnia and Herzegovina. My involvement included finding the graves, exhuming the bodies, and trying to identify them. Shortly after my arrival at the tribunal, I joined one exhumation at a place called Kevljani. By the time I got there, a total of seventy-three bodies and seventy-one disarticulated body parts had been removed and the pit partially refilled.

Identifying them was very difficult because they had lain there for seven years. Fortunately, quite a few personal documents and clothing made of synthetic fibers were discovered as well. The survivors tried to identify their loved ones according to markings or clothing as well as they could remember. If immediate identification was impossible, we tried DNA tests. Conducting autopsies in makeshift morgues with family members present was always a very emotional experience. Although I was at the site for only two days, I will never forget the piles of rotting human corpses and the sufferings of the families.

After the end of the trial against Brđanin, I was switched to the case against Momčilo Krajišnik, the speaker of the Bosnian Serb parliament. He was directly connected to Brđanin, so although another team led the investigation, I quickly became familiar with the evi-

114. (*top*) Anna Richterová prosecuting the case of Radoslav Brđanin. (ICTY)

115. (*bottom*) Anna Richterová at the mortuary in Bosnia and Herzegovina. (Anna Richterová)

116. Accused Momčilo Krajišnik before the tribunal. (ICTY)

dence. During the course of his trial, I went to Belgrade to interview Mićo Stanišić. He also stood accused, but it was interesting to hear his version of events that witnesses had already described to me. He was the minister of the interior of the Republika Srpska in 1992 but stubbornly insisted that he knew absolutely nothing of what was going on in various parts of Bosnia. He claimed that all he did in Pale was sit with other members of the government and drink coffee. Stanišić refused to admit the authenticity of documents that clearly showed his ministry issuing and receiving reports and being in close contact with the police headquarters of each municipality. His denial was dismissed by the court.

Before Christmas of 2005, Deputy Chief Prosecutor Norman Farell assigned me to the case of Milan Martić, which was ready to go to trial. For five years I had been gathering evidence related to crimes committed by Serbs in Bosnia and Herzegovina. I knew all the details and had questioned scores of witnesses. This new case would take me to the Republic of Serbian Krajina. The perpetrators were also Serbs, but this was another country. I had just a couple of weeks to familiarize myself with the evidence and make something coherent of all of it, so I took the indictment and stacks of material home with me for the holidays. There was a huge amount of documents to study, but I had to do it to prepare myself for questioning witnesses.

The events in the Republic of Serbian Krajina had occurred almost simultaneously with the events in Bosnia and Herzegovina, the major difference being that most of the victims were Croats. Arrests, beatings, murder, rape, deportation, and the destruction of churches had been going on since 1991, and one of the active participants in all of it was Martić and his police force. It was through his case that I met Milan Babić. The first time I saw him was in early 2006. He was serving his sentence in Great Britain but had been brought to the prison in Scheveningen as a witness against Martić. It was a unique experience. Babić gave the impression of someone who had lost everything, and one look into the blank stare of his eyes confirmed this. He told us how he was now the enemy of all, both Croats and Serbs: for the Croats because he's a Serb; for the Serbs because he accepted the z-4 peace plan, which led to the fall of the RSK. He had no doubt about his own guilt nor any qualms about testifying against Milošević.

A month later Babić also testified against Martić. The cross-examination by the prosecution was set to begin when, on the morning of March 5, 2006, I got a phone call from the chief prosecutor informing me that Babić had committed suicide in his cell. It was a huge shock for me, but there was nothing to do except soldier on. I spent nearly a year in the courtroom with Martić. In all that time, he never showed the slightest remorse about the fate of those who testified against him. That was pretty much the case for nearly all the defendants. Slowly their ranks began to swell. The police chief from Banja Luka, Stojan Župljanin, managed to stay on the run until June

117. Accused Mićo Stanišić and Stojan Župljanin before the tribunal. (ICTY)

2008. He was charged together with Stanišić, the minister who only drank coffee. I was assigned to the case after the trial of Martić came to an end, only this time as a senior prosecutor.

I put together a team, we prepared a full indictment with all the evidence, and everything indicated a big trial in the works. But we were subjected to pressure from the outset, mostly because of the strategy for the planned closure of the tribunal. We were advised to limit the charges and focus only on the really important things, such as the more serious crimes. Because the time for our presentation in court was also restricted, we had to calculate how many minutes to spend with each witness. It was incredibly exhausting for us to have to explain to the witnesses why their suffering was no longer the big deal it had once been.

Maybe this was the reason why I decided to leave the tribunal and accept an offer made to me by Eurojust, the European Union agency for judicial cooperation in criminal matters. It meant little change physically because it is also based in The Hague. Joanna Korner took over my case and brought it to a close. Župljanin and Stanišić were both found guilty of war crimes and crimes against humanity and sentenced to twenty-two years each.

Despite my disagreement with truncating the trials, I consider my work in the Office of the Prosecutor to have been a unique experience, and I have never once regretted coming on board at the tribunal. I have a deeper respect for people and their cultural differences, and I now notice and appreciate ordinary things that I might not have had I not encountered such monstrous and incomprehensible evil.

After seventeen years with the International Tribunal and Eurojust, Anna Richterová returned to the Czech Republic, where she works for the Supreme Public Prosecutor's Office in the city of Brno.

9

The Reckoning

Ovčara

After the arrest and extradition of Slobodan Milošević, the political situation in the Federal Republic of Yugoslavia slowly began to change, and the old Balkans changed with it. A new government strove to bring Serbia closer to the European Union. Removing the obstacles, however, was a very painful process, and one of the conditions was cooperation with the tribunal. The first of the Vukovar Three arraigned under this new atmosphere was Colonel Mrkšić, who had been in command of the First Guards Motorized Brigade and Operational Group South during military operations around the city. After the fall of Vukovar in November 1991, he was promoted to general and given command of the Eighth JNA Task Force deployed in Kordun, Croatia. Under huge pressure from the international community, Mrkšić surrendered to Serbian police on May 15, 2002, and was extradited to The Hague that same day.

The second of the trio who gave himself up to the Serbian authorities was Captain Miroslav Radić, who at the time of the conflict in Vukovar commanded an infantry unit of the brigade. He surrendered on April 21, 2003, and was extradited to the tribunal on May 17. The last was Major Veselin Šljivančanin, the security officer with the brigade who also commanded a military police battalion. After operations wrapped up in Vukovar, he was promoted to lieutenant colonel. In 1996 he was made a full colonel and transferred to the Military Academy in Belgrade. Šljivančanin had no intention of giving himself up to the tribunal voluntarily, and he made several statements to the press that he had a grenade ready for anyone who came to arrest him. During the night of June 13, 2003, a special unit of the Serbian police force arrested him nevertheless. He had boasted that no one would be able to bring him alive to The Hague, but that's exactly what happened on July 1.

The trial of the Vukovar Three began on October 11, 2005, and concluded on September 27, 2007. Mrkšić was found guilty and sentenced to twenty years in prison, Šljivančanin got five years, and Radić was acquitted of the charges. Šljivančanin appealed, but the Appeals Chamber increased the sentence to seventeen years. After Serbian military officer Miodrag Panić testified that Mrkšić had never informed Šljivančanin of his order to withdraw JNA troops from Ovčara, which was the only thing holding back the Serbian irregulars from massacring the prisoners, the chamber reconsidered and gave Šljivančanin a sentence of ten years in prison.

We were finally able to track down those who did the actual torturing and killing at Ovčara. Their names had been on a list since January 1998, but we were unable to bring charges against them. The International Criminal Tribunal had been set up to try those at the top who were responsible for these crimes taking place. The murderers themselves would have to face justice in the individual countries of the former Yugoslavia. At the end of June 2003, prosecutor Jan Wubben and I hosted a meeting in our Belgrade office with Đorđe Ostojić, Serbia's supreme prosecutor, and Vladimir Vukčević, the prosecutor in charge of investigating war crimes. Vukčević mentioned the investigation conducted by his office into the massacre at Ovčara. I told him we had a mountain of evidence, including the names of the perpetrators, but it was up to our own prosecutor to release this information. Later that year Del Ponte did just that, handing over the documents to the Serbian authorities in person so that they could go after this group.

Vukčević and his team went right to work and issued arrest warrants for the suspects on our list. They were apprehended, and in December Vukčević issued the first indictment against Miroljub Vujović and others. Then came the second indictment, eleven defendants in the case of Lančužanin and others. The third and final case was against Predrag Dragović. On December 12, 2005, the District Court in Belgrade convicted fourteen people of war crimes at Ovčara, while two were acquitted due to a lack of evidence. On November 18, 2006, the Supreme Court of Serbia threw out the convictions and ordered a new trial. On February 12, 2009, the court convicted a total of thirteen people: Miroljub Vujović, Stanko Vujanović, Predrag Milojević, Đorđe Šošić, Miroslav Đanković, Ivan Atanasijević, and Saša Radak were each sentenced to twenty years in prison. Milan Vojnović received fifteen years, Jovica Perić thirteen years, Nađa Kalaba nine years, Milan Lančužanin six years, and Goran Mugoša and Predrag Dragović five years each.

The Court of Appeals confirmed eleven of the sentences but lowered the one for Atanasijević, the only defendant to admit guilt, from twenty years to fifteen. They increased, however, the sentence of Kalaba from nine years to eleven. She was Vujanović's wife and, incidentally, the only woman among the defendants. The last sentence handed down for the massacre at Ovčara went to Petar Ćirić, whose torture and slaying of a female victim as related earlier was sickening even by the standards of this conflict. He got fifteen years.

The path to justice in this life is often a very agonizing one for victims, and there has been no better example than Ovčara. In 2014 the Supreme Court of Cassation told the Court of Appeals to reconsider, and until then the killers were to be released to house arrest with protective supervision. The appellate court returned another final judgment on November 24, 2017. Đanković and Radak also had their sentences reduced from twenty to fifteen years in prison, while Vojnović, Perić, Lančužanin, and Dragović were all acquitted. Šošić was dead by then.

It took fourteen years for this case to finally draw to a close in Serbia. Of the twenty-four accused, only eleven were convicted in the end, and some of those who were freed got off on technicalities. As for the JNA soldiers who walked away, doubtless knowing the fate in store for the victims, many of them testified at the trials, but no charges have been brought against them or are likely to be for aiding and abetting the murder of two hundred civilians. They were simply not senior enough.

Lovas

Working on our recommendation, Carla Del Ponte decided to include the incident of the minefield near Lovas in the indictment against Milošević and Hadžić. I was first told this terrible story back in 1996 by Marko Filić. He was born in 1928, married at the age of twenty, had two daughters, and lived happily in his village, where he owned a small shop. Like other Croats who lived there, he was arrested during the war. Even though he was over sixty years old, the soldiers brutally beat him and imprisoned him at the Zadruga cooperative, where he witnessed several of his fellow citizens beaten and murdered. On October 18, 1991, members of the JNA and the Territorial Defense and irregulars from the Dušan the Great unit took him, despite his serious injuries, and fifty other civilians to a field near the Borovo shoe factory. Along the way their captors randomly shot dead a villager.

Filić tearfully recalled: "We reached the field and they ordered us to form a line by holding hands and then to proceed slowly to the other end of the field, making sure we stepped on all vegetation. I knew from serving with the partisans in the World War II that they were herding us into a minefield. The guards watched from the side at a safe distance, shouting orders at us. When we safely made it to the end, we had no choice but to go back, again hand in hand, toward the Borovo factory. Suddenly, after about ten meters, I saw a mine and the wire that led from it. I shouted to Ivan Kraljević on my right about it, but it was too late. I don't know if he was shot from behind or simply fell on the mine, but a deafening explosion jolted me to the ground. I was hit by shrapnel in my leg, back, and neck. I lost sight in my right eye and fell unconscious. I came to when I heard a voice say, "Cease fire!" I struggled to crawl into a ditch beside the road. I was bleeding and lost consciousness again until someone found me, pulled me out of the ditch, and put me on the back of a truck. I vaguely remember being driven somewhere before we stopped outside the hospital in Šid, in Serbia."

The principal suspect in this atrocity was Ljuban Devetak, a trained economist who was also the director of the agricultural cooperative Zadruga Lovas. After the war broke out in Eastern Slavonia, he was appointed commander of the local militia with unlimited authority. At the end of 2003, the chief prosecutor gave the Serbian authorities the information gathered by the tribunal on Lovas, thereby allowing them to open their own investigation and try this accused war criminal in Serbia.

On May 28, 2007, Devetak was arrested by Serbian police and formally charged six months later. The trial opened in 2012 at Belgrade District Court. Since the earlier testimonies, several witnesses had died—Mate Kraljević, Slavko Luketić, Đuka Radojčaj, Andrija Balić, and Marko Filić, but those who were still alive testified again. The testimony they had previously given was used along with our evidence. Devetak was found guilty and sentenced to twenty years in prison. Convicted with him were Milan Radojčić (thirteen years) and Milan Devčić and Željko Krnjajić (both ten years). Four former members of the JNA were also convicted of this crime. Miodrag Dimitrijević got ten years, Darko Perić and Radovan Vlajković five years, and Radisav Josipović four years. The Dušan the Great irregulars were also sentenced: Petronije Stevanović got fourteen years, Zoran Kosijer nine years, Saša Stojanović and Jovan Dimitrijević both eight year, and Dragan Bačić and Aleksandar Nikolaidis six years each.

In all the Belgrade District Court gave the perpetrators of the Lovas minefield incident a total of 128 years in prison, but as with Ovčara, the Court of Appeals quashed the verdicts in 2014, and the new trials are ongoing as of this writing. In that time Devetak, Bačić, Nikolaidis, and Radojčić have all died. There is no word on whether any deathbed confession might have eased their final moments.

10

Final Words

What follows are personal reflections on the work of the ICTY and its achievements by Clint John Williamson, U.S. ambassador-at-large for war crime issues (2006–9); Stjepan Mesić, second president of the Republic of Croatia (2000–2010), fourteenth president of the Presidium of the Socialist Federal Republic of Yugoslavia (June–December 1991); Michael Žantovský, ambassador of the Czech Republic to the United States (1992–97), to the State of Israel (2004–9), and to the United Kingdom (2009–15), chairman of the Senate Committee on Foreign Affairs, Defense and Security (1996–2002), executive director of the Václav Havel Library in Prague (since September 2015); and Ralph R. Johnson, U.S. ambassador (ret.), principal deputy high representative, Office of the High Representative, Sarajevo, Bosnia-Herzegovina (1999–2001).

Clint John Williamson

On a cool, blustery morning in May 1994, I walked into a nondescript building in The Hague, which had recently become the seat of the newly created International Criminal Tribunal for the former Yugoslavia (ICTY). I came there as a secondee from the U.S. Department of Justice, where I had served as an organized crime prosecutor, and was assigned by my government for what was supposed to be a one-year posting in the Netherlands. The tribunal, which had been established pursuant to a resolution of the United Nations Security Council in late 1993, had been slow to commence operations, so in an effort to help it get started, the U.S. government sent a number of prosecutors, investigators, and analysts to assist in its work. I was one of the first to arrive, and when I began work as a trial attorney in the ICTY Office of the Prosecutor, I was only the seventh staff member in an office that would ultimately grow to employ hundreds. Having arrived so early in the life of the tribunal and having stayed there as long as I did (it turned out to be seven years rather than the one year initially anticipated), I was able to observe and participate in many of the momentous events that shaped the court. Therefore, few people could have been more pleased than I to see the ICTY achieve the successes that it eventually did and become a well-established institution by the time I left in 2001.

In the early days of the ICTY, however, success was far from assured. Very few people thought that the ICTY would accomplish anything meaningful. It had been created by the Security Council just after an uneasy peace had been established in Croatia, while the war in Bosnia-Herzegovina was still raging, and at a point when the war in Kosovo still lay in the future. In Croatia and even more so in Bosnia, the world powers had seemed absolutely impotent in the face of determined nationalist leaders in the Balkans who had introduced the world to the concept of "ethnic cleansing" and had pursued it with such vigor. People from around the world had looked on in horror as the United Nations peacekeeping force—perhaps the most powerful military contingent ever assembled under UN command—had been utterly feckless when it came to stopping the killing or even containing the conflict in a real way.

So the idea that a war crimes court could impose its authority on the region and bring to justice those responsible for the worst crimes committed in Europe since World War II was quite farfetched. Most observers speculated that, at best, the court might prosecute a few low-level camp guards and then fade away. No one realistically envisaged the court indicting senior figures like Slobodan Milošević or Radovan Karadžić, much less ever getting them into custody, especially at a time when they were thumbing their noses at the international community and getting away with it. Thus the ICTY commenced its work with very low expectations and with virtually no assurance of support from the body that had created it—the UN Security Council.

This was the climate surrounding the ICTY as I prepared to go to The Hague in the spring of 1994. Before leaving Washington, though, I had an opportunity to attend a meeting that had been arranged by the U.S. Department of State with the surviving war crimes prosecutors from the Nuremberg Tribunal. The State Department had brought the ICTY secondees together with these men—almost all of whom were in their eighties at that point—so that we might learn from their experiences prosecuting Nazi war criminals in the aftermath of World War II. It was indeed a fascinating afternoon as they recounted their participation in the trials of Hermann Goering, Joachim van Ribbentrop, Rudolph Hess, and other German leaders. It also brought home the fact that it had been a very long time since the global community had undertaken an effort to prosecute war criminals in an international tribunal; these elderly men were the only ones in the world who had had direct experience doing so.

For those of us who were about to embark on this new effort, however, the passage of fifty years since the last attempt to do something of this sort was not the most significant concern. Rather, for us the most worrying factor was the different circumstances under which we would be operating as opposed to the conditions under which the Nuremberg investigations and trials were conducted. The Nuremberg (and Tokyo) trials had taken place after an overwhelming military victory and during a period of military occupation by the conquering powers. Thus the Allies could arrest any suspects at will, could seize any evidence they needed, and could compel cooperation of witnesses and others who might assist the investigative efforts. By contrast at the ICTY we were trying to accomplish the same results as Nuremberg but during an ongoing conflict where outside military power was so limited that the UN could not even protect humanitarian aid transports. At Nuremberg compliance with the court's orders was ensured through robust military force. At the ICTY we were totally reliant on the goodwill of governments headed by the very people we desired to prosecute. We had no way of compelling anyone to do anything or of ensuring that evidence could be secured or witnesses protected. In short much of our work was conducted in a hostile environment, while at Nuremberg those running the court controlled the environment around them entirely.

So skepticism about the ICTY's potential success was totally warranted. But the challenges that faced the ICTY from the outset led to ingenuity and innovative approaches that, over time, established the court as a force to be reckoned with. Working against incredible odds and often in very dangerous scenarios, investigators and prosecutors at the ICTY invariably found ways to produce the results they were seeking. The commitment and doggedness of a handful of individuals were critical in this equation.

I had the privilege of working very closely with my team for six years at the ICTY, after they joined the tribunal in 1995. Side by side we worked to piece together the fate of two hundred men and boys taken from the hospital in Vukovar, Croatia, and murdered on a horrific November day in 1991. We worked together to unearth mass graves, to pursue the most notorious paramilitary leader from the Balkan wars all over Europe, and perhaps most significantly, to plan and execute the arrest of the first war criminal by international military forces.

The Investigator tells stories that explain how the ICTY evolved from what was perceived as a toothless tiger to an institution that struck fear in the hearts of all those in the former Yugoslavia with blood on their hands.

It is a fascinating story, but its ending was not preordained. As I have noted, few people thought that the ICTY would be successful, and it certainly had a difficult first few years. Then slowly, ever so slightly, it began to make progress. More and more of those who were indicted came into its custody, the NATO force that replaced the UN peacekeeping mission in Bosnia began to arrest suspects, the ICTY's indictments began to move up the chain of command and target those at the highest levels of leadership, the political dynamic on the ground shifted, and leaders like Karadžić and Milošević lost power. Nevertheless, there was still strong resistance—particularly in Serbia—to cooperation with the tribunal.

By the time I was appointed U.S. ambassador-at-large for war crime issues in 2006, however, only a handful of indictees had not been arrested, but these included two of the most notorious figures from the wars—Radovan Karadžić and Ratko Mladić. Although I was dealing with a global portfolio of issues as ambassador, I was understandably quite focused on seeing the remaining ICTY indictees brought to justice. I worked closely with my counterparts in European governments and spent considerable time and energy pressing the Serbian president, the prime minister, and security services to do everything they could to see that Karadžić and Mladić were arrested. Over time the pressure brought by the international community, but particularly the conditionality for further integration into Europe imposed by the European Union, had its desired effect. By 2011 all those indicted by the ICTY had been arrested and taken to The Hague for trial.

As I write, the ICTY is completing its last trial. With its conclusion the ICTY will have prosecuted 161 individuals who bore responsibility for orchestrating and executing the most heinous crimes in Europe since the end of World War II. Those responsible for the massacre of eight thousand men and boys at Srebrenica, the siege of Sarajevo, the concentration camps at Prijedor, the shelling of Dubrovnik, the destruction of Vukovar, and the campaign of persecution and killing in Kosovo have all been brought to justice. Perhaps most significantly those in the highest echelons of leadership, such as Radovan Karadžić, Ratko Mladić, and Slobodan Milošević, have all been prosecuted. These men who once seemed so invincible, whom the world perceived as being beyond the reach of the law, have found themselves confined in prison cells and standing in court to face their accusers.

This is not to say, though, that everything at the ICTY has been perfect. It has been too slow to complete its work, its judgments have been inconsistent in their findings, and I have disagreed with the reasoning behind a number of decisions and rulings.

While working at the ICTY and in the period afterward when I served as a policy official and diplomat, I have also been critical of many who have worked there, including judges, who have made little or no effort to understand the history of the former Yugoslavia, the complexities of the conflict, or the political and operational dynamics that transpired under the surface and that profoundly influenced the events that played out on the ground. This lack of understanding has sometimes led to verdicts that completely baffle the people in the Balkans who lived through the conflict and who understand all too well who was responsible for the crimes that irrevocably impacted their lives.

As a result it is hard to say that the ICTY has been a complete success. On balance, however, I think that over time history will judge the tribunal in a kind light. It has established an objective historical record of the Yugoslav conflict that will help to defuse factually inaccurate myths in future years, it has brought to justice those who bore the most responsibility for the worst crimes committed in the wars of the 1990s, and ultimately, I think that most will conclude that the ICTY got it right more often than it got it wrong in terms of its judgments. In doing so it has also established jurisprudence that has redefined international humanitarian law and has given us a body of law that is now generally accepted as the governing standard for conduct in warfare. Its greatest impact, though, goes far beyond the Balkans and is truly global in its nature, for it is the ICTY that gave birth to the new era of international justice.

When it opened its doors in 1994, few people could have foreseen that within a few short years, the ICTY would be joined by an array of international war crimes courts including the International Criminal Tribunal for Rwanda, the Special Court for Sierra Leone, the Khmer Rouge Tribunal, and ultimately the permanent International Criminal Court. What people once thought unimaginable—that a sitting head of state could be held accountable for war crimes committed at his command—has now become expected. The ICTY's prosecution of Slobodan Milošević led the way, but it has now been followed by the trials of Charles Taylor of Liberia, Saddam Hussein of Iraq, Hissene

Habre of Chad, and the indictment of Omar al-Bashir of Sudan. While these trials are still not routine, they have moved in twenty short years from the realm of the unimaginable to a very real possibility, and at the very least, there is now an expectation that leaders who unleash atrocity crimes will be held accountable. None of this would have happened had the ICTY been the failure that people expected. Its success changed the whole dynamic for international justice, and it destroyed the idea—hopefully forever—that political and military leaders can act with impunity when they unleash the worst crimes imaginable on innocent populations.

Credit is due, then, to the ICTY for bringing us to this point. Admittedly, international justice is still far from universal or uniform in its application, and this may never change altogether. Existing as it does at the intersection of global politics, national and regional interests, and law, it will be hard to overcome every challenge that the field of international justice faces. Even if we acknowledge this fact, however, we must recognize that what has been accomplished in twenty short years is breathtaking. Many people who would have escaped with complete impunity for horrendous crimes have been brought to justice, and many more will be in the future due to the framework of international justice institutions and processes that were set in motion with the creation of the ICTY. It all depended at the outset, though, on a relatively few people who made the ICTY a success, and this book tells their story.

Stjepan Mesić

The Hague Tribunal, an international court of justice established by the United Nations in order to try the perpetrators of war crimes in the region of former Yugoslav Federation and Rwanda, is a unique institution—unique because of its founders, because of the proceedings brought before it, and because of the activities of mainly anonymous investigators (at least with regard to the general public) who gathered evidence in the field and ensured (in many cases) that those who were suspected either of ordering or of perpetrating war crimes were brought to justice.

During my term of office as president of the Republic of Croatia, I had contacts with chief prosecutors of The Hague tribunal and occasionally also with the investigators working in Croatia. I supported wholeheartedly the international tribunal first of all because I knew that out there in the field there was neither the political will nor the readiness to try the war criminals and often even to acknowledge that war crimes had occurred. Each side was, of course, more than willing to denounce the crimes of "the other side," but each tried hard to hide the criminals within its own ranks, and more often than not they were celebrated as national heroes (we were witnesses to an illustration of such a mind-set when, in Bosnia and Herzegovina, Biljana Plavšić of the Republika Srpska and Dario Kordić of the Croatian National Corps respectively completed serving their sentences). It was clear to me then that in the absence of an external incentive local judicial bodies could not, and would not, tackle the problem of war crimes in a way that disregarded the ethnicity of the victims and the criminals. Such an undertaking needed an outside boost, and The Hague tribunal was just that. Moreover, a constitutional law on cooperation with The Hague tribunal was enacted during the term of office of my predecessor, Franjo Tuđman, and all citizens of the Republic of Croatia were bound by this law to provide all necessary assistance to the tribunal and to respond to a subpoena of the court. When I ensured that the investigators of The Hague tribunal gained access to certain documents that they requested, I only acted in accordance with the constitutional law of the country of which I was president.

Names such as Karadžić, Mladić, Mrkšić, Šljivančanin, Hadžić, Babić, or Martić are well known in the world. Even the infamous Arkan is not unknown, while—and to name but one example—hardly anyone had heard of Slavko Dokmanović before 1997, when he was arrested by The Hague investigators. That arrest opened a new chapter in the context of the international justice, since it became clear to everyone in the former Yugoslavia that it was indeed possible to arrest indicted war criminals and bring them to justice.

And yet even those less well known deserve to be remembered, not for positive things, but so that we know who they were and what they did and also how and why they were sentenced, so that no one will even consider repeating such actions. It is also worth remembering the hardworking investigators of The Hague tribunal who managed, often under unfavorable circumstances, to track down perpetrators of war crimes and find incriminating evidence or witnesses able to give precious testimonies at trials in The Hague. As a politician I will not and cannot give my opinion on the judges.

I am profoundly convinced that regardless of the growing criticism over the alleged politicization of The Hague tribunal, that institution played a key role in helping the general public in the region of former Yugoslavia come to terms with the atrocities that occurred during the wars in which it disintegrated. Although the Milošević trial was never concluded because of his death, I am certain that it revealed the crowning evidence of who was the attacker and who was the defender. This, of course, does not mean that those who defended themselves could not also commit war crimes. Unfortunately, they could, and they did. This is the burden from the past that we must not only face but also remove from our everyday lives so that we can move forward unburdened. The Hague tribunal—regardless of all complaints about its work—took the first significant step along this path in this process of confronting the past, including our own. It is up to us to continue. And we must never forget the victims, the criminals, the tribunal that judged them, or the investigators who worked for the tribunal.

Most of all we should not forget that a crime has no nationality and that there are no criminal nations. But neither should we forget that every crime must be paid for one day or another. If that is the heritage of The Hague tribunal, then it has achieved a great thing and not just for the peoples of southeastern Europe.

Michael Žantovský

The war in the former Yugoslavia was not only one of the most terrible episodes of modern European history but also heralded a time of extraordinary international concern about the human rights violations during the war and of determination to identify and punish the perpetrators of killings and cruelty among all parties to the war. The creation of the International Criminal Tribunal for the former Yugoslavia (ICTY) was the expression of this commitment.

The story of the tribunal shows that justice, tough, belated, and imperfect as all justice is, is possible even in situations rife with chaos, controversies, and cover-ups such as the war in the former Yugoslavia. This would not have been possible without the untiring efforts of brave and dedicated men and women doing the work of the tribunal in the field, often risking their own personal safety in the process. *The Investigator* is a worthy tribute to them as well as an ICTY investigator's valuable eyewitness report.

Ralph R. Johnson

The credible prospect of being held accountable is a necessary if not always sufficient deterrent to war crimes. The end of the war that tore apart Yugoslavia did not leave any indigenous institutions capable of meting out justice to those on all sides who had committed atrocities. The ICTY was essential to providing some measure of justice and closure to the victims of this barbaric conflict and instilling some measure of fear in those unrepentant who longed to carry on their fight.

The work of the tribunal was possible only because of the dedication and courage of its team of investigators, lawyers, and prosecutors as well as the extraordinary bravery of witnesses who came forward to tell their stories. This remarkable book offers a window on their reality. It is a touchstone for all who wish to understand the tragic end of the former Yugoslavia and who seek instruments to prevent such internecine barbarism from recurring. *The Investigator* makes a critical contribution to the historical record.

The Legacy of the International Tribunal

Since its founding in 1993, the International Tribunal for the former Yugoslavia has charged a total of 161 people. The first to pass through the gates of the prison at Scheveningen was Duško Tadić in April 1995. He was followed by many others, including people accused of one or more crimes such as genocide, crimes against humanity, violations of the laws and customs of war, and grave violations of the Geneva Conventions. Others were charged with detaining witnesses and contempt of court. It is a remarkable achievement that as of July 2011 not one of the accused remains at large.

Ten years after UN Security Council resolutions 1503 of 2003 and 1534 of 2004 established the tribunal, a three-phase plan was put into place to abolish it. All its investigations were to wrap up by the end of 2004, all trials in the first instance to conclude by the end of 2008, and the total closure of the tribunal was to go in effect by the end of 2010.

All investigations were wrapped up as planned. The difficulty of certain cases and the late arrests of some of the accused, however, meant that the initial estimates had to be adjusted. For these reasons the Security Council passed resolution 1966 of 2010 establishing the Mechanism for International Criminal Tribunals (MICT), with the goal of completing the work of the International Tribunal for the Former Yugoslavia and Rwanda.

The ICTY courtrooms were in operation for 10,800 days, summoned more than 4,650 witnesses, and generated 2.5 million pages of trial transcripts. Of the accused 90 were sentenced, 2 are in retrial before the MICT as of this writing, 19 were acquitted, 37 had their trial terminated or the indictment withdrawn, 13 were referred to the courts of the former Yugoslavia, 10 to Bosnia and Herzegovina, 2 to Croatia, and 1 to Serbia. The convicted are serving their sentences in fourteen European countries.

Epilogue

From the window of my office on East Forty-Fifth Street, I see endless columns of cars slowly making their way across the Queensboro Bridge. Helicopters are flying over the UN building to land on the East Thirty-Fourth Street heliport, and police sirens are wailing below on the streets. For almost twelve years now, I have lived in this human

118. One of the wanted posters produced by the ICTY for NATO troops in Bosnia and Herzegovina. (ICTY)

119. ID cards from various UN organizations and missions all over the world.
(Vladimír Dzuro)

anthill called New York, the city that never sleeps. On October 14, 2004, I left my work as an investigator for the International Criminal Tribunal to take up a new job, investigating corruption and other misconduct in the United Nations.

My work for the Office of Internal Oversight Services (OIOS) has taken me to destinations rarely found in the colorful catalogs of travel agencies. They range from Afghanistan, Iraq, and Syria to Liberia, Congo, and Haiti. Because these missions are assigned to areas that have suffered war, ethnic cleansing, mass rape, pillage, or famine, there is simply no escaping the need to reflect on the condition of humankind and our priorities in life.

War crime investigators have tragedy on the agenda every single day. It's a job that comes with an emotional backlog that grows with each new case, but you keep going because you feel humanity owes it to the scarred and broken people who open up their hearts to you. They have suffered so much misfortune that you become driven to hunt down the perpetrators. It's not the easiest thing in the world when you're working with a long list of mass murderers, but if you can bring at least some of them to justice, to make them pay for what they did, then you can hope that you have given the survivors some peace of mind. And yourself too, when all said and done.

I still wonder how it could have happened in Europe at the end of the twentieth century that people who had lived together for decades as friends and brothers, who had married and coexisted regardless of religion or ethnicity, were so willing to open up old wounds and demonize one another. What started off as suspicion and harassment somehow turned into a bloodlust of beatings and murder that ended in extermination. And yet even now, more than a quarter of a century after the fall of Yugoslavia, far-right nationalist parties in Serbia and Croatia are continuing to stoke hatred among frustrated youth, to provoke them into a conflict similar to the one that had only recently brought their people to their knees.

Despite all the war criminals we were able to haul before the tribunal, it's clear we have not achieved complete success, nor was there ever any chance of achieving it. No one can ever bring back the thousands of people who fell victim to warped ideologies. There isn't a single court on earth able to give the survivors the full justice they seek. That's something we all have to live with.

120. Lobby of the tribunal. (Vladimír Dzuro)

ACKNOWLEDGMENTS

I would like to thank those who inspired me to write this book or who have contributed to it, specifically:

U.S. Secretary of State Madeleine Albright

Chief Prosecutor of the International Tribunal Carla Del Ponte

President of the Republic of Croatia Stjepan Mesić

U.S. Ambassador-at-Large for War Crime Issues John Clint Williamson

U.S. Air Force Major General Jacques Paul Klein

Judge Joanna Korner, CMG QC

Czech public prosecutor Anna Richterová

Investigator Kevin Curtis

U.S. Army Colonel David S. Jones

Minister Counsellor René Dlabal, Embassy of the Czech Republic in London

Graphic designer Martina Dzurová

I also wish to thank the following friends and colleagues: Heidi Mendoza, Ben Swanson, Michael Dudley, Vlastimil and Alena Vondruška, Fernando Rey, Serge and Heidi Krieger, Dennis Milner, Marc Jeffery, Vladislav Guerassev, Radka Kotalová, Joseph (Joe) Binger, Ruth-Anne Young, Gregory Battley, Charlotte McDowell, and Tereza Nováková. My special thanks to:

Darren Baker, an American writer and translator

Philip Turner, my literary agent

Finally, my heartfelt gratitude to my muse.

APPENDIX 1
List of People

Adzić, Blagoje Serb, general, chief of staff, JNA

Agičić, Esad Bosniak, witness, ICTY

Albright, Madeleine Jana Korbel American (born in Czechoslovakia), permanent representative of the United States to the United Nations, secretary of state in the administration of President Bill Clinton

Alonso, Pablo Martín Spanish, director for coordination in the Secretariat of State Security of Spain

Anastasijević, Dejan Serb, journalist from Belgrade

Annan, Kofi Atta Ghanaian, secretary-general of the United Nations, 1997–2006

Antičević-Marinović, Ingrid Croat, minister of justice of Croatia

Apolonio, Aleksandar (Aco) Prosecutor in Dubrovnik and president of the self-declared Dubrovnik Republic

Arbour, Louise Canadian, ICTY chief prosecutor, 1996–99

Arkan *See* Ražnatović, Željko (Arkan)

Arshad, Azim Pakistani, investigator, Office of the Prosecutor, ICTY

Atanasijević, Ivan Serb, participated in the executions at Ovčara, initially sentenced in Serbia to twenty years in prison, reduced to fifteen years on appeal

Babić, Milan Serb, president of the Republic of Serbian Krajina, sentenced by the ICTY to thirteen years in prison, committed suicide in prison while serving the sentence

Bačić, Dragan Serb, participated in the minefield incident in Lovas, sentenced in Serbia to six years in prison

Bajramović, Sejdo Kosovar, delegate to the Presidium of SFR Yugoslavia for Kosovo

Balić, Andrija Croat, witness of the incident in the Lovas minefield

Banović, Predrag Serb, sentenced by the ICTY to eight years in prison for his role in the Omarska, Keraterm, and Trnopolje concentration camps

Bassiouni, Cherif   Egyptian, chairman of the Commission of Experts established by the UN Security Council

Battley, Gregory   English, UNPROFOR security officer

Beara, Ljubiša   Serb, colonel in the VRS, sentenced by the ICTY to life in prison for his role in the Srebenica massacre

Begić, Raif   Bosniak, survived the massacre in Sanski Most

Benavente, Enrique Mora   Spanish, deputy director, assistant to director general for European and North American affairs, Ministry of Foreign Affairs of Spain

Berghofer, Dragutin   Croat, survived the Ovčara massacre

Binger, Joseph (Joe)   American, U.S. Marine, security officer in UNPRO-FOR, later staff of ICTY, died in a tragic incident in Scheveningen in 2008

Blagojević, Vidoje   Serb, commander of Bratunac Brigade, Drina Corps of the VRS, sentenced by the ICTY to fifteen years in prison for his role in the Srebrenica massacre

Blewitt, Graham   Australian, deputy chief prosecutor, ICTY

Bogić, Stevo (Jajo)   Serb, commander of the SNB in Erdut

Bogićević, Bogić   Bosnian, delegate to the Presidium of SFR Yugoslavia for Bosnia and Herzegovina

Borovčanin, Ljubomir   Serb, deputy commander, Ministry of the Interior of the Republika Srpska, sentenced by the ICTY to seventeen years in prison for his role in the Srebrenica massacre

Bosanac, Vesna   Croat, medical doctor, director of Vukovar General Hospital

Bosinger, Nicolas   Swiss, Red Cross representative, deployed to Vukovar in November 1991

Boutros-Ghali, Boutros   Egyptian, secretary-general of the United Nations, 1992–96

Bowers, Terree   American, senior trial attorney at the ICTY

Božić, Andrea   Croatian, interpreter, Office of the Prosecutor, ICTY

Brammertz, Serge   Belgian, ICTY chief prosecutor, 2008–16

Brđanin, Radoslav   Serb, chief of the Crisis Committee in Banja Luka, sentenced by the ICTY to thirty years in prison

Brovet, Stanislav   Slovenian, admiral, deputy minister of defense of SFR Yugoslavia

Bulatović, Momir   Montenegrin, president of Montenegro and later prime minister of the Federal Republic of Yugoslavia

Bulić, Miloš   Serb, participated in the Ovčara massacre

Butorović, Ratko (Bata Kan Kan) Serb, businessman, friend of Goran Hadžić

Čakalić, Emil Croat, survived the Ovčara massacre

Cassese, Antonio Italian, judge, ICTY

Čech, Miloslav Czech, colonel with the Czech Military Police, force provost marshal for UNPROFOR, 1994–95

Čeleketić, Milan Serb, lieutenant general, commander of a military formation within the army of the Republic of Serbian Krajina

Cencich, John American, investigator, team leader, Office of the Prosecutor, ICTY

Ćirić, Petar (Pero Cigan) Serb, participated in executions at Ovčara, sentenced to fifteen years

Clark, Wesley Kanne American, general, commanded Operation Allied Force in the Kosovo War during his term as the supreme allied commander of NATO, 1997–2000

Cohen, William American, secretary of defense of the United States

Cokić, Jevrem Serb, lieutenant general, Second Operation Group of the JNA

Connor, Melissa A. American, member of PHR

Curtis, Kevin English, investigator and team leader, ICTY

Cvetković, Jovan Serb, friend of Slavko Dokmanović

Dafinić, Milenko (Dafo) Serb, member of SNB in Erdut

Đanković, Miroslav Serb, participated in the executions at Ovčara, sentenced in Serbia to twenty years in prison

Del Pino, David Chilean, specialist working with PHR

Del Ponte, Carla Swiss, chief prosecutor at the ICTY, 1999–2007

Deutch, John American, director of the CIA

Devčić, Milan Serb, participated in the Lovas minefield incident, sentenced in Serbia to ten years in prison

Devetak, Ljuban Serb, participated in the Lovas minefield incident, sentenced in Serbia to twenty years in prison

Dimitrijević, Jovan Serb, participated in the Lovas minefield incident, sentenced in Serbia to eight years in prison

Dimitrijević, Miodrag Serb, participated in the Lovas minefield incident, sentenced in Serbia to ten years in prison

Đinđić, Zoran Serb, prime minister of Serbia, assassinated on March 12, 2003

Di Stefano, Giovanni Italian, international criminal, spokesperson for Žejko Ražnatović (Arkan)

Divljak, Pero   Serb, member of the Serbian paramilitary unit Red Berets

Djukić, Vladimir   Croat, executed at Ovčara

Dokmanović, Slavko   Serb, mayor of Vukovar, first indicted war criminal arrested by the ICTY in collaboration with UNTAES

Došen, Damir   Serb, sentenced by the ICTY to five years in prison for his role in the Keraterm concentration camp

Dragišić, Mirko   Serb, friend of Slavko Dokmanović

Dragović, Predrag   Serb, participated in the executions at Ovčara, initially sentenced in Serbia to twenty years in prison, reduced to five years on appeal

Drljača, Simo   Serb, one of the Prijedor Three, died before he could be extradited to the ICTY

Drnovšek, Janez   Slovenian, delegate to the Presidium of SFR Yugoslavia for Slovenia

Dufková, Žaneta   Czech, member of the Czech Army, close protection officer of Carla Del Ponte

Đukanović, Milo   Montenegrin, prime minister and president of Montenegro

Đurović, Krsto   Ethnicity unknown, admiral, JNA, commander of Ninth Military Sector in Kumbor

Dzuro, Vladimír   Czech, investigator, team leader, Office of the Prosecutor, ICTY

Erdemović, Dražen   Serb, pleaded guilty, sentenced by the ICTY to five years in prison for his participation in crimes in Srebrenica

Farrell, Norman   Canadian, deputy chief prosecutor, ICTY

Fila, Toma   Serb, lawyer from Belgrade

Filić, Marko   Croat, survived the incident in the Lovas minefield

Fulton, William (Billy)   British, investigator, Office of the Prosecutor, ICTY

Galbraith, Peter   American, U.S. ambassador to Croatia

Galić, Siniša (Gaja)   Serb, member of the SNB in Erdut

Gavrić, Dobroslav   Serb, policeman, assassinated Željko Ražnatović (Arkan) on January 15, 2000

Gligorov, Kiro   Macedonian, president of the Presidency of Macedonia

Goldstone, Richard J.   South African, chief prosecutor at the ICTY, 1994–96

Granić, Goran   Croat, vice premier of the Croatian government, 2000–2002

Grujić, Ivan   Croat, colonel, head of the Croatian Government Office for Missing and Displaced Persons

Gudaš, Vlado   Croat, survived the Ovčara massacre

Gunčević, Stjepan   Croat, survived the Ovčara massacre

Gvero, Milan   Serb, sentenced by the ICTY to five years in prison for his role in the Srebrenica massacre

Hadžić, Goran   Serb, president of the Republic of Serbian Krajina, indicted for war crimes in Croatia, diagnosed with brain cancer, died in 2016 before the proceedings before the ICTY were concluded

Haglund, William (Bill)   American, forensic anthropologist, PHR forensic team

Hardin, William (Bill)   American, investigator, Office of the Prosecutor, ICTY

Hartley, Ralph   American, archeologist, PHR forensic team

Hendriks, Cees   Dutch, director of investigations, Office of the Prosecutor, ICTY

Herold, Noel   American, FBI agent

Hollis, Brenda   American, senior trial attorney, Office of the Prosecutor, ICTY

Hooijkaas, Dirk   Canadian, investigator, Office of the Prosecutor, ICTY

Hryshchyshyn, Michael   Chief of cabinet of General Klein in UNTAES

Huntered, Jack   American, ATF expert, worked for ICTY during exhumations in Bosnia and Herzegovina

Ibrić, Zijad   Bosniak, liaison officer of the government of Bosnia and Herzegovina for cooperation with the ICTY

Izetbegović, Alija   Bosniak, first president of the Presidency of the Republic of Bosnia and Herzegovina

Jevtović, Zoran   Serb, friend of Slavko Dokmanović

Johnson, Jacci   American, special assistant to General Klein in UNTAES

Jokić, Dragan   Serb, sentenced by the ICTY to nine years in prison for his role in the Srebrenica massacre

Jokić, Miodrag   Serb, last commander of the Yugoslav Navy, sentenced by the ICTY to seven years in prison for war crimes in Dubrovnik

Jones, David Sterling   American, U.S. Army major, special advisor to General Klein in UNTAES

Josipović, Radisav   Serb, participated in the Lovas minefield incident, sentenced in Serbia to four years in prison

Jovanović, Zvjezdan   Serb, member of the Serbian special forces, assassinated prime minister of Serbia Zoran Đinđić

Jović, Borisav   Serb, delegate to the Presidium of SFR Yugoslavia for Serbia

Jurela, Željko   Croat, executed at Ovčara

Kadijević, Veljko   Yugoslav, general of the JNA, minister of defense of SFR Yugoslavia

Kajtez, Daniluško   Serb, commander of a Serbian armed group during the attack on the village of Škrljevita

Kalaba, Nada   Serb, the only woman who participated in the executions at Ovčara, sentenced in Serbia to eleven years in prison

Kalapanda, Ponnapa   Indian, UNPROFOR security officer

Karadžić, Radovan   Serb, president of the Republika Srpska, initially sentenced by the ICTY to forty years in prison, increased to life in prison

Karlović, Vilim   Croat, survived the massacre at Ovčara

Kempenaars, Ton   Head of Zagreb Liaison Office, Office of the Prosecutor, ICTY

Kerkkanen, Ari   Investigator, Office of the Prosecutor, ICTY

Kilibarda, Novak   Montenegrin, leader of the National Party in Montenegro

Kita, Jacek   Polish, major, commander of special unit GROM in UNTAES

Klein, Jacques Paul   American, U.S. Army general, UN administrator for UNTAES in Croatia

Knežević, Milan   Serb, friend of Slavko Dokmanović

Knutsson, Tomasv   Swedish, member of CIVPOL in UNTAES

Koff, Clea   American, forensic anthropologist, PHR forensic team

Kolundžija, Dragan   Serb, sentenced by the ICTY to three years in prison for his role in the Keraterm concentration camps

Kordić, Dario   Croat, commander of the Croatian Defense Forces (Hrvatsko vijeće obrane, HVO), sentenced to twenty-five years in prison by the ICTY

Korner, Joanna, CMG QC   English, senior trial attorney, ICTY

Kos, Milojica   Serb, sentenced by the ICTY to six years in prison for his role in the Omarska, Keraterm, and Trnopolje concentration camps

Kosijer, Zoran   Serb, participated in the Lovas minefield incident, sentenced in Serbia to nine years in prison

Kostić, Branko   Montenegrin, delegate to the Presidium of SFR Yugoslavia for Montenegro

Kostić, Jugoslav   Serb, delegate to the Presidium of SFR Yugoslavia for Vojvodina

Kostović, Ivica   Croat, medical doctor, vice premier of the Croatian government, 1993–95

Kovačević, Milan   Serb, one of the Prijedor Three, died in the detention facility

Kovačević, Vladimir   Serb, captain of the JNA in 1991, indicted by the ICTY for war crimes committed in Dubrovnik, case transferred to Serbia for prosecution

Krajišnik, Momčilo   Serb, Bosnian Serb political leader, cofounded along with Radovan Karadžić the Bosnian Serb nationalist Serb Democratic Party

Kraljević, Ivan   Croat, killed during the incident in the Lovas minefield

Kraljević, Mate   Croat, survived the incident in the Lovas minefield

Krieger, Serge   Canadian, analyst, Office of the Prosecutor, ICTY

Kristiansen, Arne   Investigator, Office of the Prosecutor, ICTY

Krnjajić, Željko   Serb, participated in the Lovas minefield incident, sentenced in Serbia to ten years in prison

Krstić, Radislav   Serb, general, chief of staff Drina Corps VRS, sentenced by the ICTY to thirty-five years in prison for his role in the Srebrenica massacre

Kučan, Milan   Slovenian, president of the Presidency of Slovenia

Kušić, Njegoslav (Njego)   Serb, instructor in the paramilitary unit Red Berets

Kvočka, Miroslav   Serb, sentenced by the ICTY to seven years in prison for his role in the Omarska, Keraterm, and Trnopolje concentration camps

Kypr, Petr   Czech, diplomat, member of ECMM in Croatia in 1991

Lančužanin, Milan   Serb, one of the commanders of the execution squad at Ovčara, initially sentenced to twenty years in prison by the ICTY, reduced to six years on appeal

Lazarević, Nebojša   Serb, friend of Slavko Dokmanović

Leko-Roche, Vlatka   Croat, interpreter, ICTY

Limmayog, Jo   Filipino, team leader, Office of the Prosecutor, ICTY

Lopez-Terrez, Patrick   French, director of investigations, Office of the Prosecutor, ICTY

Luketić, Slavko   Croat, witness of the incident in the Lovas minefield

Lupis, Ivo   American, political analyst, Office of the Prosecutor, ICTY

Manning, Dean   Australian, investigator, team leader, Office of the Prosecutor, ICTY

Marinović, Nojko   Croat, major general, commander of 472th Motorized Brigade of the JNA

Martić, Milan   Serb, president of the Republic of Serbian Krajina, sentenced by the ICTY to thirty-five years in prison for war crimes in Croatia

May, Sir Richard   British, judge, ICTY

Mazowiecki, Tadeusz   Polish, United Nations special rapporteur on the situation of human rights in the territory of the former Yugoslavia

McDonald, Gabrielle Anne Kirk   American, judge, ICTY

McKeon, Mark   American, trial attorney, Office of the Prosecutor, ICTY

Mesić, Stjepan   Croat, second president of Croatia, delegate to the Presidium of SFR Yugoslavia for Croatia, last president of the Presidium of SFR Yugoslavia

Miguel Bartolome, Angel de   Spanish, commander of the Organized Crime Brigade in the Spanish Judicial Police

Mihajlović, Dušan   Serb, minister of the interior of Serbia

Mihov, Deyan   Bulgarian, head of the Liaison Office in Belgrade, Serbia

Milasinović, Nataša   Interpreter, Office of the Prosecutor, ICTY

Miletić, Radivoje   Serb, general of the VRS, sentenced by the ICTY to eighteen years in prison for his role in the Srebrenica massacre

Milner, Dennis   English, investigator, team leader, later commander, Office of the Prosecutor, ICTY

Milojević, Predrag   Serb, participated in the executions at Ovčara, sentenced in Serbia to twenty years in prison

Milošević, Slobodan   Serb, president of Serbia (1989–97), president of the Federal Republic of Yugoslavia (1997–2000), indicted by the ICTY, died on March 11, 2006, during the proceedings before the tribunal

Milroy, Al   Australian, director of investigations, Office of the Prosecutor, ICTY

Mladić, Ratko   Serb, general, chief of staff VRS, sentenced by the ICTY to life in prison for his role in the Srebrenica massacre

Moor, Larry   Canadian, worked for the United Nations in Erdut in 1992

Mrkšić, Mile   Serb, colonel later promoted general, sentenced by the ICTY to twenty years in prison for his role in the Ovčara massacre

Mugoša, Goran   Serb, participated in the executions at Ovčara, sentenced in Serbia to five years in prison

Mumba, Florence   Zambian, judge, ICTY

Murugan, Rajie   South African, investigator, Office of the Prosecutor, ICTY

Neel, Julian   Belgian, major, special assistant to Major General Josepha Schoups

Nereuta, Alex   Romanian, analyst, Office of the Prosecutor, ICTY

Nice, Geoffrey, QC   English, principal trial attorney, ICTY

Niemann, Grant   Australian, senior trial attorney, ICTY

Nikolaidis, Aleksandar   Serb, participated in the Lovas minefield incident, sentenced in Serbia to six years in prison

Nikolić, Dragan   Serb, commander of the Sušica camp, sentenced by the ICTY to twenty years in prison

Nikolić, Drago   Serb, lieutenant, commander of military security Zvornik Brigade VRS, sentenced by the ICTY to thirty-five years in prison for his participation in crimes in Srebrenica

Nikolić, Momir   Serb, deputy commander of military security of the Bratunac Brigade of the Drina Corps VRS, sentenced by the ICTY to twenty years in prison for his role in the Srebrenica massacre

Nikšić, Časlav   Serb, observer during the exhumation at Ovčara

Novak, Zdenko   Croat, survived the massacre at Ovčara, provided critical testimony for the location of the Ovčara mass grave

Novaković, Ljubomir   Serb, friend of Slavko Dokmanović

Novaković, Mile   Serb, lieutenant general, commander of the army of the Republic of Serbian Krajina

Oberknezev, Philippe   Analyst, Office of the Prosecutor, ICTY

Obrenović, Dragan   Serb, colonel in the VRS, chief of staff, deputy commander of First Zvornik Infantry Brigade, sentenced by the ICTY to seventeen years in prison for his participation in crimes in Srebrenica

O'Donnell, Bernard   Australian, investigator, team leader, Office of the Prosecutor, ICTY

Oliveira, Dayse de   Brazilian, team assistant, Office of the Prosecutor, ICTY

Ora, Monika   Hungarian, investigator, Office of the Prosecutor, ICTY

Orić, Naser   Bosniak, commander, indicted, later found not guilty of war crimes by the ICTY Trial Chamber

Orlović, Boško   Serb, confidant of the UDBA

Osorio, Thomas   American, head of the ICTY Liaison Office in Croatia

Ostojić, Đorđe   Serb, chief prosecutor of Serbia

Pandurević, Vinko   Serb, lieutenant colonel of the VRS, sentenced by the ICTY to thirteen years in prison for his participation in crimes in Srebrenica

Panić, Miodrag   Serb, officer of the JNA

Pap, Franjo   Hungarian Croat, executed by members of the SNB

Pap, Juliana   Hungarian Croat, executed by members of the SNB

Papalia, Guido   Italian, prosecutor in Verona, Italy

Peeters (first name unknown)   Belgian, colonel, commander of BELBAT in UNPROFOR Sector East

Perić, Darko   Serb, participated in the Lovas minefield incident, sentenced in Serbia to five years in prison

Perić, Jovica   Serb, participated in the executions at Ovčara, initially sentenced in Serbia to fifteen years in prison, reduced to thirteen years on appeal

Perisić, Momčilo   Serb, chief of staff, Armed Forces of Serbia and Montenegro

Perković, Tihomir   Croat, survived the massacre at Ovčara

Pfundheller, Brent   American, investigator, Office of the Prosecutor, ICTY

Plavšić, Biljana   Serb, president of Republika Srpska, sentenced by the ICTY to eleven years in prison

Plavšić, Ivan   Croat, executed at Ovčara and exhumed from the mass grave

Polak, Samir   Bosniak, prisoner in the Omarska camp

Popović, Vujadin   Serb, lieutenant colonel, commander of military security of Drina Corps VRS, sentenced by the ICTY to life in prison for his participation in crimes in Srebrenica

Prcać, Dragoljub   Serb, sentenced by the ICTY to five years in prison for his role in the Omarska, Keraterm, and Trnopolje concentration camps

Radak, Saša   Serb, participated in the executions at Ovčara, sentenced in Serbia to twenty years in prison

Radić, Miroslav   Serb, captain of the JNA, indicted by the ICTY for war crimes in Vukovar, acquitted

Radić, Mlađo   Serb, sentenced by the ICTY to twenty years in prison for his role in the Omarska, Keraterm, and Trnopolje concentration camps

Radojčaj, Đuka   Croat, survived the incident in the Lovas minefield

Radojčić, Milan   Serb, participated in the Lovas minefield incident, sentenced in Serbia to thirteen years in prison

Rakin, Natalija   Croat, executed by a member of the SNB

Ralston, John   Australian, director of investigations, Office of the Prosecutor, ICTY

Rambough, Matthew   Canadian, UNPROFOR security officer

Ražnatović, Světlana (Ceca)   Serb, turbo-folk singer, wife of Željko Ražnatović (Arkan)

Ražnatović, Željko (Arkan)   Serb, international criminal, commander of the Serbian Volunteer Guard, indicted by the ICTY, assassinated by Dobroslav Gavrić on January 15, 2000, in Belgrade

Rembe, Malena   Swedish, analyst, Office of the Prosecutor, ICTY

Riad, Fouad   Egyptian, judge, ICTY

Richterová, Anna   Czech, senior trial attorney, ICTY

Roćen, Milan   Montenegrin, political advisor of President Mile Đukanović

Rodriguez-Spíteri Palazuelo, José   Spanish, general director for European and North American affairs, Ministry of Foreign Affairs of Spain

Roumagere, Christine   French, team assistant, Office of the Prosecutor, ICTY

Samardžić, Dragan   Serb, prosecution witness

Samardzić, Nikola   Montenegrin, minister of foreign affairs of Montenegro

Saunders, Rebecca (Becky)   American, professor of geography and anthropology

Scheffer, David   American, U.S. ambassador-at-large for war crime issues

Scholz, Sabine   German, investigator, Office of the Prosecutor, ICTY

Schou, Jan   Danish, medical doctor, member of ECMM in Croatia in 1991

Schoups, Joseph   Belgian, major general, force commander UNTAES

Scott, Douglas D.   American, archaeologist, worked on the exhumation at the Ovčara mass grave

Seraydarian, Souren   Syrian, deputy to the UN administrator for UNTAES in Croatia

Shalikashvili, John David   American, general, chairman of the Joint Chiefs of Staff, 1993–97

Sikirica, Duško   Serb, sentenced by the ICTY to fifteen years in prison for his role in the Keraterm concentration camps

Simatović, Franko (Frenki)   Croat, founder and commander of the JSO of the Serbian State Security Service (Resor državne bezbednosti, RDB)

Šljivančanin, Veselin   Montenegrin, major of the JNA, sentenced to ten years in prison by the ICTY for his role in the Ovčara massacre

Snow, Clyde   American, forensic anthropologist, PHR forensic team

Solana de Madariaga, Francisco Javier   Spanish, secretary-general of NATO

Šošić, Đorđe   Serb, participated in the executions at Ovčara, sentenced in Serbia to twenty years in prison

Stakić, Milomir   Serb, one of the Prijedor Three, sentenced to forty years in prison by the ICTY

Stanišić, Jovan (Jovica)   Serb, head of the State Security Service within the Ministry of Internal Affairs of Serbia, 1992–98

Stanišić, Mićo   Serb, minister of the interior of Republika Srpska in 1992

Stefanovic, Michael   Australian, investigator, Office of the Prosecutor, ICTY

Stevanović, Petronije Serb, participated in the Lovas minefield incident, sentenced in Serbia to fourteen years in prison

Stocchi, Paolo Pastore Italian, investigator, Office of the Prosecutor, ICTY

Stojanović, Saša Serb, participated in the Lovas minefield incident, sentenced in Serbia to eight years in prison

Stojić, Grgo Croat, survived the attack on the village of Škrljevita

Stork, Kevin Chief logistic officer, UNTAES

Stover, Eric American, director PHR office in Boston

Stričević, Milorad (Puki) Serb, member of the Serbian Volunteer Guard of Željko Ražnatović (Arkan)

Strinović, Davor Croat, medical doctor, specialist in forensic medicine, former head of the Department of Forensic Medicine and Criminology, Medical School University of Zagreb

Strugar, Pavle Montenegrin, general of the JNA, sentenced to seven and a half years in prison by the ICTY for his role in war crimes in Dubrovnik

Tabbush, Paul English, professor, dendrology expert

Tadić, Duško Serb, first indicted war criminal extradited to the ICTY, sentenced by the ICTY to twenty years in prison

Talić, Momir Serb, chief of staff of the JNA Fifth Corps, later promoted to commander of the First Krajina Corps of the Republika Srpska Army, indicted by the ICTY, died during proceedings before the tribunal

Theunens, Renaud Belgian, analyst, Office of the Prosecutor, ICTY

Tito, Josip Broz Croat, president of SFR Yugoslavia, 1953–80

Tolimir, Zdravko Serb, general of the VRS, sentenced by the ICTY to life in prison for his role in the Srebrenica massacre

Tomašević, Vukosav Serb, friend of Slavko Dokmanović

Torkildsen, Morten Norway, investigator, Office of the Prosecutor, ICTY

Tripp, Peter Chief inspector, commander of CIVPOL in UNTAES

Trump, Nevenka Croat, political analyst, Office of the Prosecutor, ICTY

Tuđman, Franjo Croat, first president of Croatia

Tuma, Marie Swedish, trial attorney, Office of the Prosecutor, ICTY

Tupurkovski, Vasil Macedonian, delegate to the Presidium of SFR Yugoslavia for Macedonia

Uertz-Retzlaff, Hildegard German, senior trial attorney, Office of the Prosecutor, ICTY

Ulemek, Milorad (Legija) Serb, commander of the JSO, member of the Serbian Volunteer Guard of Željko Ražnatović (Arkan)

Upton, Stephen   New Zealander, team leader and later commander, Office of the Prosecutor, ICTY

Urban, Pavo   Croat, photographer, killed during the attack on Dubrovnik on December 6, 1991

Vance, Cyrus   American, lawyer, special envoy of the secretary-general of the United Nations

Van Rooyen, Deon   South African, investigator, Office of the Prosecutor, ICTY

Vasić, Miroslav   Serb, lawyer from Belgrade

Vasiljević, Aleksandar (Aco)   Serb, major general in JNA, in 1992 head of counterintelligence (KOS), also served in VJ (1999–2001), testified in trial of Milosević and other cases

Vasiljković, Dragan (Kapitan [Captain] Dragan)   Serb, trainer of Serb volunteers in the Knin Fortress in Croatia

Versonnen, Roel   Belgian, investigator, Office of the Prosecutor, ICTY

Vlajković, Radovan   Serb, participated in the Lovas minefield incident, sentenced in Serbia to five years in prison

Vojnović, Milan   Serb, participated in the executions at Ovčara, sentenced in Serbia to fifteen years in prison

Vos, Jan   Dutch, lawyer, in 1998 intern in Team 4, Office of the Prosecutor, ICTY

Vujanović, Stanko   Serb, one of the commanders of the execution squad at Ovčara, sentenced to twenty years in prison by the ICTY

Vujović, Miroljub   Serb, one of the commanders of the execution squad at Ovčara, sentenced to twenty years in prison by the ICTY

Vukčević, Slobodan   Serb, lawyer from Belgrade

Vukčević, Vladimir   Serb, prosecutor for war crimes in Serbia

Waespi, Stefan   Swiss, trial attorney, Office of the Prosecutor, ICTY

Wald, Patricie M   American, judge, ICTY

Whiting, Alex   American, trial attorney, Office of the Prosecutor, ICTY

Williamson, Clint John   American, lawyer, trial attorney at the ICTY, U.S. ambassador-at-large for war crime issues

Wubben, Jan   Dutch, senior trial attorney, Office of the Prosecutor, ICTY

Zec, Milan   Serb, admiral, indicted for war crimes in Dubrovnik, indictment later withdrawn

Žigić, Zoran   Serb, sentenced by the ICTY to twenty-five years in prison for his role in the Omarska, Keraterm, and Trnopolje concentration camps

Župljanin, Stojan   Serb, police commander of the ARK from Banja Luka, sentenced by the ICTY to twenty-two years in prison

APPENDIX 2
List of Institutions

ATF   The Bureau of Alcohol, Tobacco, Firearms and Explosives is a federal law enforcement organization within the U.S. Department of Justice. https: //www.atf.gov.

BELBAT   Military unit of the Belgian Army deployed in Croatia as part of the United Nations Transitional Administration for Eastern Slavonia, Baranja, and Western Srijem (UNTAES).

Beli orlovi   White Eagles, in the Serbian-Croatian-Bosnian language Beli orlovi. Serbian paramilitary unit that operated in Bosnia and Herzegovina.

Beli vukovi   White Wolves, in the Serbian-Croatian-Bosnian language Beli vukovi. Special unit that operated under the command of the Vojska republike srpske (VRS, Army of Republika Srpska) in Bosnia and Herzegovina.

CIVPOL   International civilian police units that are deployed in United Nations peacekeeping missions around the world. The abbreviation was derived from the term "civilian police."

Commission of Experts (also known as Bassiouni Commission)   By its Resolution 780 (1992) of October 6, 1992, the Security Council requested that the secretary-general of the United Nations establish a commission of experts to examine and analyze information suggesting grave breaches of the Geneva Conventions and other violations of international humanitarian law committed in the territory of the former Yugoslavia. On October 26, 1992, the secretary-general appointed a five-member commission, chaired by Cherif Bassiouni.

Crvene berete   Unit for Special Operations, in the Serbian-Croatian-Bosnian language Jedinica za specijalne operacije. It was an elite unit of the Serbian State Security police, which operated between 1990 and 2003. Since the members wore red berets, the unit was also known as Crvene berete (Red Berets).

323

Dayton Agreement   The General Framework Agreement for Peace in Bosnia and Herzegovina, in the Serbian-Croatian-Bosnian language Dejtonski mirovi sporazum (also known as the Dayton Accords, Paris Protocol, or Dayton-Paris Agreement), is the peace agreement reached at the Wright-Patterson Air Force Base near Dayton, Ohio, in November 1995 and formally signed in Paris on December 14, 1995. These accords put an end to the three-and-a-half-year-long Bosnian War, one of the Yugoslav Wars in the 1990s.

ECMM   The European Union had a monitoring mission in the former Yugoslavia that began operating in July 1991 under the name of European Community Monitor Mission. The mission was financed by the European Commission and consisted of seventy-five field specialists. The mission was headquartered in Zagreb, and its designated area included Bosnia and Herzegovina, Croatia, Serbia, Montenegro, Albania, and the Republic of Macedonia. The ECMM was renamed the European Union Monitoring Mission on December 22, 2000.

FBI   The Federal Bureau of Investigation, formerly the Bureau of Investigation, is the domestic intelligence and security service of the United States and its principal federal law enforcement agency. https: //www .fbi.gov.

FK Obilić   A football club based in Vračar, a neighborhood of Belgrade. Named after medieval Serbian hero Miloš Obilić, a legendary fourteenth-century knight. In the 1990s the team was owned by Željko Ražnatović (Arkan).

FRY   The Federal Republic of Yugoslavia, in the Serbian-Croatian-Bosnian language Savezna Republika Jugoslavija (SRJ), was a federal state established by the republics of Serbia and Montenegro in 1992; it lasted until 2003.

ICRC   The International Committee of the Red Cross or simply the Red Cross is a humanitarian institution based in Geneva, Switzerland. State parties (signatories) to the four Geneva Conventions of 1949 and their Additional Protocols of 1977 (Protocol I and Protocol II) and 2005 have given the ICRC a mandate to protect victims of international and internal armed conflicts. Such victims include war wounded, prisoners, refugees, civilians, and other noncombatants. https: //www.icrc.org/en.

ICTY   The International Tribunal for the Prosecution of Persons Responsible for Serious Violations of International Humanitarian Law Committed in the Territory of the Former Yugoslavia since 1991, more commonly referred to as the International Criminal Tribunal for the former Yugoslavia. It was established on May 25, 1993, and dissolved on December 31, 2017. http://www.icty.org.

IFOR   The Implementation Force was a NATO-led multinational peace enforcement force in Bosnia and Herzegovina operating under a one-year mandate from December 20, 1995, to December 20, 1996. The deployment of IFOR was also known as Operation Joint Endeavour.

Interpol   The International Criminal Police Organization, more commonly known as Interpol, is an international organization that facilitates international police cooperation. It was initially established as the International Criminal Police Commission (ICPC) in 1923. https: //www.interpol.int.

JATD   The Unit for Antiterrorist Operations, in the Serbian-Croatian-Bosnian language Jedinica za antiterorističtka dejstva, operated within the Republic Secretariat of Internal Affairs (RSUP) of the Socialist Republic of Serbia. It was established in Novi Beograd on December 18, 1978.

JNA   The Yugoslav People's Army, often referred to simply by the acronym JNA (Jugoslovenska narodna armija), was the military of the Socialist Federal Republic of Yugoslavia.

JORDBAT   Military unit of the Jordanian Army deployed in Croatia as part of the United Nations Transitional Administration for Eastern Slavonia, Baranja, and Western Srijem (UNTAES).

JSO   Unit for Special Operations, in the Serbian-Croatian-Bosnian language Jedinica za specijalne operacije. It was an elite unit of the Serbian State Security police, which operated between 1990 and 2003. Since the members wore red berets, the unit was also known as Crvene berete (Red Berets).

JW GROM   GROM stands for Grupa Reagowania Operacyjno-Manewrowego (in English Group [for] Operational Maneuvering Response), and it also means "thunder." It is one of the five special operations forces units of the Polish Armed Forces. It was officially established on July 13, 1990, and in 1997 GROM was deployed in UNTAES in Eastern Slavonia to protect UNTAES HQ in Vukovar and to provide close protection to the UN administrator, Ambassador Kelin.

KOS   Counterintelligence Service of the Jugoslav People's Army (JNA), in the Serbian-Croatian-Bosnian language Kontraobaveštajna služba JNA.

Martićeva Milicija   The militia of Milan Martić, in the Serbian-Croatian-Bosnian language Martićeva Milicija, were police units that operated in the territory of the Republic of Serbian Krajina.

MASH The mobile army surgical hospital was invented by the U.S. Army. It is by definition a fully functional hospital used on the battlefield. It first came into being in August 1945; it was used in the Korean War and many later conflicts.

MICT The International Residual Mechanism for Criminal Tribunals is an international court established by the United Nations Security Council in 2010 to perform the remaining functions of the International Criminal Tribunal for the former Yugoslavia (ICTY) and the International Criminal Tribunal for Rwanda (ICTR) following the completion of those tribunals' respective mandates.

NATO The North Atlantic Treaty Organization, also called the North Atlantic Alliance, is an intergovernmental military alliance between several North American and European countries based on the North Atlantic Treaty, which was signed on April 4, 1949. http://www.nato.int.

Operation Amber Star Originally a plan to capture General Ratko Mladić and President Radovan Karadžić but later the basis for joint special operations missions to arrest indicted war criminals.

PHR Physicians for Human Rights is a U.S.-based not-for-profit human rights nongovernmental organization that uses medicine and science to document and advocate against mass atrocities and severe human rights violations around the world. PHR headquarters are in New York City, with offices in Boston and Washington DC. It was established in 1986 to use the unique skills and credibility of health professionals to advocate for persecuted health workers, prevent torture, document mass atrocities, and hold those who violate human rights accountable. http://physiciansforhumanrights.org.

RS Republika Srpska is one of two constitutional and legal entities of Bosnia and Herzegovina, the other being the Federation of Bosnia and Herzegovina. The entities are largely autonomous. Its de jure capital city is Sarajevo, but the de facto capital and administrative center is Banja Luka.

RSK The Republic of Serbian Krajina was a self-proclaimed Serb secessionist republic, active during the Croatian War (1991–95). It consisted of a territory within the newly independent Croatia (formerly part of Yugoslavia), which was declared but was not recognized internationally.

RUSBAT Military unit of the Russian Federation deployed in Croatia as part of the United Nations Protection Force (UNPROFOR) and later the United Nations Transitional Administration for Eastern Slavonia, Baranja, and Western Srijem (UNTAES).

SAO   The Serbian Autonomous Regions, in the Serbian-Croatian-Bosnian language Srpska autonomna oblast, were the territories consisting of majority-Serbian municipalities of the Republic of Croatia that declared autonomy in 1990.

SDG   The Serb Volunteer Guard, in the Serbian-Croatian-Bosnian language Srpska dobrovoljačka garda, was a Serbian volunteer paramilitary unit founded and led by Željko Ražnatović (Arkan) that fought in Croatia (1991–93), Bosnia and Herzegovina (1992–95), and Kosovo (1999) during the Yugoslav Wars.

SFOR   The Stabilization Force in Bosnia and Herzegovina was a NATO-led multinational peacekeeping force deployed to Bosnia and Herzegovina after the Bosnian War. Although SFOR was led by NATO, several non-NATO countries contributed troops. SFOR was established by Security Council Resolution 1088 of December 12, 1996. It succeeded the much larger Implementation Force (IFOR), which was deployed to Bosnia and Herzegovina on December 20, 1995, with a one-year mandate.

SFRY   The Socialist Federal Republic of Yugoslavia, most commonly known simply as Yugoslavia, was the Yugoslav state in southeastern Europe that existed from its foundation in the aftermath of World War II until its dissolution in 1992 amid the Yugoslav Wars.

Škorpioni   The Scorpions, in the Serbian-Croatian-Bosnian language Škorpioni, were a paramilitary unit, part of the Serbian Ministry of Interior, and active during the Yugoslav Wars.

SLOVBAT   Military unit of the Army of Slovakia deployed in Croatia as part of the United Nations Transitional Administration for Eastern Slavonia, Baranja, and Western Srijem (UNTAES).

SNB   The Serbian National Security, in the Serbian-Croatian-Bosnian language Srpska nacionalna bezbednost, was a paramilitary unit that operated in Erdut, Croatia, in 1991.

SOCEUR   The Special Operations Command Europe employs special operations forces across the U.S. European Command (USEUCOM) area of responsibility to enable deterrence; strengthen European security collective capabilities and interoperability; and counter transnational threats to protect U.S. personnel and interests. http://www.socom.mil/soceur.

TO   The Territorial Defense, in the Serbian-Croatian-Bosnian language Teritorijalna odbrana, was formed in 1969 as an integral part of the

Yugoslav total national defense doctrine. The TO forces consisted of able-bodied civilian males and females. Between 1 and 3 million Yugoslavs between the ages of fifteen and sixty-five would fight under TO command as irregular or guerrilla forces in wartime. In peacetime, however, about 860,000 TO troops were involved in military training and other activities.

UDBA   The State Security Service, in the Serbian-Croatian-Bosnian language Uprava državne bezbednosti, more commonly known by its original name as the State Security Administration, was the secret police organization of Yugoslavia.

UN   The United Nations is an intergovernmental organization tasked with promoting international cooperation and creating and maintaining international order. A replacement for the ineffective League of Nations, the organization was established in San Francisco on October 24, 1945, after World War II with the aim of preventing future conflicts. http://www.un.org/en/index.html.

UNPROFOR   The United Nations Protection Force was the first United Nations peacekeeping force in Croatia and in Bosnia and Herzegovina during the Yugoslav Wars. It was established in February 1992. Its mandate ended in March 1995, and on December 21, 1995, UNPROFOR was replaced by the United Nations Mission to Bosnia and Herzegovina (UNMIBH).

UNSC   The United Nations Security Council is one of the six principal organs of the United Nations, charged with the maintenance of international peace and security as well as accepting new members to the United Nations and approving any changes to the United Nations charter. http://www.un.org/en/sc/.

UNTAES   The United Nations Transitional Administration for Eastern Slavonia, Baranja, and Western Srijem was a UN peacekeeping mission in Eastern Slavonia, Baranja, and Western Srijem in the eastern parts of Croatia. It was established on January 15, 1996, and its mandate ended on January 15, 1998.

Valkenburg Naval Air Base   A former Royal Netherlands Navy air base located just south of the town of Valkenburg. http://www.vliegveldvalkenburg.nl.

VJ   Armed Forces of Yugoslavia, in the Serbian-Croatian-Bosnian language Vojska Jugoslavije, established on May 20, 1992, and disbanded on February 4, 2003.

VRS   The Army of Republika Srpska, in the Serbian-Croatian-Bosnian language Vojska Republike Srpske, commonly referred to in English as the Bosnian Serb Army, was active during the 1992–95 war in Bosnia and Herzegovina. In 2006 VRS was integrated into the Armed Forces of Bosnia and Herzegovina, in the Serbian-Croatian-Bosnian language Oružane snage Bosne i Hercegovine.

BIBLIOGRAPHY

PRIMARY SOURCES

Information contained in the book is mostly based on the author's personal recollection of events, but for the sake of factual accuracy, the author also consulted the website of the International Criminal Tribunal for the former Yugoslavia (http://www.icty.org). The website contains useful information on the establishment of the tribunal, the rules of procedure and evidence of the tribunal, and indictments and testimonies of various witnesses and suspects before the tribunal.

Basic Documents Pertaining to the International Tribunal

Annual Reports. http://www.icty.org/en/documents/annual-reports.
Completion Strategy and Mechanism for International Tribunals (MICT). http://www.icty.org/en/documents/completion-strategy-and-mict.
Final Report of the United Nations Commission of Experts Established pursuant to Security Council Resolution 780 (1992) Annex IV, dated December 28, 1994. http://mcherifbassiouni.com/wp-content/uploads /2015/08/Yugoslavia-Report-Vol-1-Annex-IV.pdf.
Final Report of the United Nations Commission of Experts Established pursuant to Security Council Resolution 780 (1992) Annex IX, Rape and Sexual Assault. http://mcherifbassiouni.com/wp-content/uploads /2015/08/Yugoslavia-Report-Vol-5-Annex-IX.pdf.
Geneva Conventions of 1949 and Their Additional Protocols. https://www .icrc.org/en/document/geneva-conventions-1949-additional-protocols.
Letter from the Secretary-General to the President of the Security Council, dated May 24, 1994, with attachment "Final Report of the Commission of Experts Established pursuant to Security Council Resolution 780 (1992)." http://www.icty.org/x/file/About/OTP/un_commission_of _experts_report1994_en.pdf.
Report of the Secretary-General pursuant to Paragraph 2 of the Security Council Resolution 808 (1993). http://www.un.org/en/ga/search/view _doc.asp?symbol=S/25704.

Rules of Procedure and Evidence. http://www.icty.org/en/documents
/rules-procedure-evidence.

Security Council Resolution 827 (1993), dated May 25, 1993. http://www
.icty.org/x/file/Legal%20Library/Statute/statute_827_1993_en.pdf.

Statute of the Tribunal. http://www.icty.org/en/documents/statute
-tribunal.

Indictments Issued by the International Tribunal

Babić, Milan, Indictment Prosecutor versus. November 6, 2003. Prosecutor
Carla Del Ponte. Case IT-03-72. http://www.icty.org/x/cases/babic/ind
/en/bab-ii031117e.pdf.

Blagojević, Vidoje, Dragan Obremović, Dragan Jokić, and Momir Nikolić,
Amended Joinder Indictment Prosecutor versus. May 27, 2002. Prosecutor Carla Del Ponte. Case IT-02-60-PT. http://www.icty.org/x/cases
/nikolic/ind/en/nik-ai020527e.pdf.

Brđanin, Radoslav, Momir Talić, and Stojan Župljanin, Amended Indictment Prosecutor versus. December 16, 1999. Prosecutor Carla Del
Ponte. Case IT-99-36-I. http://www.icty.org/x/cases/zupljanin
_stanisicm/ind/en/Zupljanin_991216eng_indictment.pdf.

Drljača, Simo, Milan Kovačević, and Milomir Stakić, Indictment Prosecutor versus. March 13, 1997. Deputy Prosecutor Graham Blewitt. Case IT-
97-24-I. http://www.icty.org/x/cases/stakic/ind/en/Stakic_970313eng
_indictment.pdf.

Erdemović, Dražen, Indictment Prosecutor versus. May 22, 1996. Prosecutor Richard J. Goldstone. Case IT-96-22. http://www.icty.org/x/cases
/erdemovic/ind/en/erd-ii960529e.pdf.

Hadžić, Goran, Indictment Prosecutor versus. May 21, 2004. Prosecutor
Carla Del Ponte. Case IT-04-75. http://www.icty.org/x/cases/hadzic
/ind/en/had-ii040716e.htm.

———, Amended Indictment Prosecutor versus. March 22, 2012. Prosecutor Serge Brammertz. Case IT-04-75-PT. http://www.icty.org/x/cases
/hadzic/ind/en/120322.pdf.

Karadžić, Radovan, Second Amended Indictment Prosecutor versus.
February 18, 2009. http://www.icty.org/x/cases/karadzic/ind/en
/090218.pdf.

———, Third Amended Indictment Prosecutor versus. February 27, 2009.
Prosecutor Serge Brammertz. Case IT-98-5/18. http://www.icty.org/x
/cases/karadzic/ind/en/090227.pdf.

Krstić, Radislav, Amended Indictment Prosecutor versus. October 27, 1999. Prosecutor Carla Del Ponte. Case IT-98-33. http://www.icty.org/x /cases/krstic/ind/en/krs-1ai991027e.pdf.

Martić, Milan, Indictment Prosecutor versus. July 25, 1995. Prosecutor Richard J. Goldstone. Case IT-95-11. http://www.icty.org/x/cases /martic/ind/en/mar-ii950725e.pdf.

———, Indictment Prosecutor versus. July 14, 2003. Prosecutor Carla Del Ponte. Case: IT-95-11. http://www.icty.org/x/cases/martic/ind/en/mar -2ai030909e.pdf.

Milošević, Slobodan, Indictment Prosecutor versus. September 27, 2001. Prosecutor Carla Del Ponte. Case IT-02-54-T Croatia. http://www.icty .org/x/cases/slobodan_milosevic/ind/en/ind_cro010927.pdf.

———, Amended Indictment Prosecutor versus. October 23, 2002. Prosecutor Carla Del Ponte. Case IT-02-54-T Croatia. http://www.icty.org/x /cases/slobodan_milosevic/ind/en/mil-ai021023.htm.

———, Second Amended Indictment Prosecutor versus. July 28, 2004. Prosecutor Carla Del Ponte. Case IT-02-54-T Croatia. http://www.icty.org/x /cases/slobodan_milosevic/ind/en/040727.pdf.

Milošević, Slobodan, Milan Milutinović, Nikola Šainović, Dragoljub Ojdanić, and Vlajko Stojiljković-Kosovo, Indictment Prosecutor versus. May 22, 1999. Prosecutor Carla Del Ponte. Case IT-99-37. http://www .icty.org/case/slobodan_milosevic/4; http://www.icty.org/x/cases /slobodan_milosevic/ind/en/mil-ii990524e.htm.

Mladić, Ratko, Fourth Amended Indictment Prosecutor versus. December 16, 2011. Prosecutor Serge Brammertz. Case IT-09-92. http://www.icty .org/x/cases/mladic/ind/en/111216.pdf.

Mrkšić, Mile, Miroslav Radić, Veselin Šljivančanin, and Slavko Dokmanović, Indictment Prosecutor versus. March 26, 1996. Prosecutor Richard J. Goldstone. Case: IT-95-13a. http://www.icty.org/x/cases /dokmanovic/ind/en/dokmanovic_960326_indictment_en.pdf.

———, Amended Indictment Prosecutor versus. February 12, 1997. Prosecutor Louise Arbour. Case IT-95-13a. http://www.icty.org/x/cases /dokmanovic/ind/en/dokmanovic_971202_indictment_en.pdf.

Perišić, Momčilo, Indictment Prosecutor versus. February 5, 2008. Prosecutor Serge Brammertz. Case IT-04-81. http://www.icty.org/x/cases /perisic/ind/en/per-sai080205e.pdf.

Popović, Vujadin, Ljubiša Beara, Drago Nikolić, Radivoje Miletić, Vinko Pandurević, Ljubomir Borovčanin, and Milan Gvero, Revised Second

Consolidated Amended Indictment Prosecutor versus. August 4, 2006. Prosecutor Carla Del Ponte. Case IT-05-88. http://www.icty.org/x /cases/popovic/ind/en/popovic-060804.pdf.

Ražnatović, Željko (Arkan), Indictment Prosecutor versus. September 23, 1997. Prosecutor Louise Arbour. Case IT-97-27. http://www.icty.org/x /cases/zeljko_raznjatovic/ind/en/ark-ii970930e.pdf.

Sikirica, Duško, Damir Došen, and Dragan Kolundžija, Indictment Prosecutor versus. July 21, 1995. Prosecutor Richard J. Goldstone. Case IT-95-8-I. http://www.icty.org/case/sikirica/4; http://www.icty.org/x/cases /sikirica/ind/en/sik-ii950721e.htm.

Sikirica, Duško, Damir Došen, Dragan Kolundžija, Dušan Fustar, Nenad Banović, Predrag Banović, and Duško Knezević, Second Amended Indictment Prosecutor versus. January 3, 2001. John Ralston, for the Prosecutor. Case IT-95-8-PT. http://www.icty.org/x/cases/sikirica/ind /en/sik-2ai001220e.pdf.

Stakić, Milomir, Second Amended Indictment Prosecutor versus. August 31, 2001. Prosecutor Carla Del Ponte. Case IT-97-24-PT. http://www .icty.org/x/cases/stakic/ind/en/sta-2ai011005e.pdf.

———, Third Amended Indictment Prosecutor versus. February 28, 2002. Deputy Prosecutor Graham Blewitt. Case IT-97-24-PT. http://www.icty .org/x/cases/stakic/ind/en/sta-3ai020228e.pdf.

———, Fourth Amended Indictment Prosecutor versus. April 10, 2002. Deputy Prosecutor Graham Blewitt. Case IT-97-24-PT. http://www.icty.org /x/cases/stakic/ind/en/sta-4ai020410e.pdf.

Stanišić, Jovica, and Franko Simatović, Indictment Prosecutor versus. May 1, 2003. Prosecutor Carla Del Ponte. Case IT-03-69. http://www.icty .org/x/cases/stanisic_simatovic/ind/en/sta-ii030501e.pdf.

———, Amended Indictment Prosecutor versus. July 10, 2008. Prosecutor Serge Brammertz. Case IT-03-69-PT. http://www.icty.org/x/cases /stanisic_simatovic/ind/en/staj-in3rdamd080710.pdf.

Stanišič, Mićo, and Stojan Župljanin, Second Amended Consolidated Indictment Prosecutor versus. September 10, 2009. Prosecutor Serge Brammertz. Case IT-08-91-PT. http://www.icty.org/x/cases/zupljanin _stanisicm/ind/en/090910a.pdf.

Strugar, Pavle, Miodrag Jokić, Milan Zec, and Vladimir Kovačević, Indictment Prosecutor versus. February 22, 2001. Prosecutor Carla Del Ponte. Case IT-01-42. http://www.icty.org/x/cases/strugar/ind/en/str -ii010227e.pdf.

———, Amended Indictment Prosecutor versus. March 31, 2003. Prosecutor Carla Del Ponte. Case IT-01-42. http://www.icty.org/x/cases/strugar/ind/en/str-ai030331e.pdf.

Tolimir, Zdravko, Third Amended Indictment Prosecutor versus. November 4, 2009. Prosecutor Serge Brammertz. Case IT-05-88/2. http://www.icty.org/cases/party/791/4; http://www.icty.org/x/cases/tolimir/ind/en/091104.pdf.

Žigić, Zoran, Mlađo Radić, Miroslav Kvočka, Dragoljub Prcać, and Miroslav Kvočka, Indictment Prosecutor versus. February 13, 1995. Prosecutor Richard J. Goldstone. Case IT-95-4-I. http://www.icty.org/x/cases/kvocka/ind/en/950213.pdf.

———, Amended Indictment Prosecutor versus. August 26, 2000. Deputy Prosecutor Graham Blewitt. Case IT-98-30-1. http://www.icty.org/x/cases/kvocka/ind/en/kvo-ai001026e.pdf.

Župljanin, Stojan, Second Amended Indictment Prosecutor versus. October 6, 2004. Prosecutor Carla Del Ponte. Case IT-99-36-I. http://www.icty.org/x/cases/zupljanin_stanisicm/ind/en/Zupljanin_041006eng_indictment.pdf.

Relevant Judgments Issued by the International Tribunal

Babić, Milan. Judgment. June 29, 2004. http://www.icty.org/x/cases/babic/tjug/en/bab-sj040629e.pdf.

———. Appeal Judgment. July 18, 2005. http://www.icty.org/x/cases/babic/acjug/en/bab-aj050718e.pdf.

Banović, Predrag. Judgment. October 28, 2003. http://www.icty.org/x/cases/banovic/tjug/en/031028_Banovi_summary_en.pdf; http://www.icty.org/x/cases/banovic/tjug/en/ban-sj031028e.pdf.

Blagojević, Vidoje, and Dragan Jokić. Judgment. January 17, 2005. http://www.icty.org/x/cases/blagojevic_jokic/tjug/en/bla-050117e.pdf.

———. Appeal Judgment. May 9, 2007. http://www.icty.org/x/cases/blagojevic_jokic/acjug/en/blajok-jud070509.pdf.

Erdemović, Dražen. Judgment. November 29, 1996. http://www.icty.org/x/cases/erdemovic/tjug/en/erd-tsj961129e.pdf.

Jokić, Miodrag. Judgment. March 18, 2004. http://www.icty.org/x/cases/miodrag_jokic/tjug/en/jok-sj040318e.pdf.

———. Appeal Judgment. August 30, 2005. http://www.icty.org/x/cases/miodrag_jokic/acjug/en/jok-aj050830e.pdf.

Karadžić, Radovan. Judgment. March 24, 2016. http://www.icty.org/x/cases/karadzic/tjug/en/160324_judgement.pdf.

Krstić, Radislav. Judgment. April 19, 2004. http://www.icty.org/x/cases
/krstic/acjug/en/krs-aj040419e.pdf.

Martić, Milan. Judgment. June 12, 2007. http://www.icty.org/x/cases/martic
/tjug/en/070612.pdf.

———. Appeal Judgment. October 8, 2008. http://www.icty.org/x/cases
/martic/acjug/en/mar-aj081008e.pdf.

Mrkšić, Mile, and Veselin Šljivančanin. Appeal Judgment. May 5, 2009.
http://www.icty.org/x/cases/mrksic/acjug/en/090505.pdf.

Mrkšić, Mile, Veselin Šljivančanin, and Miroslav Radić. Judgment. September 27, 2007. http://www.icty.org/x/cases/mrksic/tjug/en/070927.pdf.

Nikolić, Momir. Judgment. December 2, 2003. http://www.icty.org/x/cases
/nikolic/tjug/en/mnik-sj031202-e.pdf.

———. Appeal Judgment. March 8, 2006. http://www.icty.org/x/cases
/nikolic/acjug/en/nik-aj060308-e.pdf.

Obrenović, Dragan. Judgment. December 10, 2003. http://www.icty.org/x
/cases/obrenovic/tjug/en/obr-sj031210e.pdf.

Perišić, Momčilo. Judgment. September 6, 2011. http://www.icty.org/x
/cases/perisic/tjug/en/110906_judgement.pdf.

———. Appeal Judgment. February 28, 2013. http://www.icty.org/x/cases
/perisic/acjug/en/130228_judgement.pdf.

Popović, Vujadin, Ljubiša Beara, Drago Nikolić, Radivoje Miletić, and Vinko
Pandurević. Appeal Judgment. January 30, 2015. http://www.icty.org/x
/cases/popovic/acjug/en/150130_judgement.pdf.

Popović, Vujadin, Ljubiša Beara, Drago Nikolić, Radivoje Miletić, Vinko Pandurević, Ljubomir Borovčanin, and Milan Gvero. Judgment. June 10, 2010.
http://www.icty.org/x/cases/popovic/tjug/en/100610judgement.pdf.

Stakić, Milomir. Judgment. July 31, 2003. http://www.icty.org/x/cases/stakic
/tjug/en/stak-tj030731e.pdf.

Stanišić, Jovica, and Franko Simatović. Judgment. May 30, 2013. http://www
.icty.org/x/cases/stanisic_simatovic/tjug/en/130530_judgement_p1
.pdf; http://www.icty.org/x/cases/stanisic_simatovic/tjug/en/130530
_judgement_p2.pdf.

———. Appeal Judgment. December 9, 2015. http://www.icty.org/x/cases
/stanisic_simatovic/acjug/en/151209-judgement.pdf.

Stanišič, Mićo, and Stojan Župljanin. Judgment. March 27, 2013. http://www
.icty.org/x/cases/zupljanin_stanisicm/tjug/en/130327-1.pdf.

———. Appeal Judgment. June 30, 2016. http://www.icty.org/x/cases
/zupljanin_stanisicm/acjug/en/160630.pdf.

Strugar, Pavel. Judgment. January 31, 2005. http://www.icty.org/x/cases
    /strugar/tjug/en/str-tj050131e.pdf.
———. Appeal Judgment. July 17, 2008. http://www.icty.org/x/cases
    /strugar/acjug/en/080717.pdf.
Tolimir, Zdravko. Judgment. December 12, 2012. http://www.icty.org/x
    /cases/tolimir/tjug/en/121212.pdf.
———. Appeal Judgment. April 8, 2015. http://www.icty.org/x/cases/tolimir
    /acjug/en/150408_judgement.pdf.
Žigić, Zoran, Mlađo Radić, Dragoljub Prcać, and Miroslav Kvočka. Appeal
    Judgment. February 28, 2005. http://www.icty.org/x/cases/kvocka
    /acjug/en/kvo-aj050228e.pdf.
Žigić, Zoran, Mlađo Radić, Dragoljub Prcać, Miroslav Kvočka, and Milo-
    jica Kos. Judgment. November 2, 2001. http://www.icty.org/x/cases
    /kvocka/tjug/en/kvo-tj011002e.pdf.

Relevant Indictments Issued by the War Crimes Prosecutor in Serbia

Ćirić, Petar, case Ovčara. http://www.tuzilastvorz.org.rs/upload
    /Indictment/Documents_sr/2016-05/o_2012_06_18_lat.pdf.
Devetak, Ljuban, case Lovas. http://www.tuzilastvorz.org.rs/upload
    /Indictment/Documents_sr/2016-05/o_2007_11_28_lat.pdf.
Kovačević, Vladimir, case Dubrovnik. http://www.tuzilastvorz.org.rs
    /upload/Indictment/Documents_sr/2016-05/o_2007_07_26_lat.pdf.
Pejić, Milorad, case Ovčara. http://www.tuzilastvorz.org.rs/upload
    /Indictment/Documents_sr/2016-05/o_2008_04_08_lat.pdf.
Radak, Saša, case Ovčara. http://www.tuzilastvorz.org.rs/upload
    /Indictment/Documents_sr/2016-05/o_2005_04_13_lat.pdf.
Sireta, Damir, case Ovčara. http://www.tuzilastvorz.org.rs/upload
    /Indictment/Documents_sr/2016-05/o_2008_10_17_lat.pdf.
Vujanović, Stanko, case Ovčara. http://www.tuzilastvorz.org.rs/upload
    /Indictment/Documents_sr/2016-05/o_2010_03_31_lat.pdf.
Vujović, Miroljub, case Ovčara. http://www.tuzilastvorz.org.rs/upload
    /Indictment/Documents_sr/2016-05/o_2005_09_16_lat.pdf.

Publicly Accessible Testimonies before the International Tribunal

Albright, Madeleine. Testimony in the case Prosecutor versus Biljana
    Plavšić. December 17, 2002. http://www.icty.org/x/cases/plavsic/trans
    /en/021217IT.htm.

Anastasijević, Dejan. Testimony in the case Prosecutor versus Slobodan
    Milošević. October 15, 2002. http://www.icty.org/x/cases/slobodan
    _milosevic/trans/en/021015ED.htm; http://www.icty.org/x/cases
    /slobodan_milosevic/trans/en/021010ED.htm.
Berghofer, Dragutin. Testimony in the case Prosecutor versus Slavko Dok-
    manović. February 5, 1998. http://www.icty.org/x/cases/dokmanovic
    /trans/en/980205ED.htm.
Bosanac, Vesna. Testimony in the case Prosecutor versus Slavko Dok-
    manović. February 2, 1998. http://www.icty.org/x/cases/dokmanovic
    /trans/en/980202ed.htm.
Čakalić, Emil. Testimony in the case Prosecutor versus Slavko Dok-
    manović. February 5, 1998. http://www.icty.org/x/cases/dokmanovic
    /trans/en/980205ED.htm.
Conjar, Milan. Testimony in the case Prosecutor versus Goran Hadžić. Novem-
    ber 27, 2012. http://www.icty.org/x/cases/hadzic/trans/en/121127ED.htm.
Curtis, Kevin. Testimony in the case Prosecutor versus Slavko Dok-
    manović. September 8, 1997. http://www.icty.org/x/cases/dokmanovic
    /trans/en/970908IT.htm.
Dokmanović, Slavko. Testimony in the case Prosecutor versus Slavko Dok-
    manović. September 8, 1997. http://www.icty.org/x/cases/dokmanovic
    /trans/en/970908IT.htm.
Dzuro, Vladimír. Testimony in the case Prosecutor versus Slavko
    Dokmanović. June 17 and 18, 1998. http://www.icty.org/x/cases
    /dokmanovic/trans/en/980617it.htm; http://www.icty.org/x/cases
    /dokmanovic/trans/en/980618ed.htm.
Grujić, Ivan. Testimony in the case Prosecutor versus Slobodan Milošević.
    March 4, 2003. http://www.icty.org/x/cases/slobodan_milosevic/trans
    /en/030304ED.htm; http://www.icty.org/x/cases/slobodan_milosevic
    /trans/en/030303ED.htm.
Herold, Noel. Testimony in the case Prosecutor versus Slavko Dokmanović.
    June 23, 1998. http://www.icty.org/x/cases/dokmanovic/trans/en
    /980623it.htm.
Kypr, Petr. Testimony in the case Prosecutor versus Slavko Dokmanović.
    February 11, 1998. http://www.icty.org/x/cases/dokmanovic/trans/en
    /980211it.htm.
Mesić, Stjepan. Testimony in the case Prosecutor versus Slavko Dok-
    manović. March 20, 1998. http://www.icty.org/x/cases/dokmanovic
    /trans/en/980320ed.htm.

———. Testimony in the case Prosecutor versus Slobodan Milošević. October 1 and 2, 2002. http://www.icty.org/x/cases/slobodan_milosevic/trans /en/021001IT.htm; http://www.icty.org/x/cases/slobodan_milosevic /trans/en/021002IT.htm; http://www.icty.org/x/cases/slobodan _milosevic/trans/en/021002ED.htm.

Samardžić, Dragan (Witness C-017). Testimony in the case Prosecutor versus Slobodan Milošević. June 11, 2003. http://www.slobodan-milosevic .org/documents/trial/2003-06-11.html; http://www.icty.org/x/cases /slobodan_milosevic/trans/en/030610ED.htm; http://www.icty.org/x /cases/slobodan_milosevic/trans/en/030611ED.htm.

Schou, Jan. Testimony in the case Prosecutor versus Slavko Dokmanović. February 10, 1998. http://www.icty.org/x/cases/dokmanovic/trans/en /980210it.htm.

Snow, Clyde. Testimony in the case Prosecutor versus Slavko Dokmanović. March 17, 1998. http://www.icty.org/x/cases/dokmanovic/trans/en /980317ed.htm.

Tabbush, Paul. Testimony in the case Prosecutor versus Slavko Dokmanović. June 18, 1998. http://www.icty.org/x/cases/dokmanovic/trans /en/980618ed.htm.

**Criminal Cases That Used the Arrest of Slavko
Dokmanović as Legal Precedent**

ICC. Prosecutor versus Thomas Lubanga Dyilo. August 24, 2006. Observations of Victims a/0001/06, a/0002/06, and a/0003/06 regarding the Challenge to Jurisdiction Raised by the Defense in the Application of 23 May 2006. https://www.icc-cpi.int/CourtRecords/CR2006_02991.pdf.

———. Prosecutor versus Thomas Lubanga Dyilo. October 3, 2006. Decision on the Defense Challenge to the Jurisdiction of the Court pursuant to Article 19 (2) (a) of the Statute. https://www.icc-cpi.int/CourtRecords/CR2006_03214.pdf.

ICTR. Prosecutor versus Karemera. March 24, 2009. Decision on Joseph Nzirorera's Motion for Reconsideration of Certificate of Safe Conduct. http://www.worldcourts.com/ictr/eng/decisions/2009.03.24 _Prosecutor_v_Karemera_5.pdf.

ICTY. Decision on the Motion for Release by the Accused Slavko Dokmanović. http://www.icty.org/en/sid/7458.

———. Prosecutor versus Nikolic. June 5, 2003. Decision on Interlocutory Appeal concerning Legality of Arrest. http://opil.ouplaw.com/view/10 .1093/law:icl/869icty03.case.1/law-icl-869icty03.

———. Prosecutor versus Simic. October 18, 2000. Decision on Motion for
    Judicial Assistance to Be Provided by SFOR and Others. http://www.icty
    .org/x/cases/simic/tdec/en/01018EV513778.htm.
Special Tribunal for Lebanon. Prosecutor versus Salim Jamil A Yy Ash,
    Mustafa Amine Badreddine, Hussein Hassan Oneissi, and Assad Has-
    san Sabra. July 27, 2012. Decision on the Defence Challenges to the
    Jurisdiction and Legality of the Tribunal. https://tinyurl.com/ya7tv7fo.

SECONDARY SOURCES

The author recognizes that there are numerous sources related to the collapse
of Yugoslavia, war crimes, and international justice that might be of interest
to readers of this book. Some of the most relevant books and other sources
are listed below.

Almond, Mark. *Europe's Backyard War: The War in the Balkans*. New York:
    Mandarin, 1994.
Andric, Ivo. *The Bridge over the Drina*. Translated by Lovette F. Edwards.
    London: Harvill Press, 1994.
Borger, Julian. *The Butcher's Trail: How the Search for Balkan War Criminals
    Became the World's Most Successful Manhunt*. New York: Other Press, 2016.
Bujosevic, Dragan, and Ivan Radovanovic. *The Fall of Milosevic: The October
    5th Revolution*. London: Palgrave Macmillan, 2003.
Cencich, R. John. *The Devil's Garden: A War Crimes Investigator's Story*.
    Washington DC: Potomac Books, 2013.
Del Ponte, Carla, and Chuck Sudetic. *Madame Prosecutor: Confrontations
    with Humanity's Worst Criminals and the Culture of Impunity*. Milan: Fel-
    trinelli Editore, 2008.
Donia, Robert J. *Radovan Karadzic: Architect of the Bosnian Genocide*. New
    York: Cambridge University Press, 2015.
Dunoff, Jeffrey, Steven R. Ratner, and David Wippman. *International Law:
    Norms, Actors, and Process; A Problem-Oriented Approach*. 2nd ed. New
    York: Wolters Kluwer, 2010.
Dzuro, Vladimír. "Enforcement of Arrest Warrants Issued by International
    Tribunals." *Australian Police Journal* 57, no. 1 (2003): 40–50.
Glenny, Misha. *The Balkans 1804–2012: Nationalism, War and the Great
    Powers*. London: Granta Books, 2012.
Goldstein, Slavko. *1941: The Year That Keeps Returning*. Translated by
    Michael Gabe. New York: New York Review of Books, 2013.

Holbrooke, Richard. *To End a War*. New York: Random House, 1998.

Job, Cvijeto. *Yugoslavia's Ruin: The Bloody Lessons of Nationalism*. Lanham MD: Rowman & Littlefield, 2002.

Koff, Clea. *The Bone Woman: A Forensic Anthropologist's Search for Truth in the Mass Graves of Rwanda, Bosnia, Croatia, and Kosovo*. London: Atlantic Books, 2004.

LeBor, Adam. *Milosevic: A Biography*. London: Bloomsbury, 2002.

Maass, Peter. *Love Thy Neighbour: A Story of War*. New York: Knopf, 1996.

Magas, Branka. *The Destruction of Yugoslavia: Tracking the Break-Up 1980–1992*. London: Verso, 1993.

Malcolm, Noel. *Bosnia: A Short History*. London: Macmillan, 1994.

Nice, Geoffrey. *Justice for All and How to Achieve It: Citizens, Lawyers, and the Law in the Age of Human Rights*. London: Scala Arts & Heritage, 2017.

Oliver, Ian. *War & Peace in the Balkans: The Diplomacy of Conflict in the Former Yugoslavia*. London: I. B. Tauris, 2005.

Rieff, David. *Slaughterhouse: Bosnia and the Failure of the West*. New York: Simon & Schuster, 1995.

Robertson, Geoffrey. *Crimes against Humanity: The Struggle for Global Justice*. London: Penguin Books, 2012.

Scheffer, David. *All the Missing Souls: A Personal History of the War Crimes Tribunals*. Princeton NJ: Princeton University Press, 2012.

Sell, Louis. *Slobodan Milosevic and the Destruction of Yugoslavia*. Durham NC: Duke University Press, 2002.

Silber, Laura, and Allan Little. *The Death of Yugoslavia*. London: Penguin/BBC Books, 1995.

Simms, Brendan. *Unfinest Hour: Britain and the Destruction of Bosnia*. London: Allen Lane, 2001.

Stephen, Chris. *Judgement Day: The Trial of Slobodan Milosevic*. New York: Atlantic Books, 2004.

Stevanovic, Vidosav. *Milosevic: The People's Tyrant*. Translated by Zlata Filipovic. London: I. B. Tauris, 2004.

Stover, Eric. *The Witnesses: War Crimes and the Promise of Justice in The Hague*. Philadelphia: University of Pennsylvania Press, 2005.

Tanner, Marcus. *Croatia: A Nation Forged in War*. New Haven CT: Yale University Press, 2010.

Thompson, Mark. *A Paper House: The Ending of Yugoslavia*. London: Vintage Books, 1992.

Vulliamy, Ed. *Seasons in Hell: Understanding Bosnia's War*. New York: Simon & Schuster, 1994.

INDEX